A Poetry Boom
1990-2010

Selected previous publications by Andrew Duncan

Poetry

In a German Hotel
Cut Memories and False Commands
Sound Surface
Alien Skies
Switching and Main Exchange *
Pauper Estate *
Anxiety Before Entering a Room. New and selected poems
Surveillance and Compliance
Skeleton Looking at Chinese Pictures
The Imaginary in Geometry
Savage Survivals (amid modern suavity) *
In Five Eyes *
Threads of Iron *

Criticism

The Poetry Scene in the Nineties (internet only)
Centre and Periphery in Modern British Poetry **
The Failure of Conservatism in Modern British Poetry **
Origins of the Underground
The Council of Heresy *
The Long 1950s *
Fulfilling the Silent Rules (forthcoming)

As editor

Don't Stop Me Talking (with Tim Allen)
Joseph Macleod: *Cyclic Serial Zeniths from the Flux*
Joseph Macleod: *A Drinan Trilogy: The Cove / The Men of the Rocks
        / Script from Norway*

*Shearsman titles
**Revised editions forthcoming from Shearsman.

A Poetry Boom
1990-2010

Shocked Grains Wash Up As a Beach

Andrew Duncan

Shearsman Books

Published in the United Kingdom in 2015 by
Shearsman Books Ltd
50 Westons Hill Drive
Emersons Green
BRISTOL
BS16 7DF

Shearsman Books Ltd Registered Office
30–31 St. James Place, Mangotsfield, Bristol BS16 9JB
(this address not for correspondence)

ISBN 978-1-84861-423-9
First Edition

CONTENTS

She don't dance to disco any more
She don't dance to disco, hiphop or electro
She don't dance to disco any more

from 'She Don't Dance to Disco'
composed by Love/Love/Love/Dope
for The Alabama Three

The universe is a sub-infinite array of bad data.

– anon.

Is he in raptures with a cup of good Ale? Does he prefer his own works to any of the Ancients or Moderns? Doth he despise all other languages and learning? Doth he affect low company and greedily swallow the praises of tinkers and coblers? Would he get out of bed to sing with the harp, as Gronwy used to do with me? Is he naturally inclined to buffoonery, dirty language, and indecent expressions?

– Lewis Morris, 1761

INTRODUCTION

SHOCKED GRAINS FROM A POETRY BOOM

There is an atmosphere in poetry sections in High Street bookshops. This is the poetry market. It offers a world of delicate and cultured people, low on aggression and high on conscience. The keyword is sensitivity, implying a nebula of fine structures which cannot thrive in an environment of coarse surfaces. The value is in the slight and easily damaged wisps of atmospheres, not the big and powerful feelings. The language is quiet enough for small and rare sounds to be heard. The inclination is towards personality and not towards analytical intelligence, which is more readily to be had in adjacent departments. It is towards the small scale and organic. The customers identify with the personalities of poets, relate to them as friends, rather than identifying with techniques and ideas. People who actually buy poetry approve of this atmosphere. It has the warmth and intimacy of a student house, the mixture of hope, naivety and deep interiority of a teenager's bedroom. No one would claim that the blurbs of books are fair and informative. No one would claim that the choice of books available in the shops is the best possible. But this does not matter so much. The blurbs identify what people want at the same time that they disguise the fact that they are not going to get very much of it. People come in, wander around, leave bearing the thing they want. Perhaps human beings are small scale and organic, in contrast to some of the phenomena that humans create. This art seems to favour the personal to the exclusion of anything else. If we miss those fragile and unresisting feelings, we miss the whole event. Sensitivity is what we have to write about. The *quality of care*.

I read a book about 'authenticity' in popular music which I found disturbing at many levels. It was *Faking It*, by Hugh Barker and Yuval Taylor. Part of it was one of the two saying that seeing 'authenticity' in simple musical forms, poverty, being part of a 'folk community', in naivety, etc. and in the scratchy qualities of reprocessed 78s laboriously collected by ethnomusicologists, etc., was a fantasy and an indulgence and on a par with the appeal of any commodity. Then also you had one of the authors arguing for the purity of commercial pop. He cited 'Sugar Sugar' by The Archies, which was number one for six weeks in the UK in 1969. This was derided at the time – even other thirteen-year-olds, I was 13, would have derided you for liking it. It was a poster dog for 'bubblegum'. But when this guy discussed it I could remember it really clearly, not having heard it for 40 years. That riff on the marimba or whatever it was. "Pour your sugar on me". It was shocking to find someone go into print defending 'Sugar Sugar' or anything to do with Don Kirshner. The fact that I could remember it proved it wasn't forgettable – there was something really strong about it. Love as a sugar rush and a hit record as both smeared together. The point is, most of the poets in recent anthologies are amazingly dumb. It is like pre-Beatles pop music. They have been bypassed by all the innovations that came along in the 'post repressive high' that followed the Fifties. Their project for poetry is egocentric and conservative. They have no techniques more modern than custard powder. But it's a mistake to approach them from the standpoint of someone who has read modern literature and climbed the peaks. No – it's better if you approach them as naive art, as something almost senseless but potentially heady and indulgent. The best run-up is to go onto YouTube and listen closely to records by Tommy James and the Shondells, The Association ('Windy'), The Cowsills ('The Park, the Rain, and Other Things'), The Monkees, and Tommy Roe ('Dizzy'). There is a 'reduction' involved, a vision of the poem succeeding because it is simple and can be tinted into complete harmony – fully resolved.

The figures we have tell that the number of new books of poetry published each year nearly doubled between 1976 and 1993 and then nearly doubled again by 2000, then staying at this level. In the years 1999-2001 roughly as many books of poetry were published as in the whole of the 1970s. This is a poetry boom. We seem to have a situation where there are 100,000 Eng Lit graduates and 10,000 write a book of poems and succeed in getting it published. This is the outcome of large-scale benign processes. You aren't going to take to the streets and chant *Less choice. Less access. Now!* A knock-on is that I can't survey the period; all I can do is make notes on the regions I've been to. We're on the beach and the marks in the sand get wiped away every night. Maybe 12,000 people have published at least one book of poetry. (Maybe it's only 10,000 – oh, that's so much easier. Am I an expert on all ten thousand? *What do you think?* "'I love you all' he lied and left the room.") People like what poetry has to offer. It is more plausible to describe the things people like than to describe some other cultural system which would be more free of flaws.

Not all poems work. However much you dislike theory, the sound of an emotional-symbolic structure slipping, snapping its pegs, teetering, and collapsing into cultural rubble is all-pervasive: the sound of Now. We have to listen very closely to that sound. I have included a number of chapters on critique, the thing poets dislike most.

Some poets think that equity means that *whatever I say is true*. It seems to support the statement *whatever other people say about me is true*, but in fact the rule changes at that point. The idea of softening the boundary between the self and the world does not abolish the outside world. It may be that the gift of the poet is to internalise parts of the outside world, to soften the boundary. The critic is trying to bring the processes of the self outside, into the light where they can be objectively examined. That is the reverse process, pretty much. At present the statement "justice means Me getting exactly what I want" seems to be socially acceptable. I want to reform this to say that "people who actually wrote and finished numerous poems of high quality and who didn't get good reviews, circulation, etc. are examples of Injustice". Prose has to be founded on equity.

SPECTRAL INVESTMENT

Todd Swift (of the *Eyewear* blog, http://toddswift.blogspot.co.uk/) described me as ["I just read Andrew Duncan's brilliant and provocative review of *Beyond The Lyric*, in the summer *Tears in the Fence*. Duncan is one of the best poetry critics in the UK – and one of the most radical. He is essential reading, especially because his work does not seek the texture of reassuring professional conformity that some reviews and criticism aspire to; nor is he a knee-jerk knock-about. His voice is concerned, other, and often proto-punk. His is the voice of a poetry Britain I also want to hear and know."] ... [someone emailed me this]. At another moment Swift said I was wrong 80% of the time. What is going on here? The factors which make for agreement have been weakening over the past 30 years. If we imagine six connoisseurs of poetry, with the 20% overlap, they might produce 500% of the information needed. This could be a very fertile process. But it is worrying if you think conversation is about sharing states of mind. The main impulse in the poetry scene is to contact other people and to listen to what they say. This was my goal at every point. But what about the 80% wrong? I can't capture 'the reaction that everyone finally reached' if that reaction does not exist. But I think I know what the new sound is. We have a lot of criticism which relies on close reading and excluding the ideas around the poem – but the precondition for understanding the poems better may be to understand the projection by the audience: the codes of shared subjectivity. This is a method which gets away from egocentricity. A little anyway – I still choose the texts. (I was not in Detroit in 1969 (and am not proto-punk) but I would admit that Peter Fuller is the cultural critic I feel closest to.)

I wanted a much simpler and more pleasure-based approach, and at the same time (2005) I moved away from London and to Nottingham. This kept me away from the internecine and overheated poetry scene. There just isn't much of a poetry scene here. This allowed me a much more selective approach. Since then I have been spending much of my limited free time studying Welsh and Gaelic. A residual nationalist thing, I suppose. Being involved in Gaeldom does tend to erode the distinction between 'folk' and 'literary' and make you more interested in the 'folk' thing. Just as being away from the hotbeds makes you forget what the avant-garde is for.

Partially Coded Terrain:
Eight Anthologies

A New Generation

A cluster of recent anthologies of Young Poets (around 2009 to 2013) is like this:

— *The Salt Book of Younger Poets* (ed. Roddy Lumsden and Eloise Stonborough, Cambridge: Salt Publishing, 2011)
　　Doesn't include anything avant-garde. Rule is that poets were under 26 when the book was published. 50 poets. Three stars.

— *Eighteens* (ed. Mark Cobley, Newton-le-Willows: Knives Forks and Spoons Press, 2011)
　　Markedly 'experimental' in focus. Poets are young by my standards (!) but there is no rubric so we can't say that there is a 'limiting profile'. 18 poets. Number may be a reference to the high-impact 'Ninerrors' series. One star.

— Chris Goode ed., *Better Than Language*
　　An anthology of new modernist poetries (London: ganzfeld, 2011) dwells in the 'experimental' terrain but is marked by the Avant-Garde Corporate feel. From the booklists, the first debut of anyone included is about 2008. So a very recent layer of the Underground. The introduction says that the phrase is "love is better than language". The claim to include 'new poetries' is presumably a tribute to Carcanet, but the tone is not necessarily in line with Carcanet and *PN Review*. Not sure what the term "modernist" means here but I suppose there isn't a better one. 13 poets. One star.

— Tom Chivers, ed. *City State* (London: Penned in the Margins, 2009)
　　Rule is that poets live in London and are 'new'. This is too mainstream for my tastes but is not exclusively so. 27 poets. No stars.

— Roddy Lumsden, ed., *Identity Parade* (Tarset: Bloodaxe Books, 2010)
　　Picked from poets who made debuts between 1995 and about

2008. Deliberately attempts to cross the whole spectrum and makes a very impressive attempt on that. 85 poets. Two stars. See below.

— *Voice Recognition, 21 Poets for the 21st Century* James Byrne and Clare Pollard, eds., (Bloodaxe, 2009)
     Limit is that no one included had yet published a full collection. The effect is that the poets were born between 1977 and 1986. This could be 'a generation'. Doesn't include anything avant-garde. Two stars.

I added *Freaklung* issue 6 (June 2010), which is not badged as an anthology but does include 25 poets of whom the majority are young, and is of a high artistic standard. It collects 25 poets willing to write poems in celebration of, or remixing themes from, Barry MacSweeney's *Odes* (1980). Like that original, these poets are extreme, pressurised by language. It was included partly to widen the base of observations, partly also because this was the part of the map which meant most to me. There was an incidental point that the other six anthologies didn't pick up these poets, except that Nat Raha and Linus Slug do feature elsewhere. Four stars.

I am not going to review these anthologies in detail, but most of the rest of the book will be a series of reflections on the composite picture which emerges from close reading of them. I found roughly 194 different poets in these publications. *Dear World* adds about another 45 names. Maybe a clear view will have emerged in ten years' time. This is probably the last thing you want to hear, but even the list of 240 definitely does not include all the poets from this generation who have strong claims to be heard.

Identity Parade is closest to a map, as being the first comprehensive anthology of modern British poetry for forty years. It includes modern-style poetry as well as mainstream poetry, and strives to be complete. The older book referred to is Lucie-Smith's *British Poetry Since 1945*, which really did cover the spectrum, and which Lumsden identifies as a model. It was also the basic source from which I discovered modern poetry, starting in about 1974. In 1971, Lucie-Smith included 6 women poets out of 85, Lumsden includes (allowing for my count errors) 43 out of 85. That is not a count of what *kind* of poetry they write. However, change in the sociological composition of poets as a cohort is one of the themes of the time. Young women deserted the collective norms of mid-century women who had literary interests. This was a revolution. They came to write poetry but as well as abandoning the women's poetry of the mid-century (a limited and even frustrating field) they did not start writing like men. This was innovation.

The cover also says "It offers the work of 85 highly individual and distinctive talents": my feeling is not that this is literally true but that the imperatives to conform and the inhibitions about using 'new' or 'exotic' forms are both unconscious. There are maybe 60 doing eloquent cover versions and 20 being individual. How much of this poetry would seem modern or advanced in Lucie-Smith's anthology? Given how little has changed in forty years, Lumsden's claim that "exploration and individualism" are the salient features of the era is questionable. Clearly the question of change over time is a problem that will repay further thought.

There is a package which involves defining the personality as the freight of the poem. The audience are supposed to love the poet and the words are there just to teach them how to do that. Everything that would distract from this bond of attachment forming is rigorously segregated from the text. Curiosity about psychology is contraindicated and attachment is not meant to be distracted by descriptive accuracy. Huge numbers of people write in this way – it's *contemporary* but not *modern*. The bewildering simplicity of modern English poetry, and of most of the poets on show here, is hardly unrelated to a notion of authenticity and even documentary. Any wish to use language originally and even critically is perceived by many, certainly by the poetry managers who speak for the market, as a treacherous lurch away from authenticity, away from the direct presentation of the self. The proviso that society is not of any interest allows a belief that the poet's daily round is of great interest. How can you express your personality adequately when your writing accepts every convention of how bits of language are meant to fit together and includes no element which by being original could, even notionally, express your originality? How is it that your wish to be different is the same wish that 50 other poets cherish and is expressed by identical linguistic, that is poetic, means?

The difference between conservative and innovative in the present dispensation is simply that conservative poets want to reduce the poem to their personality. The code-name for the anti-personal lot used to be underground, is now 'process oriented', was also 'critical'. They start out by not identifying with ads and pop songs and TV. This line generated a lot of new information: when it started, it was didactic and uncomfortable – disenchanted. Poets born since 1970 are desperate not to be cold or didactic, and there is a new sound which says *in a new world I am infantile and tactile and my sensations are new.*

Swimsuit Universals: Dear World and Everyone in It: New Poetry in the UK (edited Nathan Hamilton, Tarset: Bloodaxe Books, 2013)

To the 194 poets in the seven anthologies we dealt with above, *Dear World* adds another 45. Rumour has it that there is a 'response record' called 'nowhere and nobody in it', involving cut-ups of parts of *Dear World*. We even acquired a copy of this through the usual fences. It seems to be one-take improvisations inspired by gabba music. (Like music by The Ramones – *Suzy* is a headbanger, *her mother* is a geek, etc.) The authors were not in *Dear World*.

Hamilton says that the concept began with a series of features on (individual) young poets which he was doing for *The Rialto* magazine in Norwich. They aren't all under 35 because the publication date of the book was a bit late in the curve – each poet was probably that age when their feature in *The Rialto* was published. The title may come from a poem by Jonty Tiplady from his 2010 book *Zam Bonk Dip* (previously published in a 2008 pamphlet), and Tiplady is representative of a sound or style which arguably features with quite a few other poets in the book. I will start with a blog post on him by Joe Luna because I think this is a 'first-person participant' talking about this new style of poetry and the people who write it:

> Things make us happy. But this is not always true, and even if it is, emphatically true, what kind of 'things' are we talking about? Objects? Commodities? Beer? Holidays? Lovers? All these and more undoubtedly make our lives more complete than they otherwise would have been, regardless of whether that standard of completeness has been pre-programmed into our relations of exchange by those things themselves.
> [...]
> What avails a sense of idealized empathy from subjects otherwise incomplete, weakened or damaged by desire, is the complete thing, the bounded, constant, secret, composed thing, held out

to us with all the sublime grace of macro-life, supernumerary, brilliant chrome, the miniature gestalt containing all the crucial elements of style and faith to make it the ideal companion, the soundtrack to our lives, gliding effortlessly along beside us & life in impeachable parallel design, offering.

[...]

Thinking about pop songs is immensely difficult because the residue they leave is short-circuited, a kind of 'self-destruct in 5 seconds' sonic memory that only works by imparting the double dream of future listening bliss and the abject melancholy at the parallel objectification of the world that the pop song enacts (more on this melancholy later), and because, most importantly, they are emphatically not *built* to be thought about, or thought with, or thought on, or in fact done anything *with* except bopped, tranced, head-banged, slammed and smiled with. To.

[...]

Jonty Tiplady's poetry takes what Pop proposes, mendaciously, coercively, and attempts to make it real, vulnerably live, and loveable. It can, after all, be real. We can, for the moment, really believe in the hook, verse and chorus, the rising minor key synthesizers of 'Dear World and Everyone in it', primed as it is for super-realisation of the fully-blown burgeoning reality of life composed around us, forging an intenser real from the cacophony of Pop-sexuality, Pop-social performance and Pop-cataloguing than any smarmy neo-Romantic blitzkrieg of luddite pretensions could ever believe possible, let alone confirm, let alone betray. [...] the poem achieves grace not by cynical or ironic citation, but by actually re-investing its material with the hope, or if there is to be a concession to at least a modicum of restraint, the wry hope, that the affirmatives of its lyric appeal might truly be believed, or at least trusted in until the poem either frowns in belated emo majesty or squirms in pathologically persuasive climax.

(retrieved from http://fallopianyoutube.blogspot.co.uk/ 2012/05/world-is-for-this-on-poetry-of-jonty.html)

Luna edits *Hi Zero* magazine in Brighton and blogs at fallopianyoutube. (Emo is short for emotional and is a genre of music, also more vaguely a kind of person who is emotive all the time and whose opinions are projective and quick to evaporate. Musically, I think it is a term without a genre to go with it, but as far as critics go I think Luna is a little bit emo.) It is reasonable to think that Luna's highly expressive description of Tiplady's situation is indicative of where other poets in the book with their sophistication and their 'problems of modernity', are. Joe names an array of low-level desires which animate our patterns of gratification. If we want to characterise the mind by its visible objects we could envisage it by means of a supermarket: as thousands of object-sensation loops – our selves are not unified but symmetrical to the supermarket shelves – which are there because we want them. If you switch off the voice of theology (and the metanarratives, the *grands récits*), you may release a swarm intelligence, and maybe what becomes audible is a thousand decentred and simple voices, self-starting programs beneath the level of consciousness. In parallel, language encodes a vast array of subtle sensory distinctions, for example between different kinds of fruit or textiles, a world on the periphery of which is the body and its nervous surface, and poetry is made of these distinctions. The poets in *Dear World* are releasing these peripheral but vigorous voices and swarming into a thousand interstices left empty by an older poetry.

The book covers 70 poets and I am going to claim that it embodies a style, which must be inaccurate, because the poets don't all identify with one version of melody & sound. Yet among anthologies this stands out as projecting a distinctive sound, as the inclusions support each other. We don't have wrenches and lurches as we move through the pages. *Dear World* has 4 names in common with *Identity Parade* – also an anthology of young poets, from the same publisher, and published 3 years earlier. 4 out of 72. This suggests that the two editors had radically different views of the scene, and further in fact that Hamilton is in love with one section of the spectrum. There is some kind of envelope that his poets fit inside. If you look in the opposite direction, at the poets in *IP* who didn't make the cut in *Dear World*, it seems plausible that they are the most conservative, realistic, and prudent of the crew. It would follow that Hamilton is going for the most innovative style segment – and we have to keep our antennae switched on to check if this style, which is new as the time is new, is the style of the time – the music we will identify with the period when looking back in 20 years' time. Is it then typical of the time (i.e. of a thousand other young poets not inside its covers) or rather a signature of the era – but atypical?

Hamilton defines a *product*-based aesthetic which is largely reaching a preset level of finish which is marketable and which the public is supposed to recognise. In contrast – "After that let's say 'Process' is the approach that instead enjoys nonsequitur surprises aimed at high-lighting formal relationships between words. Fundamentally uncertain about the reliability of the self as organising principle, it is concerned with poetry as a way of speaking about the world that simultaneously presents the difficulties of doing so. It feels suspicion towards, or attempts to make strange, subject-object correlatives. Rather than represent a self-contained thought, it enacts the poem's or poet's own processes; highlights or ironises these processes, or the thinking that produces the poem-text. So 'Product' seeks to build in mimesis while 'Process' seeks to enact in and through language. Product would understand realism as representing the physical world through verisimilitude in 'good language' or 'the best words in the best order'. Process would define realism as a textual performance of the drama of language, self and world." This distinction seems to me to be 40 or 45 years old, not indicative for 2010-13.

Out of thirteen poets in *Better Than Language* (Chris Goode's anthology, named for another line by Jonty Tiplady), five make an appearance in *Dear World*. This makes things clearer. Goode's anthology is connected to the main institutional corpus of the avant-garde or Underground – these are poets who can write their own footnotes, to put it uncynically. This would imply that Hamilton also is hearing that avant-garde music. It is remarkable that this book should come out from Bloodaxe, known as a conservative and anti-innovative shop. But things can change, and Bloodaxe may now be trading up their retail success into rather higher standards of quality.

I also feel that *Dear World* is the great anthology, the one which is worth arguing about at length. It has a momentum which lifts the reader into a heightened state of insight and which acts as a bright light that flashes through to the structure of apparently difficult poems. After a point, it is hard not to feel part of it. At the least, the contributions from Nat Raha, Katharine Kilalea, Chris McCabe, Kate Potts, Toby Martinez de las Rivas, Mendoza, Oli Hazzard, Marianne Morris, Emily Critchley, Heather Phillipson, Rachael Allen, are important poetry and demand a rewriting of the map. I thought to define the new sound, even though the various poets in the book are so different, because I can't describe 72 poets individually.

Was this Sound around in say 1995 or is it literally new in three or four years leading up to 2013 and the editor's deadline for collecting poems? I think that Emily Critchley's pamphlet *How to Make Millions* (2005) was a breakthrough into a new stylistic world, but I am not sure it arrived in a vacuum. I think the situation is more that there had been failed runs at the new sound earlier on, maybe in 2000 or even just tipping into the '90s, but Critchley actually heard it clearly and could put it in tune.

As Joe points out, the idea of absorbing pop is basic. To produce poems that you could set beside pop records and which wouldn't seem inhibited, complacent about educational capital, pinned down by objectivity, hostile to the reader's desires and willing to be the manager rather than participate in the fun. Perceiving the last 50 years of poetry as one long failure to compete with pop music, with sorties into dumbing down and political righteousness being no more than convulsions which made the trap more secure. Reacting, finally, a bit late, to the realisation of how smart pop musicians are in manipulating shared forms. Taking in, also, at least thirty years in which pop music had been intelligent, escaping the limits of folk music and Tin Pan Alley, and when reflexivity had leaked into what had once, a long time ago, been rural and even non-professional dance music. Pop songs have an amazing lack of information, but what they do have is the idea of being carried away, not by rational proofs but by a feeling, visible in fragments of language which are instantly persuasive and involving.

The new environment favours an emphasis on texture. Complexity can't be delivered by accumulation because that means that the good stuff punches the button after say fifty pages of build-up. You may have fabulous levels of information but you can't make that work by writing very long and concomitantly slow poems. Instead you have to mutate the texture. This goes live instantly even if the first reaction may be incomprehension. This texture is like a still from a film – if the film produces great stills, it is credible that it is a great film. These poets are very good at producing exciting textures. Some examples:

Souvenirs of the millennium shrouded with dark linen. They gathered together with anatomy transparent. They spoke with coarse voices, conversed with anaemic lips. They listened with elastic lobes stretched by heavy silver earrings for many years plaiting otherworldly tête-à-têtes about the heat that flooded those late summer city afternoons. That brimmed over the rims of porcelain. They predicted one everlasting summer storm, they said it was on its way. Then their words die away into quiet murmurs about lichthofs and enormous fire walls exposed vertically to the world. Silhouettes of ghost trams, their unostentatious midnight apparitions every winter clad in a thousand silver light-bulbs. But these tête-à-têtes weave the vegetation of the world, you decided.

(Ágnes Lehóczky, from 'Rememberer', originally published in *Rememberer*, Norwich: Egg Box Publishing, 2011)

(*Lichthof* is a large room lit from a glass roof and without windows.)

The sky is threaded with tree limbs
and electric lines
and the cross hatch detail of cranes,
train lines and more trees.
The direction of each thing bleeds into the direction of another thing,
making the directions subjective and laughable.
This a metaphor for purpose, which is

<surely all of those things>.
(Marianne Morris, from 'Who Not to Speak to')

We make up for it by making things up, spilling our adventures to anyone who'll listen. Some share life, like two unequal halves of a Chelsea Bun, with a stranger. Some release the sugared non-half into the mouth of a stranger. Some realise the unequal-half-fiddle once the sugar's all swallowed by a mouth that won't be around forever. The inventions of the back workshop may be the high-spot along the damp bricks of years, Claire would deduce, if Claire could be here.

(Heather Phillipson, from 'Although You Do Not Know Me, My Name is Patricia'; since republished in *Instant-fLex 718*. Tarset: Bloodaxe Books, 2013)

It is 1968 and there's the woman before my mother
behind that flimsy bank glass. She is called Miss Heather
and is a delicately translucent clerk, rinsed out but luminous
with hope. One work evening, dating, you are to take her
to that forest of satellites, where the future ideas of us are
        mocking you
from behind whacked-out nuclear trees.
        (Rachael Allen, from 'Goonhilly', since republished in
            revised form in *Faber New Poets 9*, London: Faber
            & Faber, 2014)

He was one of the last when the talents
were handed out – skulking as usual, purple fist clenched and
    held low.

The other gods jostled and elbowed for their powers:
muscular flight, velveteen invisibility, the whittled cogs and
    pulleys

of super-strength. His own gift was small,
misshapen like a dried-up bean, a dulled skin-curl of tan
    leather.

He held it to his ear and heard – death rattle,
a distant meddling of breeze in grass, grating of worn and
    hollowed bones.

He cupped it always – little, ugly pod – in his broad palm, in his
    pocket.
Nothing, it seemed, transpired. The other gods tautened,

grew luminous [.]
        (Kate Potts, from 'The Runt', originally published in *Pure
            Hustle*, Tarset: Bloodaxe Books, 2011.)

There was a wave of reviews. Peter Riley produced a review (in *Fortnightly Review*) in passive-aggressive style. He writes as if the arrival of new writers and new readers were a scheme of some evil and calculated ideology rather than an organic and biological process. He seems to feel that it can't be genuinely new if it hasn't got the old poets in it to supervise. He does not have new reactions and is willing to conclude that the poetry also is not new. He talks about 'clearing space' as the purpose of the introduction as if he were being physically cleared out of the way to make space for these young poets. But linguistic space is free – as much as you create, it's never exhausted. The book is an abundance – the space isn't suddenly going to run out and arrest the poem. The artistic space will give you as much as you have time to take. The labour of writing has become much less important because this is an era of cheap information. The poem is being fed by the flows and so is easy. We don't have to be grateful because someone highly educated has condescended to write us a poem which is actually tedious and which we are vaguely guilty about not liking. Maybe that condescension belonged to a time when there were only a few thousand graduates and so being a graduate actually did make you Important, which stopped being true around 1960.

This poetry is anti-didactic and yet open to torrents of information. The information, the vital flow of the poem for obvious reasons, avoids didacticism by being overtly anti-realistic. The literati gave up ideology. But still wanted to own documentary and enlightenment as bulwarks against ideology. They still retain authority. There is a logical next step in which they give up that too, and become scatterbrained and aesthetic. Why should poets be exact witnesses sifting through everything for the truth? Isn't that a claim to superior lucidity, another claim to social authority, to unnatural influence over legislation and government decisions?

Authenticity might be a feather-like lightness rather than slowness and stubbornness and resistance.

Rawnsley's book about the declining years of the 1997-2010 Labour administration says that Gordon Brown prepared decisions very thoroughly but as prime minister was making them ten times too slowly. He wanted to wait for the facts and for proper research. In the meantime, he wasn't making decisions. Certainty would only arrive late in the cycle, when the possibilities had disappeared. Certainty was indeed the mortality of possibilities and ways out. Blair took decisions at the right speed. He had a low guilt quotient and limited interest in the long term: but he was the star prime minister; Brown couldn't actually do the job very well. One version of the older poetry is that it only dealt with long-term positions – the moral stances which poets spent too much effort digging and occupying. This implied that there was no present moment ever – every moment of poetry was the demonstration of the permanent and theologically grounded rigour of the poet. The poet was passing an audition to be a bishop, or a commissar, or something. This left free a whole realm of sensations, ideas, states of mind, etc. which were short-term. The new thing has a different sense of time. It seems that older critics have a detection apparatus which just isn't rapid enough to pick up the new poetry. The new poets have discovered a whole spectrum of missing sensibility in the keys of fluffy, harlequin, unassimilated, pastel, pop, beachwear, ornamental, babbling, uncoded, scatty. As an aside, the recording may be finding human character in fine details of muscular activity, delicate facial gestures, verbal quirks, all transient and low-energy patterns. This is where the personality is found – different from either heroism or moral-ideological commitment, long-term and high-volume. (Or even visionary flights – which can be interpreted as akin to sequences of ideology.) In this space of short time intervals, the poets are attuned to social and emotional possibilities which exist briefly, and are not going off-line to ponder all the implications. This means being emotionally available to other people. It means the abandonment of power over the situation. This condition, considered as something that vanished but keeps recurring, can be considered as the new sound of lyricism, the music of lyric poetry once you move out of post-Renaissance conventions. This is the **second naivety** and it exhibits **scatterbrained authenticity**.

The recent evolution of the internet as a vehicle for 'social media sites' may be a breakthrough, a new form of intimate speech that affects self-consciousness. It soaks into the core, the melody and the prosody, and it then spills over into poetry as an utterance of inner speech. The web forum links are selective and allow you to become much more specialised. It is less like social contact being a levelling or normalising influence and more like a projection of inner impulses that reinforces and exaggerates them, so that the poetry scene breaks up into myriad spatters getting faster and lighter as they hurtle away from all the other spatters. The poetry is committed to social life. It possesses *non-narcissistic intimacy*, the idea of a self-made world from which the poet rarely gazes out on the real world outside has been sidelined or got rid of. The element of subjectivity is social rather than 'owned' and this may be to do with the prevalence of the Internet of which one form is a mighty sharing of transient and subjective feelings. Where it presents autobiographical material this does not show 'personality conquering and shaping experience' but the reverse, a self which is involved in fluid situations shaped by other strong personalities, by improvisation, by unexpected and unanswerable events, by chance and inattention.

The group feeling is new, disembodied but the home of language. The poets are writing less as individuals than before, more as participants in an intimate group reality which is the home for very developed kinds of speech. The 'inner' has got larger and louder and the 'outer' has faded away, jammed by an excess of data. The poems are reproducing group feeling rather than a personality. The specialised textures may  be a reflection of this level of existence, and a shift away from accurate autobiographical narrative, which seems to be in decline. This shift makes it radically easier for the reader to participate in the poem. The group feeling is just more available for participation than the system in which a poem reflects a personality. The more personal the poem, the less the reader's personality is reflected in it. This version of texture gets ever closer to a game, one many people can participate in. The move away from hard experience – experience as a possession, experience as an anatomical part of the self – gives the poem ever greater qualities of spontaneity, of openness to being taken over by the reader, of repeatability. Some of these poets are thinking about writing programs to generate programs rather than just running programs to generate poems.

The new time sense explores states of mind which you can call scatterbrained and dizzy. Anyway, the new poets are not demonstrating their knowledge or qualifying to be managers or disproving anyone's ideology. This is a kind of figure-ground reversal where the unconscious (of short-term, feather-light, alluring, sensations) subverts and replaces the conscious structure of principles and inhibitions. So the rule of what segments a poem from the life of language in general, is no longer selecting the permanent (weighty, rigid, predictable?), but may be selecting what is light enough to fly. So with Marianne Morris the key adjective is dizzy. Her poems are going into areas of life which are unstable and uncertain, and which it is reasonable to think involve the whole resources of the mind – instant and all-over reactions. Her poems deliberately avoid certainties because the point is to get to the live tissue, the line of pure now, and to lure the mind out of its comfort zone. This is not naivety but a program to push the self into a zone where all its intelligence is needed. The unmediated present is not easy to find but the rule underlying many of these poems is to get to that zone and stay there.

One moment in Luna's blog is where he is talking about Chris Goode's website:

> One massively good thing on the internet has recently come to an end, but thankfully remains stuck to the lining of the contra-sphere like the best gob of virtual love-juice ever spat into the system, and that is, of course, Chris Goode's blog. Chris's blog has consistently provided some of the most passionate and believably truthful soliloquies, mix-tapes and pornography ever channelled through Blogger's succulent tubes[.]
> (retrieved from http://fallopianyoutube.blogspot.co.uk/ 2012/01/neutral-facial-expression-internets.html)

What struck me was that triple structure: *soliloquies… mix-tapes… and pornography*. It's as if the first two words weren't exciting enough on their own. This is an AB! structure because the third element doesn't belong with the others. It is there to signal "Hey! we are so uninhibited! We are not academic in any way!" I doubt that Goode's blog has any pornography – the third element swerves off into gaga territory because to be objective and accurate is already too old-fashioned. The Internet has been constructed around play – its ambience incites people to show that they are playful. That triple structure incorporates a sugar rush, of melting out of rigidity and discipline. The promise of being free from any inhibitions reflects the wishes of a young generation which is not much impressed by their elders, at the same time as reflecting the institutional or technical fact that blogs have no editors and no committees, so that writers can get stuff out which an editor would demand to be organised more carefully. The 'mix-tape' is a cassette-era personal tape of favourite pieces of music – foregrounding the non-musician as promoter of cultural consumption and of shared pleasure, at the same time of course as bypassing control, the 'party tape' is something you don't have to pay for. (I don't see how a mix-tape can be either believable or truthful, or untruthful, this is just froufrou.) One step beyond is the idea that the poem or book of poems is going to be like a mix tape, a sequencing of fabulous and unheard of and super-vivid sensations and textures which the poet and reader share, and which emphatically has the boring bits taken out. Why should the poet go on investing boring and old-fashioned skilled labour in building poems inch by inch when you can capture data online, as 'screen grabs', and so on, and sequence them in a rush of amusing and catastrophic juxtapositions?

The fear of inhibition leads someone to pursue the text to its ultimate stage, to the brink of excess and beyond, or to offer to make that pursuit. The Internet makes people scared of appearing rigid and of holding back on delivering less than everything.

The 'screen grab' approach is a source of radically distinctive textures. Of course the sample might be more interesting than you are – this is definitely a way of losing. The sampling thing got big in the 1980s (Cold Cut's remix of 'Paid in Full', date 1987) and poets have had a long time to get intimate with the problems and to practice tilting or tinting the captured data, how to make the juncture between two contexts work, how to master the silent art of framing. The poets in *Dear World* are very, very good at this stuff. This stream of activity has had a confluence with the avant-garde stream of capturing and recontextualising source texts as part of a political and art-political programme.

Tiplady's poem 'Eskimo Porn Belt' seems to be quite literally a poem about sex. There is no anatomical detail – it functions in the layers of meaning which basic anatomy bashes into and cuts out. It is pretty determined and pretty sensual though. The pleasure to be drawn from it has various limits – I didn't want to join in so I felt detached. I think Barry White records suffer from the same limitation, he did sell a lot of them though:

> Like little spanners rising and shining, like the rat, like don't do what Donny does, like Jimmy does it, like Miles does it, like ants are back in, like I wear swastika pants, on the stars on the floor, like I wear orange and red fur, like switch, like you fucking chess fag, like spring in my anus, like summer in yours, like sleepy animals that don't make phone calls, like Buffo only emerged when you stopped sex and gooed her back together [...]

Is this about someone imagining you to be Donny Osmond (OR you imagine *yourself* to be Donny?) while making love? Channelling

Donny? *Get Donny on me baby?* Don't tell me. The implication of seeing the act of making love as like a karaoke performance (full of hyperbolic, drunken, essentially tacky gestures, and yet mythical and splendid) is largely unacceptable.

Dear World is so brilliant that I possibly have to warn against being hypnotised by it. We should remember that the individual poets have an existence outside the magical and monumental context of the anthology, and that there are good poets who are not in it. While Hamilton does not give a 'product description' for his book, it is clear that his poets were, largely, born in the 1980s, and (to repeat) that it is much more original than *Identity Parade*. But, of all the anthologies I have just read, *Dear World* is the magnetic one, an awesome synthesis of a scattered and mutinous data plot which creates a total present which we can all go and live inside and which everyone has to work out their relationship to.

Hamilton says that some people think there are divisions but not a spectrum. Is there a spectrum? I would like to imagine a magnificent sweep of poets standing in a line on some chalk hillside with Prynne at one end and Sean O'Brien at the other. I can find the ends but it is difficult to fill all the niches in between. This is a one-dimensional division but you could post poets on 10 or 20 different spectra according to line length, level of parataxis, political commitment, originality, etc. I do not think these postings would all give the same results. The spectrum can be imagined easily but it may not be very helpful. If poets form in clusters then they aren't formed up in a spectrum. It would be good to have a weekend school where we took huge amounts of coloured Lego pieces and built a model which displayed 240 poets in the right relative positions.

I suspect that there is a division between O'Brien and Prynne even if there are some poets intermediate between them. Oppositions? Surely the scene includes differentiation, contradiction, protest, and in this way is structured by division. The kinetic energy of swarming hatred for Andrew Motion (for instance) is surely one of the great fuel sources of modern poetry. A certain amount of poetry is still 'denial of what poetry X asserts'.

THIRD STREAM

Another formative historical moment, barely within our period, is the collapse of The Movement, which had formed a hegemony in official English poetry between the 1950s and some point in the 1980s. Most of the poetry being read, indeed, belonged to other affiliations, but the mixture of formalism and domestic anecdote had authority from being linked to so many critics and academics. It summed up educated values in a certain period; the migration of the academic elite onward to a different set of values, no longer anti-consumerist, more 'post modernist', hedonistic, theory-oriented, pluralist, has been important for poetry. I suspect the poets who graduated in the 1950s are little read today.

As we count 240 new poets across these eight anthologies, it is obvious that there is a Poetry Boom. My impression is that the scene has been dominated, *generally since the early '90s,* by new figures who have little experience of the scene. This accounts for their enthusiasm, it also puts into question the relevance of the recent past. If you don't know what the shared past is, you don't share it – and the historian dragging that past up may be finding patterns that *aren't there.* What the poets share is knowledge of pop culture, the Internet, and, mostly, exposure to university culture as found in Humanities departments. They don't have a shared understanding of modern poetry – the thing they are writing.

Lumsden is keen on poets "on the cusp between conventional and innovative", and perhaps a score of poets in *Identity Parade* show a new way of emerging into a linguistic future. We could call this 'homely-modern' or 'artisanal-modern'. In the 1980s, the work of producing poetry which was highly intelligent and yet had an organic feeling and psychological continuity was carried out to a very high degree by poets like Frank Kuppner, Ian Duhig, and John Hartley Williams. Maybe this was the big thing that happened in the '80s, if hidden by more noisy processes. Rather than the intellectual Underground taking over, or disappearing, what we see here is a 'midstream' of poets who have absorbed modernist furore but deploy it in much more palatable terms. This is a grand theory but there are other story lines running.

The main thing I came away from this campaign with is Clare Pollard as an absolute star. The extreme risk-taking of her poetry as totally personal freezes out as extreme vividness by dint of being quite astonishingly inventive and sustained. The fundamental proposal that the poem represents a brief but dizzying exchange of your ego for the ego of the writer, seeing through their eyes and feeling through their skin, is proven to be most successful when the writer reacts so intensely and has the power, apparently, to articulate everything. Even when writing about politics, this approach comes off brilliantly, because the primary intensity of identification with a pair of eyes turns out to be the doorway to experiencing political problems directly and coherently, with a sense of community being demonstrated by this identification, as its most basic and predictive unit. Pollard's poems represent the vividness of the mainstream poem as a theoretical truth in the face of however many other poets whose minds are duller and who are merely self-centred.

Lesley Saunders deals in each poem of *Cloud Camera* (2012) with a moment of scientific or technological history, and the phase of intense absorption by a human subject which is offered as the zone for very closely shared attention by us, as readers, is the specialized knowledge. That is, the poet is making a bet on shared attention, empathy; but supporting this by pushing the human subject into a zone of high alertness and intellectual exertion. Simultaneously, the poem summons up empathy and presents a high information flow. This is a good bet, I think, a strong concept. The fact that Saunders has composed sixty poems all using this concept is quite extraordinary, this is where she goes beyond what rivals could manage and even beyond what seems possible. I suppose the lesson is that if you want to write poems about the history of science you need a good knowledge of the history of science. Information is the fuel. Anyway, the range and vividness of these poems are a wonderful thing. The poems are very lucid and we are allowed to think here of the third stream, a poetry which is neither underground nor mainstream and is not vitiated by an inherited ideology of style.

> They experimented on themselves, no longer believing
> in god's perfect-circle certitudes. Not knowing limits,
> they had to invent them – what the terrestrial body can stand,
> at what point the mind turns itself inside out. Those heads,
>
> those shrunken leathers shovelled up from peat-bogs, rotting,
> are they theirs, that we looked on with awe and revulsion?

Was it from these we got the base metals of our earth, the art
of working them, the propagation of root-cuttings, or the beautifying

of the eyelids, the classification of clouds, not to be unlearned now?

(from 'The Fallen Angels', from *Cloud Camera*, Reading:
Two Rivers Press, 2011)

Post-modern is not the dominant sound of the time. Actually it seems to
work out that a post-modern manner is only available to an elite – it is
difficult and risky. The vast majority of the poets on view do not attempt
this style or array of devices. Various attempts to isolate the sound of
today have failed because in reality the centralising mechanisms have
failed and the scene is extremely diverse. There is some confusion about
what this means for a text. Because the landscape of 200 (or 1,000?)
poets is diverse does not mean that the volume written by one poet is
diverse or surprising.

Some people who wrote about the 'post-modern' thing presented it
as a way of eliminating almost every writer and of qualifying the 'really
significant' ones. Thus it could not be the typical style of the times,
because its 'price-setting' function was to qualify an elite in whom
capital could be invested. This pattern is not unique, there are maybe
a dozen other mechanisms for identifying winners. I want to show this
mechanism briefly, because it is old-fashioned even though the sheer
volume of young poets available means that every critic wants to get
most of them off the stage. The point of finding winners is also that the
winning critic is defined as the one who invests in the winning poets.

EPIPHANY AND VOICELESSNESS

In the film *Gravity* there is a point where the 'mission specialist' Dr Ryan Stone, is alone in the fuelless re-entry module, having accepted the certainty of death. Then she sees and hears the mission commander, Matthew Kowalski, who she knows to be dead, kick open the hatch, enter, and explain to her that she can use the fuel designed for deceleration against gravity prior to landing as a source of thrust and save her life. This idea does save her life. Because she recently had a prolonged episode of hypoxia during which Kowalski's voice was in her headset the entire time and he was offering technical ideas, an idea of hers voiced itself in her mind as an apparition of Kowalski. Such apparitions are recognised, if rare, and tend to happen in moments of physical and psychological strain. They may form a real substrate for the stories of meeting a non-human being-god, nymph, angel – which feature in surviving mediaeval and Classical literature. The beings often have a message to deliver. (Often, they leave an object behind which then supports the story.) 'Epiphany' is a Greek word for the *appearance of a god* which appears in the New Testament to describe the appearance of the Angel to Mary. It is quite common earlier, in Hellenistic times, when someone compiled a 'catalogue of epiphanies'. The Marxists liked to use that word in the context of 'this poem claims to be the product of an epiphany and I can barge in from my position of ineffable superiority and kick the poem to bits by sneering at its source'. Since the Renaissance, most artists have not seen their creativity as the product of divine intervention, so the word is not correctly applied in modern times. But poems do come from somewhere.

Much of 'theory' was by origin arguments in favour of communism and against the media consensus of the Cold War. As more information about conditions under the Soviet Union leaked out into common knowledge, ever more ingenious ways were found of shifting the argument to where it did not have to be lost. There was a collective Freudian denial of the evidence of dictatorship, militarism, loss of liberty, mass incarceration, in the Soviet world. It was a protective fantasy on a global scale. All the same this meant a certain creativity. The most systematic treatments of modern poetry in Britain have been Marxist. Christopher Caudwell, Jack Lindsay, George Thomson, all wrote memorable and dazzlingly wide-ranging interpretations of poetry and society. The 'bourgeois' writers could not produce anything so global, so symmetrical. Or so totalitarian, I have to add.

We will mention John Berger in discussing the 'nonist' Andrew Jordan. Berger, one of Uncle Joe's last nephews, was an influential art journalist in the 1950s and his famous TV series was broadcast in 1967. Is he really relevant to poets and readers in 1995 or 2005?

Blocking out the subjective views of readers or citizens offers the idea of experiencing 'social process' *objectively*, through a hundred different minds at once. Apparently there is a 'blank space' where individual feelings are cancelled out, or there is a 'gathered' view which is everyone's feelings at once. I think this is totally suspect. It may be the goal but no one has ever got there. The main concrete result is that you invalidate individual feelings. You can eliminate bits of the spectrum but that doesn't get you close to seeing the whole of it. You can't be a hundred people at once. Having a bookshop with a thousand different books in it is OK but having a bookshop with only one book but expecting that everyone read that book is not OK at all. Close attention is not compatible with reckless subversion. Poetry in this era is primarily egocentric and subjective. It lives in the realm of intimacy. Poetry strengthens the self, the ego-illusion if you like. Discarding individual experience crushes this poetry to bits in the first moment. My goal here is not to open a door onto the whole spectrum of human experiences but to give familiarity with contemporary poetry, which is virtually unknown. So we are going back to a singular subject.

The nightmare for poets is that the information unique to their poetry will be crushed and thrown away as 'atypical', while what is 'common knowledge' is consumed from prose and television and appears in their poetry too late.

The poets never used the word epiphany – the attack was on something that didn't exist. Their repetitive dishonesty was one reason why the Marxists became so unpopular. Yet some prestige still attaches to this genuinely vile and arrogant form of behaviour. It is as if we feel adult when demolishing a feeling of closeness to the essential and feel good when we are saying yes to exactly that feeling.

To find modern poetry we need keywords like *insight, empathy, creativity, symbolic utterance, every fact transforming into idea, complex associations, aura, sensitivity, idealism, clarity of pattern, imagination, breakthrough, myth*, sight of *greater wholes*. Meeting a god? We would think rather of moments when the brain is working in a different way, where more rapid and richer associations breach into sight, and perception of new and intense patterns breaks out of tired and frustrating routines. A modern poem is expected to deliver such powerful and new insights and associations. The threshold for detecting new patterns is lowered. The share of 'knowable things' that fit smoothly into a pattern goes up. The silent rules of poetic style have as their latent purpose to bring about these states of mind, through intuitive identification.

Scotland is to the north of England. Norway is at the edge of the North Sea. Holland is at the mouth of the great rivers. Modern poetry is *here*, where what prevails is intuitive identification and belief in the gifts of individuals able to reach higher ground. It is wholly based on a belief in individuals and on attraction to them. That is where it is. The fact that the dominant style of theory rejects intuitive identification is a problem. That theory prevents you from reading contemporary poetry (and regards contemporary poetry as bad data).

The idea of some commissar striding in and demolishing this state of mind, ridiculing the patterns it makes visible, is not altogether pleasant. More pleasant is the idea of writing poems that mediate these zones of experience. Rejecting the knowledge that is brought back from these journeys is problematic. It is the stake that you win if you win the game. But it seems likely that the Marxist type wants to refute this knowledge because it competes with their rigid schemas and also they want people to be unhappy so that they can be recruited to overthrow society. *You aren't being unhappy enough. Be more unhappy by next week.*

I feel that the radical rejection of the insight of the artist, which Berger put over so glibly, is still a presence on the scene, through whatever channels. Jordan's work has at its core a satire on moments of intense insight concerned with feelings about landscape, about social continuity, and about the deep past as recovered – evanescently – through archaeological finds. This kind of egoism has led to interpretations of archaeological data which are now widely accepted to be mistakes. If Marxism solidly sticks it to individual egoism, and the projection of the self and its insubstantial interests is the main source of errors in the study of human culture, then Marxism is going to be proved right time after time and will persist as an entity even if it has abandoned the working class, liberation, Stalin, Marx, and so forth. There is another reason for looking at it. Just possibly this rather abstract mode of rejection of the great show of an artist reflects and represents a more intuitive rejection by the mass of readers. Is it not true that most poets *fail* to achieve aura, grace, veneration, or credibility? They want to be liked but most of them aren't likeable. They offer their precious insights and we discard them – taking their states of enhanced perceptiveness as phoney. Everybody wants that enrichment but mostly it isn't there. So maybe the criticisms the Marxist bosses were announcing are similar, with whatever distortions, to the real reasons why poems fail to achieve conviction or autonomy.

You reach that enriched psychological state and when you speak from it people hear it as a rush of higher truths. That is the goal but the norm is *failure*. Originality of language is the accepted sign of individuality but most published poetry has no linguistic originality.

Whatever we don't know about empathy, we know that it is domestic and developed in the Stone Age. Because it is the central thing with poetry, the critique of empathy is an important task to carry out. Empathy can also be soft authoritarianism, where someone imagines your state of mind but does that inaccurately and misrepresents you. Without powers of imagination, empathy gives an inaccurate result. Someone conventional will imagine you with all the unconventional parts of you silenced, blocked, nihilated. In this case empathy is a way of neutralising someone's voice. There is an idea of poetry as where empathy stops being repressive and becomes receptive; but to a conventional person everything sounds the same. This is where the idea of the 'mainstream' comes into conversation.

I suspect that one impact of a greater female influence in the scene is the decreasing fashionability of alienation. Women are more sociable and less interested in going underground. The chatter of the times, the media babble, is trying to tell me that feminism is demolishing poetry written by men in general. This would be a modern re-run of John Berger. I am not convinced this is actually happening. Was there an exchange whereby feminism in 1985 to 2013 occupied the premises previously tenanted by the Marxists and their progressive critique, while the Marxists moved out (and disappeared)? It seems unlikely to me – the geography has changed rather than just exchanging tenants. I feel that that position of superiority with respect to the social order and its cultural institutions, combined with alienation, burning resentment and a cold inability to identify with popular cultural expression, a position which was so prominent in Britain between (say) 1930 and 1984, has become less fashionable. It was never popular and never occupied a position of dominance in the small world of poetry.

I believe that the poetry boom was partly caused by the collapse of both cultural Marxists and of the neo-con perimeter guards who made culture over into a war to defend capitalism. The quality of the era may be the absence of something – of ideological warfare.

It is important to know that some poetry excludes empathy – even if the result is like treating a radio so that it can't receive signals any more.

DIFFICULT TEXTS

the/ sorry/ pence/ that/ illiberally/ squandered
dropped/its/ pocket/ ran/away/ as
lead/ under/ a/ blowtorch/ newly/ minted
to/ another's/ purse/ it/ will/ find
new/ companies/ there/ new/ satisfactions/ new
redress/ and/ accounted / for/ again/ may
courier/ forth/ the/ best/ intentions/ these

---

are/ capable/ of/ sodium/ burns/ on
contact/ with/ water/ caesium/ violently/ explodes
this/ drop/ of/ nickel-brass/ is/ no
different/ but/ fires/ the/ glutted/ heart
of/ a/ fortress/ all/ the/ paper
burning/ in/ sequence/ one/ little/ spark
carrying/ its/ flame/ to/ the/ next

(Piers Hugill, section 6.1 of 'Il Canzoniere' in the volume *Shuddered*)

The moment when everything was
washed into the Thames
inside a filthy refrigerator. A poor guy
staring at the blurred, little faces,

upper-class women in the black winter
if silence crumbling away like the heavy
upper-class women in the black winter
with glued-on cloth, painted black. The

of rooks and jackdaws following the
revolutionary policy committee, a
shorter rectangle, two rectangles next
a rocky patch. The furore over the taxa-

reflections, the swamp water and ice,
shorter rectangle, two rectangles next
And here we finally break through
through the ice with an axe, a man

(Antony John, from *now than it used to be, but in the past* at p.23)

You don't have to like this poetry. But I am offering it because I wanted to show something which doesn't respect the silent rules of contemporary poetry, and which also shows what the rules are, by breaking them. I see variation in form as restricted by respecting anatomy: everything which produces a personality has to accommodate itself to the inherited form of a person. The parts fit together in a preset way and if you try to redesign that the reader will *restore* the data to the preset form. Most of the data space remains empty. Outside that is a *viral* realm where the form of a poem covers the entire space of possibilities because it is not regressing to an organic form. It has no organs and its shape is not stable. Even, it is not functional, it varies uncontrollably.

A spectrum is a wonderfully simple notion because it finds a single variable which all the data objects possess. This is inadequate for a viral realm. The faithful elements of comparison are missing. The variation is too total to yield a spectrum where differences follow a simple pattern.

It is fair to add that in the original of *now than it used to be* the master copy was visibly made up of clipped-out lines of print from some source. Some pages of the book have three texts side by side. It consists of fifty-five A4 pages. Some entire stanzas are repeated.

Hugill's poem has a subtitle 'after Adrian Clarke', so it may take its method from 'translations' by Adrian Clarke, an Italian-speaker who has translated European poetry, in a very radical way. A *canzoniere* is a rather nineteenth-century word for collections of poems by mediaeval poets, which at a basically oral stage of culture would not usually have been collected in the poet's lifetime. *Canzone* is 'song'.

The following passage is from a poem by Rob Holloway:

Called them Fisher-Price dog toys
a twice-preferred second method
how loud plastic cracks in the gallery space
dreaming of instantaneous civilian transport
call it street fighting for distressed features "if
cut watermelons shine take
        these guards" its walls
        splintered muster
        exceptional insects
        walk with us
        rubbing their
        red legs rimmed

by a once-English
riddle for
glass music.

A porcelain boat, a military bowl
ran aground and limbic-lobed
will sniff and dig. Red
hot after sex, rearrange the cell
membranes switch
memory leave beggars feeding worms
to within seconds of the well-licked King.

(Rob Holloway, from 'The Concrete Float' in *Permit*, 2009. This
    is one page of a twelve-page poem.)

This seems to be a 'gateway' passage – it opens a way out of familiar patterns of perception but is not channelling the reader into a preset 'new' pattern. Instead it is a gate to an uncoded area – where the reader can choose their own route of travel. The one recognisable moment of intent is "well-licked" which is probably a variant of 'well-liked'. The couplet possibly goes back to a 'traditional' topos on the lines of 'beggars and kings are both eaten by worms in the end', I can't recall the source.

The quoted poems share a voicelessness. The cultural landscape has everywhere a flow of language, like background music, interpreting everything and usually asking us to make a purchase. Everything is personalised even where the application of a human face is clearly disguising what is really happening. The temptation to shut the voice off and recover a landscape before language is just overwhelming. Poetry is mainly pouring a comforting voice over everything, but some poetry is actively doing the *opposite*. We can only carry out an act of understanding of something that is not already understood.

I don't want to pour my voice out at this point, to leave the poems in a rationalised and consumed condition. Perhaps though we can reconstruct some of the reasons for the composition. Take the theme of 'stripping out teleology'. By 'teleology' we mean the doctrine that a process (history, for example), has a purpose (*telos*). This is an example of a fallacy: if someone thinks that the purpose of history was to lead up to the Russian Revolution (or to the victory of Nixon in 1968) then it is a fallacy and the role of critical thought is to unmask it and to unweave all the patterns made in verbal creations by someone following this false reasoning. In poetry, teleology is, or can be, the patterns imposed by the ego on the material of the world which becomes the material of the poem. Thus someone who uses nature as a metaphor for their feelings may be subduing birds, trees, etc. to a purpose – of which the birds and trees are unaware, and which is valid primarily from the point of view of one human ego. So there was a project undertaken by the avant-garde in the 1960s of taking found texts and stripping out all the teleology. The logical end goal was a surface of zero teleology. This was a competitive process and so we can say that Holloway has produced a text which has won the game or at least produced a creditable score.

Another game that all three passages win is about predictability. Check it out – given lines 1 to 8 you really can't predict line 9 and given lines 1 to 6 you really can't predict lines 7 to 9. Objectively, these poems win this game. If you apply a secondary rule that a poem has to be coherent as well, the point score is not so good.

As an overall concept we would have 'scraps which have been reduced to a minimal but integral state and which are presented as the raw material of cognitive or behaviour patterns which haven't been invented yet'. It isn't quite right to call them "meaningless" – rather, the proposal is primary units which can perfectly well be organised into a meaning. If we walk through a town, all the things or people or bits of speech we pass are not meaningful but they are the contents of daily awareness. This can't be so difficult in a poem if it is what we experience as we walk into town. Indeed, it could well be that we could take a conventional poem, knock out all the connectives, and end up with a string of isolated sensations (objects, etc.) which would resemble 'Concrete Float'.

Critics tend to search for patterns in poetry because there is a feeling of frustration if none is found. But a poet may not be offering finished patterns. Someone may be happy to offer sensations that haven't been sorted and stored and neutralized, and distrust the other kind. Simply a belief that the consensus is politically repressive and has blanked out important problems and possibilities which are growing increasingly urgent could lead you to that position. The design is of course not explicit in the text that we have bought – but if you look at the text thinking that the writer has that feeling, you *might* find that the text rolls well. The problem here would be looking for a 'finished' pattern and being unhappy until you found it. The poet has made up the rules by which the poem is generated. They have a purpose and so do fail any test that would show them as *arbitrary*. You have to guess what the rules are but you can prove your guess right as you go on reading. They are secret if you fail to guess them. There is no negotiation between you and the poet because he is only going to make the same bid over and over.

Permits may be 'generated' by a set of time limits – the allowances of the title where Rob Holloway found material from media stories, the Net, etc. within predefined and tight time limits and then cut them up and assembled them into texts – also under restrictions, possibly of time or possibly based on chance. There is no documentation of this in the book but Rob explained them at some readings which I attended. Watching the generation process (almost as a layer of the text) is like watching film of musicians playing. Seeing the effort and the success can make you identify and so get closer to the music or the text.

These texts are high on spontaneity. This is something else they win at. They are low on being beholden to outside agencies and bodies of propositions – and win at that. They assert nothing that they have to defend.

These poets are constitutively not epiphanic. They are not claiming intense insight brought back from exalted states of consciousness. They believe in Process, which functionally replaces the personality (along with personal experience, a personal verbal style) as the device which generates text. But what would a Marxist make of all this? Claims to unique and particular understanding of culture and social relations, reached by experimentation. Sited in a tiny and self-selected group, without submission to Party textbooks or to collective and inherited art forms. They would accuse these poets of believing in epiphany, just as they accuse everyone else of doing that.

The people who read modern poetry believe in the creative imagination, in talent, in personalised language. There is an advantage in studying poetry which rejects all that, in order to understand the nature of the collusion of the era. There is a hegemony of silent rules which allow poetry to be composed and read. You can see this collusion as an asset, a welcoming shared space where all the individual stories can unfold. But there are reasons why you would want to be aware that it exists – to see the frame as well as the picture.

I don't have much knowledge of the avant-garde after I left London in 2005. Does that imply I can write the history up to 2005? Hardly so. This is a history hard to write. But in the '90s I was hearing avant-garde poets all the time; some of it soaked in.

It is virtually impossible to frame a form of words which an avant-garde poet would sign up to as a description of their intentions. I may put words in their mouth but it is very hard to make them drink. I mentioned Berger but does all this come from a Marxist critique of 'individualism' as offered by *Ways of Seeing*? I can suggest other possibilities. First, the task of representing a personality is a form of rigidity. If you stop even trying to do that, much wider possibilities open up. This is attractive in itself. Secondly, it is plausible that not only is modern Western poetry excessively specialised into the individualist quadrant of the linguistic space, but also that English society, especially, has pursued a goal of individualism so unhesitatingly that it differs from almost all historically existing societies and may be repressive of parts of the human personality. If this is where the unused possibilities are, then it is attractive for poetry to go there. More simply, if you count all the people who are radically opposed to the social order, only a low percentage of them now are Marxists. So it is not a given that a poet who wants to question everything is coming from a Marxist background.

For completeness, I should say that I know of one poet who is writing 'apparition' texts, in a sense in which this is obviously a Latin translation of the word 'epiphany'. This is in a Tantric-occultist tradition. Most poets are not occultists.

Archipelagic Fulfilment
— a Sign of the Times

Randall Stevenson cites the figure of 2,700 new books of poetry being published annually by the end of the 1990s. Some poor devil crawled through the trade list of all books to recover this data, bravo. The 2,700 figure (fabulous as it seems) points to a Poetry Boom and everything I am going to talk about must be visualised as happening in the middle of this boom. There must be a 'sugar rush' to create quite so many books and so many printed objects. More specifically, the volume of publication seems to have jumped up in 1990-94 and then stayed consistently at that high volume, with perhaps a dip in 2010-12 following the banking crash. Whatever the idea of poetry is that poets and readers have a craving for, it must actually be available for so many people to rush along the 'sugar trails' that led to it. While it would be unbalanced to dislike the 'ground tone' of a poetry scene that people are flocking to, I suspect that maybe 2,600 of *the cold 2,700* were of low quality, and I give notice that my role is to aim the limelight at the good ones rather than try to redeem the bad ones.

The figures imply that new poets rapidly began to outnumber 'battle-hardened' poets. This further implies a clean-up – the new scene is not dominated by the recent past, which has been simply washed away by clean downfalls in the hills. Specifically two main cultural positions lost identity: the post-'68 generation with their idealism about a future state, and the neo-conservatives with their dream of rolling back all the cultural changes of the post-war years. The decline of the mutual hostility implicit in that confrontation of cultural ideologies may have been the trigger for the poetry boom.

Have those deluging books been assimilated by a tier of connoisseurs who read them, found the good ones, and shared the knowledge with a wider public? That's a no, and don't be so optimistic. The boom has brought more funds but this is still an overwhelmingly amateur world. Most parts of the infrastructure that you can point at are broken – the scene relies on unpaid work by enthusiasts who are rarely thanked. Readers are scarce although poets pile up in heaps. People want authoritative reviews for their books but these are unlikely to be forthcoming. 'Crowd-out', that silent disappearance of data when a mind is impinged on by too much, is the key event in the whole landscape.

EVERYTHING IS ALREADY HERE

We can start on the new time-sense by thinking about the idea of revolution. This had a sharp breach in time – an asymmetry. The present time is nullified by alienation. Within it, there is a project of willpower – a war against the apparatus of the alienating regime. Heroism is the key quality of individuals. Hardly less obviously, theory is the means of planning for change and itself has heroic qualities. Critique is what offers to bring the end of alienation, and poetry is often a way of demolishing experience, of reliving and negating the personal experience and the emotional attachments of others. The radical opposition has to acquire the means of power in order to take on and defeat the power of the regime. After the revolution follows a liberated time which is blank because it hasn't happened yet (and which is present in poetry only as a kind of patch of shimmering colour, without distinct form). It is not true that poetological activity was simply critique of living poets, reducing the poetry people were writing to another dose of alienation, and praising only what made people discontented (or, aware of contradictions). It just felt that way.

Suppose someone is sharing this idea of Time and migrates out of it. Alienation is re-analysed as what is denied and this breaks down into all the things that are denied, simultaneously into the project of living them all out. The idea of fulfilment flows back from the indefinite future and starts to infect present time. It loses its link with arguments about social organisation and with propaganda against the regime. As it stops being the single culminating moment of winning the war, it subdivides into fulfilling all the things which the human mind wants to do. At this point the poetry they write no longer contains the single central message of subversion. Instead it takes on a thousand different sensations and ideas, dissolving into constant diversity. Everything is already here. Instead of a New Era at the end of a war you have a cloud of droplets of time in the present. You no longer have the redemption knowledge. Revolt fades into style – the revolt is not going to work but you still have a style, an aesthetic stimulus field, which might be only a fragment from the wreck of hope. You no longer have the statue of the heroic you but instead you can take on a thousand forms.

A supermarket may stock 8,000 different commodities. Each is distinct and if we see those 8,000 sensations as words we get a glimpse of what language is, as a mass of information. Poems are made of such words, but are not restricted to the chemical senses, the 'virtual space' of taste is just a metaphor for the larger 'virtual space' of the brain, which can locate or represent millions of ideas. At the same time, of course, a thousand poets differentiate from each other, they form into a market where (artistic) commodities appeal and compete with each other. The poet has to offer the reader a fulfilment not already present. This distinctiveness is the replacement form of the new: no longer the end of oppression but a series of new sensations. The series apparently never ends but we feel frustration if the next moment fails to arrive.

The claim is not that at some unspecified date (1973?) everyone was planning for revolution. This is though a story that many people lived through. It explains how we get to archipelagic fulfilment.

A MILLION MILES OF BEACH

We spoke of poetry based on care and compassion. There is another kind of poetry which is lyrical, inconstant, spontaneous, narcissistic, and which is obviously not compatible with the 'quality of care' poem, just as the care-preoccupied poem finds it difficult to raise itself to lyrical heights – to be enthusiastic at the same time as reliable. To raise the stakes somewhat, it may be that the quality of pop music which makes its songs more acceptable to a mass market than poems is linked to carefreeness, and what could also be seen as a narrow focus on the self – where the feeling you're having is the most important thing in the world.

I find a cluster of significant works in the spontaneous-lyrical realm in roughly the past ten years, and I think this is one of the most interesting developments of the moment. In fact, poetry is not acting as a defended territory of literariness barricaded off against billows of popular culture that might erode it, it is dissolving under those billows and blissfully reconstituting itself, downstream, as islands in a generous sea. This conscience and sensitivity naturally get in the way of more basic functions of art – or spontaneity, lyricism, play, pleasure. Literary culture is not pop culture. We have to consider the interaction between care and self-control, and the sugar rush of pleasure, in the dialectic of the scene. So many styles of poetry have as their goal the withdrawal from complex states of mind (and complex inhibitions) into a simpler state. The 'underground' has always had its lyrical component, and at present the 'Second Naivety', the return to spontaneity and the present moment by highly intellectual poets, is a very important position. Prominent examples of this are *fetish poems* by Marianne Morris, *Her Various Scalpels* by Sophie Mayer, and *Love / all that / & OK* by Emily Critchley. In this work I have to explain why a sugar-rush can be good – not in order to banish the mountain ranges of J.H. Prynne and Geoffrey Hill from view, just to protect biodiversity.

The idea I am fronting for is that everything is present simultaneously and this is called archipelagic fulfilment – there are a thousand islands with a million miles of beach. Everything is already here, you just have to swim to it, but each island is out of sight of the other islands, immured by a horizon of cultural enclosure which means that your poetry is insular rather than public.

I was lying in bed listening to the radio and thinking about getting up and going to work when a feature about the life of Ray Harryhausen, who had just died at 92, came on. As he was a visual effects artist, the medium of radio was having difficulty explaining him, but they played a sound clip from a film – it was *Babes in Toyland* and I knew that meant it was the voice of Annette Funicello. Never mind the economy, it's Annette! It was a sugar rush. I knew I could write about archipelagic fulfilment by writing about beach movies, usually starring Ms Funicello, who had the same initials as archipelagic fulfilment.

The originator of the post-modern, Nietzsche, wrote *Zarathustra* on an Alp, 6,000 feet above the world. *6.000 Fuss jenseits von Mensch und Zeit. Die Mitte ist überall,* he wrote. The centre is everywhere. The goal of history is all around us. Zarathustra descended from the mountains into the plain, and so must philosophy. Mountain sports are not democratic enough. It must be updated to the beach. When Friedrich said, "Das Meer stürmt: Wohlan! Wohlauf!" he wasn't quite saying, "Surf's up!", but it's close. Friedrich's noon becomes the eternal sunshine of the Great Beach. The world-historical beach. Of the thousand islands. *In jedem Nu beginnt das Sein,* everything is in the here and now, on this beach. Nietzsche would have learnt from Las Vegas. Or from San Tropez. The centre of his work, had he completed it, would have been *der Grosse Mittag* – the Great Noon, blissful and inconsequential. *Mittag – Mitte.* He would have written a great work about Noon. It would have been like surf music. Sun sun sun. In the AF concept, there is no centre or future time, poetry is post-derepression and has flowed out into a thousand islands where people can get everything they want. It is post-

Nietzsche but the great philologer's burden of knowledge and stance against nationalism have been replaced by beach culture. Dithyrambs unfold to surf music. There is an 'eternal present', time is only the tide rolling in and out. The cycles of the sun god. It has no consequences because everything is already here.

The buoyant state of the contented beach person hardly arrives without bringing along emotional openness and attraction to other people. Humans released from care and stress naturally socialise and identify with each other. The critique of identification is something that starts when you leave the beach. Something else necessarily present is idealism – you can hardly have self-idealization without a set of ideal political arrangements swimming into view. Each island is also a New World. The ideal society is a form of breach with the past, the eternal present breaking free of the dominance of unjust decrees. *What does your heart say? I don't listen to it any more. Maybe you'll hear it on the beach.*

BOX: VARIETIES OF THE PRISTINE & THE ETERNAL PRESENT

Pastoral	This was the 3rd century BC's equivalent of surf music. Learned poetry imitating rural and illiterate innocence. Written in an artificial dialect associated with a backward hill province. Revived in the Renaissance (mainly in Italian and Spanish) and continued into the 19th century. Basis for Marxist poetry about the innocent and uneducated.
Naive	Line of art, primarily visual art, by untrained artists with access to older modes of perception or depiction (and limited access to 'high' stylemes). term for art (mainly visual) by people with limited technical knowledge but also outside the collective opinion of the art world and so much more integral and optimistic. Can look like advertisements and in recent times ads have been a main influence on naive art. Makes the world of 'art insiders' look weary and disillusioned. Most art by children is naive.

Outsider art	May include naive art but also includes 'psychotic art', art by those subject to religious visions, and spiritualists, zones of creativity detached from a receptive audience, shared language, or market. Has been described as 'an intense event without horizon' because the creators have no idea of cultural context. Generally used of visual art but this often incorporates words (in what may be an older mixed form of creativity). Often has the visual as a weak equivalent for elaborate and compulsive symbolism. Typically fulfils itself as a creative act and not by reaching other people. Often encouraged by art therapy. Arguably all religion has outsider art at its core.
Myth	Symbolic narrative embodying pre-rational thought. Can be seen as raising of folk motifs to 'high' cultural forms. the breakthrough to original (and geographically local) myth has been a source of anxiety for rational poets worried about the limits of disenchantment.
Folk	Lower tier of W. European cultural tradition embodying partly pre-Renaissance modes of expression (or feeling) and partly imitations of these created since 1960. Favoured by Marxists and Christian poets for whom the Middle Ages were the age of piety.
Oral	Limited by memory and yet freed by improvisation. Time works differently in oral art, which prefers the exigencies of the present moment over knowledge, than in literature. Divides into low oral and high oral (which includes oratory and verse drama). Rhetoric inheres in the oral world, as does pop art, and is a store of archaic exuberance. The Sixties saw a shift towards oral modes and a shift away from the domination of the past. Oral creativity is based on formulae that can be re-linked ,and the development of 'learned' poetry has been to get rid of the formulae but fumble for new ways of signalling to the audience a shared mood or direction. Can include very old material but only within its formulae.
Primitive	A range of psychological modes which to some extent can be summed up under 'myth'. The word is generally used to refer to illiterate cultures and is no longer used by anthropologists in that sense. Illiterate cultures are likely to be thousands of years old as opposed to 'early'. The word is more frequent in the sense of 'western artists jettisoning Renaissance technique'.

Ludic	Art partaking of the serene energy of the game. Arguably a feature of the most sophisticated art but its point is to create something more controllable which is thereby simpler than real-life structures. Is generated by rules rather than by capture of experience.
Dogma	Dogma is simple and aimed at children and represents a blissful ignorance about ideas. There is a close link between didactic verse and the childhood state. Any art which does not deal with ideas is likely to express trust in a rigid form
Propaganda	Totalitarian states and churches have rather consistently used forms of verse that exclude information and rely on stalwart repetition and 'group feeling', voiced by someone naive and whole-hearted
Stupid	'Dumbing down' is the main feature of the era. Being stupid makes you write poetry with restricted information, which can look like the lyric condition
Pop song	The 'retarded twin' of poetry, never completely separate from the popular song. Song lyrics are poems. The choice to go without music is almost willed alienation.
Lyric	Most attempts to partition poetry from prose end up with the idea of the 'lyric' with its implication of personality structures which evade the calculating to achieve wholeness, love, exalt-ation, joy, innocence, etc. Leaving us with the problem of how then to partition 'poetry' from 'song'. Poetry has the inter-mediate position between prose and popular song. Lyric also deals with pangs of loss and longing, experiences taking over from naivety. Represents the marriage of poetry with the song tradition.
Dithyramb	Pre-literate form of Greek poetry in free metres associated with ecstatic states, dancing, rituals. Used by Nietzsche for his 'Dionysos-Dithyrambs'
Pure present	The Sixties had a special preoccupation with the immediate present of which the pop song was one form. It offered an escape from memory into the New. Improvisation in art was one form of this. The dominance of film art, perpetually showing the present moment, assisted this.

Advert-isement	Presents ideally uninhibited and spontaneous people enjoying impressive contact with an object of consumption in an 'eternal present'. Spontaneous art endlessly generates new ideas which are recycled by endless admen. It is hard for poetry to be more hedonistic, more carefree, more self-indulgent, than advertisements. But it can learn from them.
Infantile	This includes the non-discursive – genres like concrete- and sound-poetry which jettison the structures of language that you learn after early childhood is over. These were important forms of the avant-garde in the 1950s.
Dialect	Until recently most people spoke dialect so folk material before 1960 or so tends to be in dialect. Associated with naive characters. The original pastoral poetry used a non-literary dialect (Doric). Patois poetry tends to use pastoral and oral modes.
Hymn	Meeting of the lyrical (even dithyrambic) and theology, present as a kernel set to be memorised and so close to propaganda. Was where learned poetry met a folk audience.

The point of these withdrawals is largely to escape the servitude of running the weary systems of government and business, of rationality, disenchantment, and adult carefulness.

The poetry boom was founded on optimism and propelled by ignorance, in a deluge of new poets and new readers making it less likely that rules acquired by conscious artists in, say, 1976, would even be remembered in 1996. That includes the clauses of the stylistic 'little wars' of the era post-1968. Historicism relies essentially on artists remembering rules that say "you can't do that", and in an era of derepression and the dominance of youth that negative memory is likely to be washed away as the tide comes in – to leave smooth white sand. The most stylistically conscious poetry was on the Alternative scene, which was remarkably hard for young poets to find, due to its absence from the bookshops, public libraries, standard textbooks, and so on. Poets who were unaware of it could hardly build it into their 'collective memory'.

HISTORICISM, ANOTHER THEORY OF TIME

A lot of poets own the belief that there is a style which embodies the
time, a kind of bullet speeding ahead of everyone else. If you are inside
this bullet, everyone else is out of date. Critics would search for this
Now thing and feel unsuccessful if they didn't find it. By proposing
an archipelago, I am failing to find the forefront. I am saying it is an
illusion. Comparison: every guitar band took a big hit in radio play,
record company interest, and so on in 1988-90, when guitar-free dance
music took over. Things changed. But... guitar bands came back. By
the thousand.

Historicism is conservative, it believes that past stages of the game
dictate future ones. Claims to the influence of the Past on events
combine significantly with claims to status, viewed as a result of having
won the game (and so *won* dominance). In such a highly educated,
highly examined, society, the arrays of verbal anxiety reach very high
complexity. Historicism in its explicit form was generally abandoned,
roughly in step with the abandonment of Marxism by the relevant
group. It was a very clear line of thought and has been replaced by
confusion. Things can still be out of date. To this extent, time does
destroy the potential of certain artistic devices. It is much more popular
now to run through the argument of the post-modern laws of time,
where there is no progress and every style is simultaneously possible.
This still doesn't mean that clichés have begun to work. It is noticeable
that some poets don't use clichés. In the end, some things are out of
date. If you don't understand this you can't do art.

The idea of styles becoming obsolete has a flip side. The person who
says poetry giving lyric expression to the feelings of an individual who is
excited and emotional inside the experience they are having is obsolete
can equally well be accused of *dissociation* – exhaustion, inability to
react, being blasé. This position suits especially well the claims of an
elite – the only fashionable restaurant in town is the one we own and
everywhere else is just passé and impossible. Groups which aspire to
cultural elite status are structurally forced to build such a claim to title
by vocally denouncing everything they do not (symbolically) own. It's
like the military – go to the enemy, *break his stuff, degrade his assets.*
It's also no secret that a lot of the people who jeered at lyric poetry
were Marxists who wanted a monopoly of cultural production for the

workers' choruses of a State, real or future. The inability to feel is in the beholder. Dissociation is a personal gesture.

Is There a Time?

Question, is there a cultural field? The idea of a field is that all the parts relate to each other, even if they relate by dissimilation. The D word means that a faction are acutely aware of what another faction are doing and go to great pains to find the common ground and to evacuate and devastate it. In Faction A, the preferred values are, and were chosen to be, values which faction B rejects and sets at naught. Perhaps there really is an invisible field structuring cultural creativity and whose ornate yet firm patterns can be 'uncovered' from every text we look at – given that we have the right level of expertise. Tracing these fields is deeply enjoyable, so much so that I suspect that we may be doing it just out of self-indulgence.

In the 1950s, I believe, the 'stratum' of cultured and educated people was so small and so prestigious that young people writing poetry wanted to assimilate to it and so there was a style of the times which both signalled belonging and delivered it, for two or three hours, to the reader. This was actually a way of competing. The expansion of the universities which was beginning already in the late 1950s produced mass higher education. Within this mass, competition was realised by differentiation as well as assimilation. The new volume of cultural production also meant that the perception of norms became blurred. People necessarily assimilated norms, this could hardly be avoided, but because there were so many different norms in the stylistic market-place the assimilation made contemporaries travel rapidly away from each other.

Ideas cannot disperse across the whole scene so there can be no 'time-style' which creates a brand of the period. Twenty styles, we may suspect, could be proposed as typical of the time. People rarely speak of the '80s, the '90s, the Noughts – there is nothing typical of the time. It follows that as I write I cannot succeed in finding something 'typical of the time' nor fail in identifying styles which were practiced by some fraction of poets in the time. Everything you pick up is true for a finite extent of time and a finite extent of the stylistic field. The typical feature of the Eighties is the regression away from the heroic leftism of the seventies – but the same leftism still persisted during the Eighties, as the background to everything.

When I checked back to what critics were saying at the time, I realised that there were two styles available in the '50s, summed up by John Press as *rule and energy*, with the latter including Kathleen Raine, David Gascoyne, George Barker. But there were also volumes of modernist poetry by Graham, MacDiarmid, and Jones. Memory has produced a sharper and more coherent picture than what was actually there. Even in the '50s there wasn't only one style happening.

I propose that the landscape is one of archipelagic fulfilment. There are a thousand islands and a million miles of beach. There is no 'historical time' because there is a different time prevailing on each island. No impulse can ever roll across all the islands. They are isolated. There is no 'now' but time rolls on each island separately. The archipelagic division into many small islands over the horizon of invisibility from each other *is* the quality of the time.

A text has to contain time and to do the work of drawing the reader into this shared time. We can identify the time in which each concrete work unfolds its gestures. No style can be made to disappear, but also everything is already here: the loss of boundaries which was announced by commentators around 1965 had by 1980 allowed an exploration of the stylistic space which had reached every part. The next step was – apparently – to disappear into the oceanic reaches, leaving language and meaning altogether. You cannot have progress if all you can do is travel out to an existing island and if all that ever follows is travelling back again. The modern condition could also be archipelagic frustration.

If there is a cultural field which engulfs a poet, or animates him, that field is partly composed of distinctions and affinities. By reaching back into the prehistory of a poetic biography we could recover the *reasons* for differences and explain how different parts of the spectrum relate to each other. That fore-time is not there, or recoverable only in a fragmentary way. More concretely, the field has patches of concentration, where coherent styles or feelings emerge, and each of those represents a poetic ideal and has an audience who presumably share that ideal. In fact the parts represent 'stakes' and have histories, in which their assets rise or fall in value. The gifted poets are scattered widely over these domains, and it is not difficult to see that if you wanted to find the largest amount of good poetry you would wander widely, ignoring the border fences. The project followed by readers follows (also) an opposite principle, of locking into a certain pattern and rejecting anything that makes it weaker. Like tuning into a radio station.

All the organisms which were there on the beach a hundred years ago are dead. There is a past and it follows that Time passes. The crabs, sea anemones and humans care little for their forebears. This may be a game that really resets to zero.

Another question which is rarely discussed is who lives in the territory of the New. The charter condition of the avant-garde is to open new cognitive territories and configurations in which we do not yet have reaction patterns and we revert to infantile states of fascination and wonder. This is the 'wow' factor which poets like T.S. Eliot and David Jones certainly offered on first encounter. It was a new land.

How do we compare the biological newness of young people whose experience is of acquiring new reaction patterns, with the artificial newness and youth of *learned innovation*? For a sensation to be new it is sufficient to have a young brain. The condition of being fascinated, wondering, of perceiving unfamiliar and elaborate patterns and of learning noticeably resembles ignorance, and this is supplied structurally in every year that the species lives simply by *youth*. It is hard to believe that the lyric state can be abolished by collective cynicism or that we can only reach it in the unusual genre of the lyrical avant-garde.

Western popular culture rotates around teenagers partly because their emotions are simpler and less refracted. Has poetry lost impetus by committing to less simple and more refracted modes of being? Reflexivity and critique shape the place where you say No, without also offering a new life which could fill the measures of a new poetry. No – it's the same old capitalism but you live without identifying – or saying Yes.

What Is the Scene Like?
Some Generalisations

The theories aren't some Supreme Court that gives a final ruling in 100 years' time. They are indirect codifications of the doubts that readers harbour and which induce them to eject poems as not tasting right. In this sense there is no point in theory being original. It is 'reported thought' and strives to be accurate as a reconstruction. So much of this is an attempt to reconstruct and put into words the reading reaction. This is closely related to the set of processes that a poet goes through in appraising a line or a structure.

Theory is a separate domain and this is a descriptive work from which much of interest had to be discarded to limit the size.

People new on the poetry scene tend to ask many questions reflecting a perception that it is deeply damaged and dysfunctional. I stress that I am not able to answer these questions – saying "why is it like that" is much more difficult than describing what is, verifiably, there. People less new on the scene ask fewer questions. Presumably, this is because they have got used to how things are and just accept them, and because they identify with the scene and see the criticisms as criticisms of them. The 'big picture' is that modern poetry has a tiny share of the cultural market and it is hard to define this as success.

Looking at the landscape invokes the idea of *subjectless action*. The plurality is subjectless. The wide gap between poets and a general readership is subjectless. No individual devised these things. No individual can dispose of them. The supposition that the landscape is the result of conscious design leads to paranoia, as everything bad becomes a conscious act. The supposition that you can redesign the landscape leads to megalomania – and claims to have designed, and to be designing, the whole landscape.

It is psychologically easier to lurk in the position of revolt and withdrawal than to join the management and claim that everything is going fine and no policy mistakes have been made. Fairly obviously the revolt of people arriving in 2010 includes a protest against the practices of people who have been in a state of official revolt since 1973 and are integral parts of the landscape. It is conventional to judge poets by the quality of their critique.

GENERALISATIONS

In this period poets are unlikely to:
— write either drama or narrative, things prominent in English poetry at least until 1905;
— use dialect;
— support the government;
— regard what they do as conventional;
— write with a cast of kings and dukes. (The poet-self fills the position in the centre of the text formerly occupied by saints and kings. A philosophy of unimportance guides poets towards the small scale.)
— write propaganda;
— claim insensitivity or wish to write insensitively.

I think 'quality of care' is plausible as the organising concept which would appeal to the largest number of people in the poetry world. The core area would be 'warmth, sensitivity, intelligence, expressivity, lucidity'. This is what people care about. Arguing about the sensitivity thing must be good because this is the focus of poetry and it is theoretically underdeveloped. Theory seems to start by switching empathy off.

THE METABOLISM OF A GENTLE ANIMAL

Every day of the week, typescripts are falling onto the mat of two hundred or so editors. The gatekeepers with real jobs are faced with a weekly chore of going through a large number of typescripts that are never going to reach the public and which will not make the gatekeeper famous. The job involves overwork, as a basic condition. Mostly this work is carried out in a state of insensibility, as bad poetry numbs the reader's ability to react. The chances of a poem breaking through this dutiful dullness are slim. This is a machine where meaning is generated; the editors are carrying out a duty to poets and to readers, making primary judgements and definitions (although the artistic choices of poets are even more primary).

Poetry prizes based on open entry tend to be won by writers who already have a book about to come out from a publisher one of whose employees is on the prize panel. It is likely that almost all the poems thus rejected are conventional and unoriginal: the dispute between stylistic innovators and the gatekeepers is a small sound buried beneath this noise. If you give up the prestige outlets, there is a bewildering variety of little magazines which take on a huge quantity of poems, perhaps also yours. They are not easy to find but they are numerous – perhaps less than 200. Their impact is low, since the bookshops are unwilling to stock them (which may be because they can't sell them). The corollary of finding acceptance there is that few people are going to read your poem. Editing such a magazine is not a real job: the gatekeepers do not read the little magazines, they are too numerous. Essentially unpaid, the editors are also free agents, what they do is pretty similar to what they like to do. Because economic rationality is not really a factor, this sector is amazingly responsive: nothing holds it back. The few people who are keeping up with it know many things that the managers do not. It is like the Internet before the Net: hundreds of providers, more or less domestic, each reaching a very small radius of listeners. There are two views of the little magazine scene: either that it is where everything new happens, the non-corporate innovative sector; or that everyone who is going to have a career bypasses it, going straight to the national prizes, the High Street publishers, the visible magazines.

The quantity of good poets is extraordinarily high, but so is the quantity of books coming out. An article in *Agenda* 28:3 by Roy Blackman (year 1990 or '89 I guess) says that January-April 1989 saw 480 new poetry titles and this figure was supplied by the Poetry Library. He extrapolates it to 1,400 titles a year. The 'executive summary' of the Arts Council's poetry survey counts 1,797 new titles for 1994 (as quoted in the *Times Literary Supplement* for 5/7/1996.) This was a 23% increase on the previous year. That implies that 1993 saw 1,461 titles. An annual survey in *The Bookseller*, issue of 31/1/1997, counts 2,311 new titles for 1996. (128 of these were translations and 192 were 'revised and new', so presumably a mixture). Randall Stevenson gives a figure of 2,700 new titles each year "by the end of the decade", part of a boom which saw "poetry's readership almost doubled during the decade" (p.266). Blackman estimates 6000 people writing publishable poetry. That is for 1989 – does this mean double as many in 1999? We don't know. An estimate of the overall population of poets by the year 2000 must be up on 6,000, perhaps 10,000. So people on the scene in 1990 were at the start of a poetry boom. The ideas in circulation were new and undamaged, the proportion of idealistic and energetic people was high. The assets lying around were going to increase in value. The cultural impresarios were producing moves that impressed the audience and rolled new people in.

Poets who actually got books published are not the whole extent of the writers active. These figures are based on assumptions that could be varied a great deal, the conclusions are accurate only with a possible 50% or 75% error. They may help to indicate the size of the 'poetry world', and also to let me point out that only a tiny minority of these books actually got reviewed or got into the 'elite spot of light' enough to be consulted by anthologists. I thought of collecting reviews together, but most of these books went into print and out of it without being reviewed. There was a tier of readers who knew what was going on by the prickling of their fingers, and it seems they were the only ones who knew what was really going on.

Heat diffused over a large space means cold. The poetry world is large and also cold. These poets relatively rarely interact with readers, or get reviewed, or get recognition from the institutions. The sheer amount of information prevents individuals from reaching eminence and from 'winning'. Average sales of each book are astonishingly low and the lifestyle is based on poverty – no matter what you want to do, the resources probably aren't available. Poetry works for people who are willing to be alone for long periods of time and to pour a great deal of that time into an activity without obvious rewards. The lack of commercial rewards is also a lack of constraints. This favours the long haul of patient development into the unknown. Surprisingly, most poets do not believe in experiment or originality.

INSIDE AND OUT

Even in these vast distances, there is the possibility of a reader and a poet entering into a shared state over bursts of language and swirls of information. Against the cold we pick out 'rhyme' moments of togetherness and simultaneity. The weakness of institutions persuades us to look at these isolated clusters of emotional unity as decisive, although they cannot be institutions – as too fragile and intermittent. When there is no building which belongs to poetry, its site and home is intermittent – flares of high-energy interactions which could almost be said to destroy themselves by dissipating the energy which is their anatomy.

Robert Hampson said in an interview that "I would see my work as situated within a community of 'London-based' poets [...], who would describe similar influences and would see themselves as part of a similar dialogue. I am thinking of people like Robert Sheppard, Adrian Clarke, cris cheek, Harry Gilonis, Gavin Selerie, Peter Middleton, Caroline Bergvall". Thus someone builds a tiny cell of warmth which stands out against a wider society which is completely indifferent. These groups of friends store a knowledge which is very far short of an aesthetic appreciation of the whole scene – but that expertise in the whole scene does not exist, whereas the coteries do.

It is hard to see the content of poetry as being objectivity when the subjective acts of acquiring and internalising are so important. The self has a boundary and that boundary has a vital chemical function of sorting and assimilating. Writing a poem may be an act of enclosing.

There is a key difference between an individual being territorial, self-centred and self-referential and a group being territorial, self-centred and self-referential.

Digital

What about the internet? If you had 2,700 books being published in 1999, then making it easier to publish poetry does not change the direction of travel – it simply facilitates the qualities, of archipelagic fulfilment, elegiac solipsism, etc., which already prevailed. If you have total saturation in substandard poetry then adding any amount of extra substandard poetry makes no difference.

It is possible that the new technology can add to selectivity by targeted searches and so on – that is, you belong to one notch on a great spectrum and you find other people who belong in the same notch. They can be your primary writers and your primary readers. Open access reduces the quality of the product and the market but the *selectivity* raises the quality. There are indications that this may be happening here and there. The significant thing is the conversation around the poetry, allowing connoisseurship and design to develop. Hampson met his 'reference group' in London, but via a stylistically narrow-beam forum you can locate people of like minds on the Net without ever meeting them.

VOWS OF POVERTY AND ANONYMITY

On average, new poetry has very, very low circulation. There seem to be few connoisseurs of the time. There is instead a wealth of experts in dead culture, the Death Cult. Deep knowledge and the contemporary hardly seem to go together. It is as if living culture could not assume the passivity of cultural wealth. Low circulation does not imply that the readers you have are experts or that their judgement is well thought out or impressive to other experts.

In order for a 'poetry war' to take place the protagonists would have to find each other; instead of clashes, the scene is rather dominated by a loss of audibility, as huge amounts of bad poetry block the channels. Why publish all these books? Certainly not for money. Barely for prestige. The publishers were motivated, very often, by benevolence. This was a sector outside capitalism. The night side of meritocracy. A land of free actions. This kindness without condition was hard to combine with consistent application of artistic standards and even rejected the latter as not matching the charter values.

The climate has been described as warm indifference. The publishers didn't believe that what they were publishing was great or brilliant. They just didn't like to say no. The sound of yes was what they really liked. They felt anxiety about quality control and were happy to put out stuff that *wasn't really very good*. They had a cottage ideal of authenticity. The idea of being anti-capitalist and anti-marketing was deeply attractive to them. Being a published poet has come to be almost meaningless.

Few people had the wish to plough through large amounts of this generally bad art. The question of why you would want to read most of it is quite urgent. The role of a historian in this field is perhaps to consign the bad poetry to silence, so that gifted poets, perhaps a hundred in number, can emerge into full sound. Perhaps the predisposition of poetry is to be the night side of a business society, so it is the mirror image of daylight rules of rationality. This is something quite different from the idea that one day you would wake up and the daylight world would have been replaced. So if you work in a meritocratic system interminably measuring people and identifying talent, maybe you want to go home and run a micro-publisher where *talent doesn't count*. An economy without profit. Without marketing machinery. The slowing of metabolism allows for survival in an economic winter which is like a post-industrial world. Or like the 1940s, with people growing their own food. Where capitalism doesn't work. This feeling could have expressed itself in almost any way: the link with poetry was unnecessary but became very solid through habit and tradition.

Going somewhere without the language of marketing hype was so attractive. Everyone was appalled at one publisher gorging convulsively on marketing hype and releasing insults to anyone who wrote differently from their little treats.

There was a kind of zombie crew, frighteningly numerous and dehumanised, of neo-con cultural critics who were trying to destroy anything that did not directly serve capitalism, but they were not noticeable around poetry. The most significant point in the period is a silent one, and it is the turning-point where neo-conservatism ceased to expand and to seize all vulnerable cultural assets, and the legislative programme of favouring corporations and doing down the worker stopped rolling forward and halted on fixed positions. This is hard to date, but by the 1992 general election in the United Kingdom the wave had clearly broken. The cultural world was not in fact dominated by neo-cons but the passive majority had rolled back from any Left propositions and was quite tolerant of, unable to resist, neo-con propositions about cultural choice and how the cultural process occurred.

There is a certain ambiguity about the neo-con label in poetry. A good example is *The Black Rainbow*, a 1975 collection edited by Peter Abbs and subtitled 'essays on the present breakdown in culture'. This shows a large Left component: the new thing of the period 1965-75 is being interpreted as the product of capitalism getting out of control. Coincidences of position with a neo-conservative programme which hates socialism and wants to roll back the State can be misleading and need careful sifting. The local anti-modern current in poetic opinion was not pro-capitalist. This area needs further research but probably we need different terminology. (I apologise for not having a recent anti-modern text to cite.)

Most of this output was mediocre. To understand this mediocrity you have to have a knowledge of certain texts which is humiliating and numbing to acquire. It can be acquired *only by reading them*.

The volume of work would seem to say that originality is necessary. But most poets were anything but original. They clung to familiar and banal ideas with a certain terror which is almost distinctive in its plenitude.

THE DEPOLARISATION PROJECT

In 2001 there was a series of talks under the label 'Binary Myths' organised by Andy Brown at the Spacex Centre in Exeter. The idea was that most people on the poetry scene divided the cultural field into two halves (the Good and the Bad) and that this could be corrected by benevolent talks on the theme. This was a part of a 'depolarisation project' which ideally would have dissolved all prejudices and enabled readers in general to spend the rest of their lives enjoying a magnificently wide spectrum of cultural pleasures. Great idea! I think most people on the poetry scene believe that *other* people are victims of crippling aesthetic prejudice and that the institutions of the poetry world are helplessly vitiated by the implacable forces of opposition and contradiction.

Why resist this campaign? I got very excited about it. On reflection the idea of a binary division in the collective realm was unconvincing, and the evidence for any particular division is depressingly weak. There has been a certain amount of discussion about the opposition between the Alternative scene and the mainstream, but I very much doubt that a large proportion of poetry readers see that division as paramount or even prominent. In fact endless divisions could be suggested. The word binary is treacherous because it forecloses argument by suggesting that anyone who believes in divisions can only perceive black and white distinctions. Evidence is not to hand that anyone sees a binary division in the poetry world. Sweeping this division away may not, therefore, make any difference.

The real binary division may be between poetry I want to read and poetry I don't want to read. Trying to abolish this is alarming because it is trying to take away the very basis of aesthetic choice. It is distinctly likely that people know what kind of poetry they are going to enjoy and that their whole knowledge of a lifetime's reading is summed up in these acts of preference. If you see eight major divisions in the poetry world, the binary thing just fades away. My research suggests that there might well be that many factions. If you try to erase those groupings, you are surely eroding free artistic choice.

The *Binary Myths* talks often had the tenor of "the crucial problem on the scene is that people don't read My poetry enough". Testimony on the lines of "I changed my reading habits and my whole set of existing opinions collapsed and I liberated myself by proving myself wrong" was noticeably absent. The idea of repentance and entering a new artistic world retains its attraction.

There is, we hear, a test for brain damage which asks the subject to draw a clockface. Subjects with damage to one side of the brain draw a clock in which one side is distorted, shrunk, badly drawn. Similarly, we can imagine a test for poetic bias in which someone draws a map of the poetry world and if they draw a one-sided map then we can point to damage to the cognitive organs. The problem with this is that we have to start with a complete map – a dial with 12 numerals, metaphorically. This offers certain difficulties. If the reference map does not have a credible status, then no one need pay attention when their 'mental map' turns out to have major differences from it.

The 1970s were a period of notable differences of opinion on social and political issues. Arguments were inflamed, and alliances, formed to defend territory or to advance into new territory, became tight and enduring. This situation led to polarisation in poetic opinion – where seeing only 15% of the clock face was accepted as a virtue. The poetic community has been diluted by new people arriving in each year since, and the poetry being argued about has been modified by the publication of thousands of new volumes. We don't need to worry about washing away the aged hostility of the Seventies. However, new oppositions are establishing themselves, hard to see because they are essentially blocks. In one room full of the poetically interested, a certain named poet does not exist and their poetry does not even exist – and no-one there even reads it. This block can't be made conscious. Essentially, even if you read 50 books of new poetry a year then you are ignoring the other 2000. The idea of covering the entire clock face is a poetic myth in itself.

SUBVERSION

You have someone write that there is no political poetry around. It's irritating because she is just erasing all the political poets from the map. Off-mapped, sound erased from the air. Negated. You up to say "you don't mean there is no political poetry you mean that you don't like political poetry and have constructed a small world in which that poetry is blocked out and mistaken it for the big real world." This is the *relativising* manoeuvre. It is happening *all the time*. But it is also hostility. It makes you feel cold. People are only happy when not being relativised – and shoved from centre ground into somewhere barely visible. Do I have a right to my opinions? It would seem so. I am wondering if this attitude is simply aggression. Visit my place, break my stuff. Destroy the good parts. Rip the joins apart. Turn it to powder. Degrade my capabilities. How can I be happy while someone is doing that to me?

If someone does that to a poem is it an act of *criminality*?

We need to define a balance between the impact of a concrete narrative about the illogical bases of a real-life situation and the impact of an avant-garde and conceptual text-structure which has a damaged version of conventional patterns and so (in optimistic theory) dislocates them. I'm talking about the lead, so the difference if you subtract impact-1 from impact-2. Im-2 minus Im-1.

Compare a feminist poem in conventional language and a post-textual avant-garde thing. In the first, you show someone being treated badly, humiliated, excluded, not allowed an opinion. You look at the person doing the humiliating and think how come he's in charge. Because other people accept him in that role. How did they learn to accept? by constant experience. Why don't they change things? etc. As you keep on asking questions you figure out how inequality maintains itself, how arbitrary it is. Subversion through language can't actually do more than this very simple story. If it lacks concreteness and vividness it may not even achieve that much. If you start the poem from biographical and concrete experience, you may find it hard to get people to see any wider implications. If you start from theory, with no concrete instances, you encourage people to think conceptually but they may find the whole project thin and unconvincing.

This might be a way of describing the era: that everyone wants to write a poem inside which the reader sees everyone flying out of social roles, possession dissolving, signs of status dissolving, people recapitulating entire routes from birth to an acquired 'personality', soaking up behaviour patterns and shedding them again, by turns imitating and dissimilating from the key patterns that they like and dislike, everything whirling around and then recombining in a new way and breaking that up and recombining in a hundred different ways. This is 'the poem everyone is writing'. So the history of the period might be a catalogue of a thousand different ways in which people write that poem and it fails. The audience just sits through it waiting for the next thing to come along.

It is touching how the avant-garde are convinced that if you build a pile of broken language the audience are going to think, "Aha! Society has been dislocated and I must rethink the basic assumptions of the social order", and not, "Wow, this language is broken and I must find some working language somewhere else". Certainly there is a fine time to be had rethinking how society is put together and how people reached the social roles they inhabit. But this might be hard to induce the 100th time someone is asked to partake of it. It might be that you can only induce it by something highly coloured with exciting characters and narrative. To be honest, the idea that you can subvert anything by using damaged language may be just a theory. What happens when people read avant-garde texts may be something quite different and using much less energy.

When I was a kid people used to get this kind of experience from acid trips. Which were notoriously hard to control. I don't know why people think poetry is so much easier to control. Actually acid lost almost all its popularity because people were too lazy to turn their heads inside out and rebuild everything. They wanted a convenience food equivalent that wouldn't take all weekend. Reading complex poetry is unfashionable the way lysergic acid is.

You think you can write 'reimagine the world' and the reader will do the work. They aren't going to do any work unless they get paid. You do the work.

Less written about is the feeling of being subverted, but all those feelings being subverted belong to someone. When it happens to you it's a feeling of being frozen out. You lose everything that made you warm. This coldness is not unfamiliar because it's always possible, every time you do a gig in another town you look at the audience and wonder if they are going to go with your stuff at all. At least with a gig you can win people over. What's new is the idea that the disenchantment is *progress*.

John Berger can stand for the line of critique of art which makes most Western art illegitimate. Berger was a Stalinist who was influential in the 1950s in formulating a Marxist critique of art for England. While Berger is still influential, it would be too simple to attribute ownership of this line to him. *Ways of Seeing*, a 1967 TV series later turned into a book, put things in an especially crass and exaggerated and emotionally aggressive way. This is why it had an abiding impact. Berger turned Stalinism into populism.

There is an anomaly of theory being dominated by Marxism. This anomaly implies that believing in the existing order of things makes it difficult for your feet to leave the ground. It is still the Cold War legacy. Theory as an area of endeavour is not written by poets about composition and not aimed at poets.

I don't even think the disenchantment is subject to conversion and control. The emotional landscape keeps dividing up into the enthusiastic and the indifferent, in a million different ways, it swirls around but it always comes down to the same pattern: some like it some don't. No theorist is going to turn this into a basically different pattern. That *is* the pattern.

As soon as you're indifferent to some art that you deal with for a protracted period of time, you see inside it the whole vortex of egoism, egocentricity, acquisition, self-regard. Everything. Berger's critique doesn't give you anything new.

Suppose you could turn this negativity into a ship that you can ride on. We can imagine someone *riding* the energy waves of this subversion and aggression. How rare is that? If you just fall out into the coldness, then people inside your art are just wandering a featureless coldness looking for something that they can touch without it dissolving into powder.

ACQUISITION OF ASSETS

The history of self-consciousness was written, in the grand German philological manner, around a century ago, by Georg Misch, in his many-volume *History of Autobiography* (published 1907-69). He draws our attention to the elaboration of biography into "romanticized writing of history" in the Hellenistic period, giving the centre stage to individuals, who deliver soliloquies with full rhetorical colouring; this unfolding of complexity and sensibility within history, no doubt holding up the exposition of the events, naturally affected the self-awareness of poets, so that an autobiographical poetry became possible for the first time. Ovid's love poetry and the late Hellenistic romance were both influenced by this richer and more introspective historiography. In the Baroque literature of the 17th century, tragedy, history-writing, and romantic story-telling once more came together in a single work, coloured by an interest in psychology, which isolated and exaggerated passion and fancy as subjective factors in life. History thus reaches a peak twice, as the recovery of command over language, of the willingness to handle in public speech so much that is slight, fanciful, and contradictory, produced again literature of psychological depth equivalent to that of the few centuries around the birth of Christ. For Misch, this mixture gave rise to both autobiography and the psychological novel. It is the current which flows into modern autobiographical poetry and its stress on the personality. It seems like the way a poet behaves is to acquire objects, drawing them into an interior space, where they change into some things which are part of the poet as well as parts of themselves, and the load of the poem is the way the poet has transformed these things. Afterwards, the things remind people of the poem. Not just objects, not just verbal patterns, but also people, also entire atmospheres, the feelings the people have about some phase of experience, are drawn into the poem, signed by it. It seems as if a poet who doesn't do these things, drawing a boundary around a sector of floating emotional objects, can't write a poem. But it seems as if what the Bergerian critique is doing is exactly the reverse – acting to *reverse* all these minimal, invisible, mighty, transformations and disperse the grouping which allows the poem to happen.

Look at this atmosphere of doubt. If I read a book of poetry, I am having feelings and judging the feelings in the poems and evaluating the lines as I read them. I possess the experience because it's mine and the poems become my possession as I read them. Suppose you let this doubt in, all those reactions are frozen. You can't trust them. In that situation I wouldn't get past the first page. Being dispossessed of the poem means it is no longer property, I suppose, but it means that the reason why you want to be inside the poem, inside the book, has evaporated – it's just one more landscape of surveillance, cold, being controlled, being anxious.

I am not sure if this dispossession has anything to do with people actually reading poetry. It seems to belong somewhere entirely different. I'm not sure either what happens if you amp up this dispossession, if you multiply it by a million, release it into the mainstream. Is there anything good about it? There seems to be a superstructure of high-flown discourse around art which has nothing to do with creating art, or what people enjoy about it, or where to find the good stuff.

High Burbly

A certain area of alternative poetry is based on an over-consumption of data. Maybe I can try a partial sketch of youth culture as a way into this poetic arena. Projection onto artist figures. The assembly of bafflingly complex tests which art has to pass (to be able to be projected-onto). Structuring of the artworks by the tests. Desperate fear of being left behind. In this regime artworks are incredibly important, but only for a very brief time. The febrile consumption of art products tied to the wish to define oneself through the display of virtual commodities which advertise a way of living and offer a shared framework of manners in which to live it. The constant shifting, the over-consumption of such products, many in the course of a day, and the latching together of compound assumptions, inside which songs or poems are then written, hard for anyone else to trace effectively. Helpless consumerism masked by a search for authenticity. Judging people by their clothes and forever trying on clothes to escape judgment. The exit from shared frames to achieve individuality, competing via stylistic offsets, permitted by the structure of the commodity system (which calculates on it). The converse of such 'fever' is an attachment to real (personal) experience which is slowed down, predictable, and includes the possibility of failure. 'Fever' is in fact the opposite of authenticity. University libraries as equivalents of record shops, where a similar regime of reckless grabbing of resources, of searching for worked objects that externalise the (wished-for) self, gobbles up entire poetic systems. The glimpse of a liberty where you become whatever you say and say whatever you think. Being terrified by the slowness of adult poetry where basic personality structures have cooled and hardened. Identifying instability of identity with the rhythmic unpredictability, the swing, which differentiates a good pop record from a bad one.

We may deploy a parapraxis of the poet and impresario Kevin Nolan to define an area of *hyberbole*, which is to be understood as a combination of hype, attention deficit hyperactivity disorder, and burble. This rather dry word describes the state of poets who snatch successive gobbets of information from various sources, the Internet, television, advertisements, textbooks, etc., and stitch them together without any kind of coherence. The transformation of the disparate scraps by a 'personality' function is wafer-thin and unimpressive. But then integrity is interpreted as a slowing of the body clock.

The poem is a bid at the spectrum auction. The consumption of high culture (as of youth culture) relies on overall semantic frameworks by which the individual signs are related to behavioural gestures and interpersonal exchanges. The fever regime produces constantly new frameworks (by mixing and matching), and the problem is then of making the framework current at any moment visible, so that the reader can find out what the poem means. Over-consumption (youth dutifully listening to the radio or CD player many hours a day, 7 days a week) makes following rule-shifts easy; the lack of 'programmed consumption' in small-press poetry makes a complete failure of communication always likely. Predictability is linked to intelligibility but could actually be seen as a failure of communication: as speed was the *burden* of the message, the true intent.

It is hard to tell the difference between anxiety and rage. The disaffected reject culture because of rage or because of anxiety. Lack of trust, lack of firm & beneficent relationships, condemn them to fury. Lack of shared context makes it hard for them to write. I think perhaps we can draw a link between media fever and the life of the intellect. Abstract ideas similarly move at far, far higher speeds than real life (than your *body*, I suppose) and are similarly irritating to the fogey-ogres who run the shop. In fact, we could define poetic conservatives as people who hate ideas. This hatred is one of the great features of English culture. Belief in the possibility of personal change, the energy to abandon your investments and redraw your maps, are youthful traits. The idea of continuing to learn and improvise in adulthood is quite seductive. It's quite a long path from the instability and imitation of a 'media freak' to being an intellectual – but *thought is instability*.

In some of these texts the failure of logic in an arbitrary jump is being used as a replacement for lyricism. It is supposed to demonstrate subjectivity and excitement.

What is the opposite of blank logic? Is it darkened logic? Chromatic logic? Gloss logic? Logic matte? Logic *latte*? If you are going to cut very rapidly it is useful to develop a way of making the images arresting and recognizable in a short space. If the individual snatches are blurred and uninterpretable, the overall effect is like a camera bouncing down a flight of steps one by one. From handheld authenticity to what? The impression made by hyberbole on me is one of indifference and frustration. The 'feel' of the eye constantly being distracted by a new thing from the old thing which it didn't really engage with may be 'contemporary' in that young people are having this experience while watching TV, flipping through racks of CDs, wandering around shopping malls, patrolling university libraries, etc. However, we suspect that one part of the future is being interested. The hyberbolic text gives off messages like "skittish", "fear of commitment" or "not taking things in". The Stooges, of course, were able to take states of boredom and indifference and make you emotionally identify with them. But they knew how to fill the subliminal channels. Not use them as garbage chutes.

THE RECEPTION OF MODERN POETRY: VIEWS OF THE CONTEMPORARY SCENE

BIOLOGY TAKES ITS COURSE; THEORIES OF TIME, ONE

I went through Jonathan Barker's bibliography of *Poetry in Britain and Ireland Since 1970* extracting all the books published in 1990. The list when typed up is a dreary one, arousing thoughts of death, dissolution, the climactic cold which is the final phase of decay. But at that, publications listed by Kelvin Corcoran, Robert Crawford & W.N. Herbert, Peter Finch, Raymond Garlick, Hamish Henderson, Brian Jones, Judith Kazantzis, Mimi Khalvati, Tony Lopez, D.S. Marriott, Peter Redgrove, Robert Sheppard, Ken Smith, and John Hartley Williams show that something good was happening. Looking at the whole list, it is possible to doubt that the 'scene' had anything to do with the excellent poets, who were *notoriously* atypical. Perhaps study of 'the scene' has nothing to tell us about the islands of excellence.

I also made a list of debuts by five-year groups, in the hope that this would yield some periodisation. Finding the first publication by a poet is not a simple process and this list, while based on the British Library holding which has only a few thousand lacunae in the relevant area, may be fraught with errors. Which flimsy pamphlets do we count, which do we pass over. Etc.

POETS MAKING DEBUTS DURING THE 1980S
Alison Brackenbury, Adrian Clarke, Kelvin Corcoran,
Robert Crawford, David Dabydeen, Peter Didsbury,
Vicki Feaver, John Goodby, Robert Hampson,
W.N. Herbert, Paul Holman, Frank Kuppner,
Hilary Llewellyn-Williams, D.S. Marriott, Maggie O'Sullivan,
Peter Philpott, John Seed, Jo Shapcott, Pauline Stainer

POETS MAKING DEBUTS 1990-94
Moniza Alvi, Tim Atkins, Michael Ayres, Elisabeth Bletsoe,
Ian Duhig, Mark Ford, Mimi Khalvati, Jamie McKendrick,
Kevin Nolan, Deryn Rees-Jones, Robert Saxton,
Robert Sheppard, Simon Smith, Susan Wicks

POETS MAKING DEBUTS 1995-99
Sean Bonney, Andrea Brady, Giles Goodland, Graham Hartill,
Dan Lane, Nic Laight, Helen Macdonald, NS Macias,
Peter Manson, Alice Oswald, Clare Pollard, Niall Quinn,
Lesley Saunders, Karlien van den Beukel

POETS MAKING DEBUTS 2000-2004
Emily Critchley, Jeff Hilson, David Kennedy,
Carola Luther, Sophie Mayer (then publishing as Sophie Levy),
Marianne Morris, Jeremy Over, John Stammers,
Vittoria Vaughan, Matthew Welton

POETS MAKING DEBUTS 2005-09
Zoë Brigley, Christopher Brownsword, Mark Goodwin,
Chris McCabe, SL Mendoza, Nick Potamitis,
James Sheard, Carol Watts

POETS MAKING DEBUTS 2010-13
Rachael Allen, David Ashford, Steve Ely, Oli Hazzard,
Katharine Kilalea, Francesca Lisette, nick-e melville,
Cris Paul, Heather Phillipson, Kate Potts, Nat Raha,
Luke Roberts, Rhys Trimble, Samantha Walton

LIST OF POSSIBLE DESCRIPTIONS OF 1990-2010 AS A PERIOD

LABEL	COMMENTS	PERIOD OF APPLICABILITY
Solipsistic banality	An error rather than an intentional artistic outcome. Includes use of colloquial language as the home of banality. Flatness of language may correlate with flattening of social prestige (and the democratic current since 1945). This descriptor may include several thousand published poets	Mixture of The Movement and the singer-songwriter current; was barely there before the 1960s.

Boom	Correlates with growth in numbers of people with (or in) higher education. Electronic typesetting and printer control also important. New cohorts of poets are larger (and more influential?) than old cohorts	1993-2010 (subject to better research)
Vitality of the Underground as an alternative to High Street and conservative poetry	Is an index of the health of the scene even if the 'parallel distribution networks' and parallel audiences remain small-scale	Said to have started around 1960. Has not stopped but it would be useful to have new classifiers to point to later generations of it
Ludic/ hedonistic approach to the text	Means abandoning that package of moral authority and claims to documentary truth. Makes it possible to reclaim the 'figures of speech' and reverse the laying-bare of language.	Key works were published in the early '80s although Edwin Morgan and George MacBeth were doing it in the 1960s.
Indeterminacy	Related to art placing itself on the plane of ideals rather than realism. Has been linked to a 'de-ideology' project so that a good citizen builds knowledge by an active and critical process and the poetry reader is forced to do this too. This is virtuous but it is not clear why it is pleasurable. Many other links.	Indeterminacy was highly developed by various poets in the 1960s. Not clear it is a feature of the era post-1990.
Reliance on process (as opposed to self-expression)	Rival sources in surrealism and in mathematical approaches to language. Overlaps with ludic current. Relies on idea that the personality repeats itself and a far wider domain of patterns exists	Ideas available in the 1950s, key works being produced in the 1960s. Oulipo founded in 1960.

Singer-song-writer influence – dominance of intimacy and empathy.	Standard style of the time, is at least better than Cold War disenchantment. Reaches huge audience in music. See Privatisation.	Got going in the 1960s and by now most bad poetry is written in this style
Rejection of rhetoric	The 'New Criticism' made 'rhetoric' a dirty word and was the most successful academic current from the 1950s. Link with 'laying bare' both self-deception and the claims of propaganda possible but not necessary.	Inspired by the New Criticism from 1930 on, became mainstream in the 1950s. The avant-garde has followed the same 'stripping down'. But modernity meant simplicity of language already in 1910.
Privatisation; a belief that no object or sensation can be owned by more than one person; a withdrawal from the public realm.	Loss of intellectual interest in any formation outside the nuclear household. Much the same as singer-songwriter thing but also sees public space as corrupt and the attempt to enter public space as corrupting. Correlates with the 'end of rhetoric' seen as the loss of collective symbols.	Arguably begins with The Movement in the 1950s. Obeys the basic logic of a consumer society, reduced to a conscious ideology also in the 1950s.
Feminism	Radically split between poets who think that self-regard is feminist if you're a woman and poets who think that politics involves a critical tendency.	Consciously feminist poetry barely there before 1975.
Decline of ideology	Most significant feature may be the decline of a 'social ideology' in which a few gate-keepers tried to exclude most poets and destroy their assets. Could be that withdrawal from general truths is part of the loss of prestige of writers. Can also be described as the rise of data.	'End of ideology' was proclaimed in the 1950s.

Detection of ideology everywhere	Seeing art as the cells of ideology, a form of brainwashing into a social system with its power elite. Has a variant seeing art as ego-projection rather than part of a system.	Was a tenet of Marxism in the whole 20th century but had a revival in 1968 with the New Left.
New lyricism	Key feature is mingling in ideas as part of the fabric of everyday consciousness, so could be seen as the personalisation and reduction to spontaneity of essays about exciting modern thinkers. Is distinguished from the 'domestic anecdote' current by being intense, subjective, excited.	Not totally separate from the old lyricism. Key reference point is Frank O'Hara's work of the 1950s. Arguably is also the main new feature since 2000.
Influence of pop songs	Hard to quantify, e.g. Pop means both 'soulful empathy' and 'brazen power-assertion'	Began with Pop poetry in about 1965.
Destruction of the prestige of the writer	Along with the discrediting of ideology comes the discrediting of unsystematic ideas, projections, memories, etc. produced by poets. Yet there is a poetry boom.	Hard to periodise because bad writers are always failing to convince.
Use of sampling (i.e. acquisition and modulation of pre-existing and continuous stretches of language) as basic component of texts	The ability to manage and design junctures between discrete samples becomes paramount. Failure to transform source material becomes a distinctive and tacky way of producing bad poetry.	Arguably this interest in found material goes back to surrealism, but the popularity of sampling in pop music (since 1987) and the habit of dipping into multiple data streams on a screen linked to the Internet (since the mid-'90s roughly) are new and distinctive

Move away from theories of historical progress in the arts.	Replacement would be a belief in the personality as the source of original linguistic moves and a trust in exploration at a micro level. Anyway a significant number of people believe in progress and that they are its very arrowhead and that everyone else is obsolete.	Dating disputed but there was clearly an anti-Marxist wave from circa 1975 which brought a rejection of formalist progress ideologies with it.
End of trad-itional course of assimilation to a shared norm of the cultured tier; so that a period style is not there to be found.	Means a larger elite rather than the end of elites. Poets still assimilate to the stylistic patterns of their sub-group even if the poetry world as a whole no longer has coherence. Also, these subgroups may have lines of growth and change measurably over time.	We would have to date this pattern to the boom of poetry, cultural revolution, etc. in the years after 1968.
The end of formal inno-vation. Loss of the link between polit-ical radicalism and poetic innovation in the long-term eclipse of the Left signalled by Conservative government from 1979-97. End of the progress ideo-logy means poetry has nothing to offer except what is already there.	Hard to distinguish from a tendency of poets to regard younger poets as insignificant and slightly older poets as charged with meaning (a silent rule). An unpopular thesis. Could also be that the Underground recovered after c.1990, i.e. with the decline of the New Right.	There was a crisis of confidence already in 1977, dates otherwise confusing.

It is noticeable that none of these descriptions of the present would be recognised as important by a majority of the people on the scene. I don't have any trump card which would allow me to invalidate *all the groups except one* and name a winner. So far my attempt to locate a style of the time is a *defeat*. There is an operative version of the present in which any poet identifies *people who like my stuff* and *people who don't like my stuff*. Following on from that defensive awareness, poets may well develop explanations *of why everyone who dislikes my stuff is wrong* and even *who and where their wrong ideas come from and what they eat*. This is the content of conversation in bars filled with poets. The scene can get along without an objective view of stylistic change.

A while ago, I talked about archipelagic fulfilment – a million miles of beaches where there is no centre and no future time. If we now come back and find stylistic progress, that rebuts the claim about a thousand islands in the sea – we have to throw that idea away. The idea is also an excuse for not writing about everything – just ten islands out of a thousand.

In 1990, poetry written in the style of the 1950s seems out of date. This implies that something might be changing. It is only with difficulty that we could find a style suited to 1990. Certainly poets are asking themselves all the time what style they should use. So many poems collapse on the page that people are tempted to find an underlying pattern to the failure. Because the scene is littered with styles which have visibly burnt out, and imitations of these styles work very badly, one view is that innovation is needed to avoid being out of date. The way that things change over time – society, the media, women's hats – suggests that the failure of a poem has to do with its relation to Time and to the language of the time. This remains unproven. Poets who adopt a method may simply be switching off the whole battery of doubts that go with a self-critical process, in favour of speeding up the line. This may be no better than a bet on the roulette table.

The fact that so many poets write in a broad vulgate which has not changed in their lifetimes does not mean that their work is timeless – or that it is adequate and appropriate to the times. If we abandon historicism, we do not abolish change. This is inevitably happening in a parish register way, as poets either arrive or die. Poets have individual breakthroughs, they write a new book. We could look for stylistic progress by taking poets in the innovative sector and comparing new work with what was present in the 1970s. Maybe something new is there, although not to the extent that grant applications are suggesting. I could mention Rob Holloway and Piers Hugill as poets whose work I find rebarbative but which could be crossing boundaries for that reason.

In 1990, Raymond Garlick was noticeably using a style which people liked to use in the 1950s. Drawing the line between period and personality is difficult. Garlick's poetry certainly suits his personality. Which features are reflecting an era and which a personality? or is it true that certain personality types were produced by certain social climates?

How does style relate to time? The most typical artistic moves of the time are also among the most worn-out and irritating ones. The typical has to have a great swathe of overlap with the banal. What will be remembered from this time includes the most original works, which are quite obviously atypical. The search for a modern style is not quite the same as rejecting every device, idea, turn, that is over-familiar and worn-out. Poetry has to avoid the worn-out but that is a negative rule which simply leaves us with a vast undefined space full of possibilities which do not resemble each other. The remaining idea of 'history' is perhaps of the separate development of thirty or so strands which are not especially close to each other. The idea of a single flow of poetic style probably has to be abandoned, and the idea of simple reckoning of what has changed since 1980, or 1960, or 1940, has crumbled before we can touch it. The confidence of some people in defining such changes is not well sustained by the material. As for a stratum which is typical and original at the same time, the answer is probably that there are several such styles, and that they are quite separate from each other.

THE CONCEPT POSTMODERNISM; OR, FUN IN ACAPULCO

The introduction to the 2004 anthology *New British Poetry* (the 'only definitive anthology of modern British poetry') describes the poetry which Don Paterson hates as 'post-modern'. He does not name any names, which limits the interpretability of his claims, but he believes that this group have procedures which they follow instead of making artistic choices or representing autobiographical experiences. I pointed out in an earlier essay that several of the poets Paterson and Simic select to promote are widely described as 'post-modern'. The word is short on validity and shared meaning even if the froufrou around it points to real issues, hidden by unthinking use of terms – or by the stiffness and incoherence of the supposed 'community' of poetry, if you prefer.

Tim Woods' book *Beginning Postmodernism* (2009, originally 1999) lists a number of British poets whom he sees as "post-modern". They began publishing between about 1965 and 1983. This is already a problem. First, if "post-modern" refers to that generation, or swathe, of poets, its accuracy as a descriptor for younger poets must be in question. Secondly, and this is something Woods does not offer any thoughts on, if the newest tier in 2009 can be subsumed under a description valid in detail for poets who were publishing in the 1960s, like Thomas A. Clark and Tom Leonard, the question arises of whether the 'innovative' poetry has gone on innovating enough to replace itself. If not, the question then is "when did the forward flow stop", and this is not something the literature offers much of an answer on. It seems likely that there has been a forward flow of change, but that a warm 'sense of cultural identity' mercifully protects the poetically active from noticing this, so that even when you identify it it is not recognizable to the active audience.

To be specific, Woods lists at page 89 "Robert Sheppard, Barry MacSweeney, D.S. Marriott, Denise Riley, Gavin Selerie, Tom Clark [mistake for Thomas A. Clark], Bill Griffiths, Peter Middleton, Maggie O'Sullivan, Alan Halsey, Fred D'Aguiar, Allen Fisher, Tom Leonard, cris cheek, Adrian Clarke, Clive Bush [has Bush ever published any poetry?], Wendy Mulford, Bob Cobbing and Ulli Freer." Almost none of these made a debut after 1980, so analysis of them is not likely to give us the flavour of the period *after 1990*. I am suggesting that they may be the poets Paterson is thinking of (since the poets he selects also belong to that generation, born *circa* 1940 to 1960), but there is no guarantee of this. Neither Paterson nor Woods mentions the word 'Left' at any point, but there is little doubt that almost all the poets named fit in on a reach of the spectrum to the Left of the Labour Party, roughly in an area scrapped over by anarchists and Marxists, or that the poetry is fundamentally influenced by this site. I don't have a database of 1,200 British poets showing what their politics are, since I think that would be a breach of privacy, and I am not saying that everyone on the 'small-press scene' is sceptical about capitalism, but you can take my word for it that the scene is part of the Left. (As I have pointed out elsewhere, the 'official' poets are not in agreement with the Conservative Party or the City of London about how society should work, but the nature of their disagreement with the Underground could also be connected with disagreements within the Left milieu, for example between people trying to make the Welfare State run without springing too many leaks and people who want a revolution. All sides agree that poetry starts with the command, "imagine the place where you want to live".)

To substantiate this, Woods offers an outline definition of what he sees as "post-modern" poetry:

1. a resistance to preconceived forms dictating the arrangement of language and ideas;
2. a resistance to closure, espousing open forms like 'open field' composition, the 'new sentence', and forms other than those handed down by orthodox poetry;
3. a challenge to the 'lyric subject' [...];
4. a suspicion of the 'poetics of presence' embedded in the priority given to oral forms, and a rigorous exploration of the written or textual dimension of language;
5. an insistence on the materiality of the signifier, and a delight in opening up the possibilities of that recognition;
6. commitment to a 'politics of the referent'; in other words, their 'play' with language and its 'rules' is a deliberate challenge to the ideological power invested in dominant linguistic formulations or patterns;
7. an insistent emphasis on the shared practices of a poetic community, as opposed to the ideology of individualism.
    (page 93)

There is no guarantee that any other theorist would agree to this list. In fact, the most likely thing would be for them to launch a seminar in which they discuss at length their own position and how it is more valid than everybody else's. To make my own position clear, I see the term as one which has a honey-like attraction for academics and which has gradually had so many objects added to it that it has no internal consistency and therefore cannot be used in meaningful statements. I am discussing it merely to explain some of the language practices around it. Its lack of meaning, or the possibility of changing its meaning on a daily basis without being called out by any stable body of scientific opinion, may be one of its key attractions. When Charles Jencks launched it in 1977, in his book *The Language of Post-modern*

Architecture, it had a definite meaning with relation to architecture, and his arguments are not inconsistent or diffuse. Since then, though, forty years of exploitation sequels have followed. The word is hopelessly split between (a) a description of the new styles of art on the scene in 1977, (b) a description of one style of art only, applying to one in a thousand works of recent art, (c) a description of what features distinguish art of the 1970s, in its totality, from previous art, (d) a description of art in its totality from about 1966 to 2010, inclusive, (e) a whole state of being ascribed to Modern Man which yet eludes most people. I suspect that any sentence containing the word 'post-modern' could usefully be disassembled and rewritten after asking the questions, 'What do you really mean? What concrete analogies are you drawing? Is there a more precise category you could use? What are you trying to say?' Even though an individual may have a clear idea of what they are meaning by the word at a particular moment, it is improbable that this meaning would overlap with the meaning received by the listener. If we wanted to describe the culture of modern times, in the way that for example scholars talk about 'the culture of the Baroque' for a period of the 17th century whose borders are agreed, I am sure that we would want an inclusive definition, containing perhaps forty traits of style; further, that it would refer to all works typical of the period, and not just to an ambiguous subset of them; further, that there has been a succession of styles over a 40 or 50 year time-span, and that we would want to devise terms that capture the vital shifts of fashion and intellectual project.

Lyotard's classic book on 'the post-modern condition' does not even mention art, so that the current which analyses 'modern knowledge' in a way which Lyotard was summing up, already in 1976, may be completely independent of the line which addresses art, and which uses one or two of the same terms. Quite probably if you piled up, in a room, all the books which use 'post-modern' in their title, that room would contain descriptions of most of the interesting art and theories of the past 50 years. My problem is more old-fashioned: how to identify the best of recent British poetry, and to evoke a subset of it, in prose, in a way which is accurate and memorable.

Woods' list of features is strikingly negative: it doesn't say anything about what the poetry looks like or why it would be enjoyable, and the position it defines could easily be occupied by someone who writes no poetry at all. The applicability of these qualities as a test to actually existing poems is puzzling and liable to failure: because they do not describe aesthetic or linguistic structures, it is hard to say whether an actual poem passes them or fails them. The list is single although the chapter clearly covers both American and English poets. This puzzling fact bears thinking about. 'Similar interests have developed in British poetry', he says. Does it mean that the British are just wannabe Americans? Given the dominance of Americans in the field which they invented, it seems on the face of it unnecessary for any British poets to try and swim in the same waters. A second possibility is that the theory which Woods is summarising is exclusively American: poets like Silliman, Watten and Bernstein have piled up whole rooms full of theory, and Woods' list is robust because it is a credible paraphrase of what they have written. I am much more doubtful that there is any significant prose theory explaining what these British poets are doing, and I think evidence is missing that the British poets he mentions either follow these theories or regard them as salient for what they do. The third point, as you will already have guessed, is that evidence is missing that these poets are even a group in any salient sense. The capacity to create theory *once dogma and tradition have fallen away* is of all things fertile: it is possible that each poet has developed their own theory and that it is culturally necessary to read, or in the first place to write, their work only because it did not exist before and is not similar to what did exist. The manoeuvre of compression whereby you describe a cultural wing in the USA and then tack on a list of British names as a sort of 'franchise of the brand' destroys any political force the latter may have had: it is quite noticeable that Britain is not America, has different corporations and owners, a different social or class structure, a different government, different possibilities of reform, so that something can only be political if it is specific to the State it is attacking or the social abuses it wants to reform. A critique of American media/government/ business, as developed by American Marxist academics or whoever else, cannot also be a critique of British media/government/business.

While the features describe the attitude of an academic essayist, much more than of a poet, they seem to stop short before we get to the first line: they don't explain what you have to do to produce the first line, or how the second brilliant idea is going to follow and replace the first one. The features listed may really have been important to some poets, in this country, at a certain stage of their learning process, but their scope is much more to define a detachment from other people, from real life experiences, from relationships, even from older poets you admire, than to describe a poetic situation which lives in a poem and which readers share. This stress on the moment of cutting attachments and becoming an individual strikes me as part of an early stage in life; I would suggest that what is likely to happen, slightly later, is that you form new attachments, develop new poetic forms of identification, acquire experiences you identify with, and in fact rebuild social and psychological bonds. The phase of detachment, which could be multiple (e.g. five relationships that you 'move through and on from') is no longer visible in the poem that actually gets written – it had to stop before you have something to write a poem about. So more useful for us is a set of features that we could detect within actual texts and show to people and win their agreement that, yes, these features are there, in the text.

Older poetry didn't have a problem with the dominance of the artist because it had a realist foundation in the characters and situations of other people. The suggestion would be that the 'monologic' situation arises from the retreat into theory, abolishing character, and that this problem is specific to the intellectual poetry and does not arise in empirical, mainstream poetry. If you describe a real life situation, its control is shared by all the people participating in it. Thus, the issue of whether your Romantic intuitions dominate it does not have any relevance. The issue of Romantic dominance arises when you are describing situations you haven't lived. There is a strange anecdote about the actor Michael Redgrave. He was to play the inventor Barnes Wallis in the war film, *The Dam Busters*. This is a terrible film and the scenes with Redgrave are the only interesting bits. He spent several days with Wallis as part of his preparation and based his performance on the man, although there was no physical resemblance and so an impersonation was excluded. Wallis said that the performance was 'disturbingly accurate'. (*British Cinema of the '50s*, page 228) The structure of the great body of art before Modernism was based on real-life experience and inhibited by that from bolting off into areas where the fantasy of the artist had control. Memory and plausibility intervened to guide the narrative back to the real and so added a substance which the conscious intent of the artist could not provide. Just as visual artists drew from life, *sur le motif*, so also poets reverted to real-life experience to provide most of the information in their poems. Limited by stylisation, the texts contain the outlines of real people, just as Redgrave captured the real Barnes Wallis even though it was unnecessary to the plot of the film.

Thus I would suggest that (a) the decision not to write about real-life experiences already cuts you off from communal life and from a rich flow of data that shapes and stabilises the poem (b) the critique of the immediate data of consciousness is the equivalent in poetry of abstraction in art, it is visibly prestigious but it may strike the onlooker as excessively cold and their experience inside it may be one of alienation rather than freedom. The stress on originality leads to a single voice dominating because the other people met in daily life obviously do not speak in this strange and original way. Steps to weaken the dominance of the authorial self are needed in this new poetry because other characters, other voices, have been silenced in order to allow the author to speak, a problem which the older poetry did not have.

A range of the features described by Woods serve to inhibit identification and emotional projection. That is, distrust of the immediate data of consciousness is a key factor in this poetry. The elemental acts of wishing, identifying, sympathising, imagining, etc. are 'frozen' because they are held to contain a legacy of ideology. Liberation is held to come through detachment from this primary material. The reader is likely to sense that the immediate data of their consciousness is likewise under attack. The 'progress line' of modern poetry can be seen as running up an ever increasing level of distrust of primary consciousness – the substance from which the older poetry was built. This distrust is not identical with humility.

Attention is drawn to these features because after all they are widely disseminated. As we identify a maxi-level of them in one group with very few readers, we should bear in mind that a mini-level of them may be present in a much wider group who do reach a large audience. Some of these features have had a long time to filter through the geology. The self-set task of a mainstream writer may be precisely to dish up 'avant-garde' techniques in tiny doses and integrated into a poem of older design – based on the 'lyric self' and not saying that "your consciousness is an illusion". The difference between poetry of the 1950s and poetry of the 1980s or 1990s may precisely be that the latter has absorbed 'distancing' 'alienating' 'doubting' etc. techniques into the tried and tested, and partly worn-out, structures.

The Dam Busters serves a sneaky spare function (did I hear 'double coding'?) as defining the stiff-upper-lip patriotic view of social function (and by implication politics) which almost everyone in the 1960s was rebelling against. Because it belongs to the 1950s, it defines another

problem, namely that social protest in art depends on what it is criticising: the 1950s have disappeared and recent art has the problem of
having to show what it is a protest against. The coherence of British
social mythology in the 1950s was remarkable; it seems quite plausible
that the multiplication of media products since the arrival of a second
(!) TV channel in the late 1950s has produced a 'capitalist mythology'
so diverse that any attack on part of it is only a partial success. The
critical thinking which underlies Woods' list of features is very clear
when put up against *The Dam Busters*, not least because the whole genre
of war films was so monotonous and mutually supporting. Criticising
them as art and as politics is a 'clean shot'; you are likely to hit. It
is doubtful that this applies to modern narratives, to the media since
1965 really. 'Detachment' is hardly such an asset given that everyone
born since 1950 is detached from the 1950s style/ideology, simply by
having lived through the 1960s or their sequel.

A suggestion would be that Postmodernism as a term is a kind of
sumptuary closure, that is, it creates an elite of super-artists, or super-
people, who fit inside this category, while everyone else is on the outside
looking disconsolate. (Closure in archaeology means a possession
which defines a limited group, so for example a certain ornament in
an assemblage of grave goods might signify that the individual buried
was male and a king. Sumptuary laws forbad people of low status from
wearing luxurious clothes which were suitable to people of high status,
thus 'cleaning' the signifier and preventing it from being widened.) This
would hand the power of a gatekeeper to the cultural managers who
deploy the term. The less meaningful the term, the more complete their
power to exclude or include people, following the momentary ebb and
flow of alliances. The implication is, pervasively, that artists who are
not post-modern are out of date and that critics who know what 'post-
modern' means are in the swing.

Jencks' polemic about the "post-modern" [*The Language of Post-
modern Architecture*, 1977] was essentially a plot to replace the
supremacy of Neo-Brutalism, the sheer modern architecture of high-
rises and office blocks which is associated most of all with the name
Le Corbusier. As it includes pictures of hundreds of very beautiful
buildings which are 'post' this modernism, he was not pioneering
the idea but cataloguing a world-wide implementation of it. Jencks'
critique has largely been accepted by the profession of architects, or
by their patrons. Surely there is a good match between Le Corbusier

and Modernism in poetry, and the cluster of poets which Woods offers us as 'post-modern' is actually the heir and functional equivalent of Modernism, and so doomed to wither and perish if we accept Jencks' polemic. Jencks illustrated and described rebel buildings, scenographic and ornamented, promising a departure from modernist bareness *also in other forms of art*. Jencks centrally denied that 'ornament is crime' (Adolf Loos' phrase of around 1905) and promoted decoration, scenographic effects, glamour, colour, play. He rapidly followed his seminal 1977 book with *Bizarre Architecture* and *Daydream Houses of Los Angeles*. I don't see how this line of gorgeous and often *nouveau riche* daydreaming maps onto Woods' 'post-modern poetry' at all. I think there is poetry which matches it, but it has nothing to do with the list of poets he is foisting on us. (By scenographic I mean 'resembling stage scenery', i.e. beautiful to look at but without load-bearing/ functional/ three-dimensional reality, or a triumph of surface over mass. It is hard to see how poetry is ever 'functional' or has any mass at all, so it seems that all poetry is scenographic in this sense.) The polemic of Philip Johnson, Jencks, and that whole line, must be directed against the *critical* poetry defined by Woods. Instead the rejection of ornament visibly matches, mirrors, the 'critique of the immediate data of consciousness' which is central to the critical poets. A postmodernist is, surely, someone who masters lyricism and irrational ornament – even if not learnt from a visit to the Liberace Museum.

In the British universe of discourse, the rejection of neo-brutalism was most likely to connect on to the line of attacks on modernism which had been articulated almost as soon as the first skyscrapers were built in Chicago, after the American Civil War, and which had not retired and fallen silent in 1977. Jencks' line had in fact, to defend itself from a conservative takeover by forces which wanted every new building to look like a nest for 18th century gentlefolk. He attracted patronage from people who were in touch with big new money, and who thought that the mansions in which New Money lived should look exactly like Old Money, and not like something connected with European Marxists and avant-gardists, and the century of the Common Man. Jencks had no share in these plutocratic ideas and wanted to liberate the designer to make beautiful things. This neo-conservative take-over is something almost violently present in the poetry world, and the curve of Jencks' critical architecture tells us all kinds of things about the curve followed by poetry. One of Jencks' books in fact is about Prince

Charles and architecture, a direct self-defence against the most publicly visible critic of modernist building. Charles of Wales also had patron connections with *Temenos* and Kathleen Raine, an anti-modernist and anti-Enlightenment line in poetry, as I have documented in *Origins*.

Randall Stevenson's *The Last of England?* (2004), covering the years 1960-2000 as volume 12 of a series on English literature, deals with poetry at pages 165-270. In other chapters Stevenson discusses post-modernism and feminism, obviously key parts of the literary world. He deals with poetry from five miles up in the air and so makes out general features without dealing with individual works. Stevenson's account is hard to fault, although not pitched at the level at which poets usually argue. His perception of the field is as one where conservative and empirical poets dominated the public realm but where something more interesting was lurking beneath the surface. He gives credit to two anthologies (compiled by O'Brien and Tuma) as revealing this underworld, at the end of the period – but his account does not give much detail about them, because his mandate is to describe what was most official, most public, and indeed most read. He speaks of "a range of modernist and postmodernist influences" (p.270) as part of this underworld – suggesting that there is a range of poetry which is untouched by modernism or by anything new since 1960.

Stevenson offers a good description (pp.230-37) of what he is calling postmodernist poetry. The description absolutely does not match up with the primary definitions of postmodernism by Jencks and Lyotard. Using the same term is therefore a source of confusion and it is better to use a different word. He cites *A Various Art* and *Conductors of Chaos* as key anthologies in this area of style. Almost all of *A Various Art* was written before 1980. *Conductors* is a later generation but almost everyone in it had worked out their artistic line before 1990. As an idea of what was new in poetry after 1990 this group of poets, about 50 over the two anthologies, do not qualify. They are really the central and dominating figures of the *alternative* sector whom new poets after 1990 had to compete with (and frequently got edged out by). Quite a few people feel that *the history since 1990 is that the great innovations of the 1970s became institutionalised and were rolled out smoothly and in high volumes*, but relatively few of them were born after 1960. As an aside, these Fifty Figures are the poets of the Underground and I don't see the value added of re-labelling them as "post-modern".

The meaning of "modernism" in 1960-2000 (in statements like "this is an example of neo-modernism" or "all these works were in the tradition of modernism" or "this poet's work is quite untouched by modernism") is also vague and in need of discussion.

He reports too poets "practising a poetry unostentatious or colloquial in its language, minimal and unobtrusive in its use of poetic device. Movements in this direction were more or less progressively apparent throughout the period." Indeed, for many observers, "a variety of contemporary pressures were eroding the range, resources, and poetic potential of the English language." We can very rapidly see why dumbed poetry is uninteresting, but that exposes the question of why people were dissatisfied with the good stuff, undumbed and fully functional. Stevenson says at p.159 that "poets could hardly remain unaware of the minority readership for their work, favouring private discourse and inward vision partly as a result." Intriguingly, this hints that the short range, intimate tone could include the flat colloquial *and* obscurity. Obscurity is simply the ultimate personal tone, a mind talking to itself, regarding mediation as valueless. The flat tone was certainly emerging in the 1950s, only held up by the Formalism which was so important from 1956 to 1964. I suspect we would have to go into the nuts and bolts of language and trace a set of inhibitions, when people see figures of speech and refuse to get on board them. This opens up even more difficult questions of legitimation, acquisition of patterns of reactions, and social cohesion.

I really wish Stevenson's strictures were not true. But they are. All the same, the response to him is that the dumbed down poetry surely does not cover more than 90% of the field, and 99% of the attention of the artistically committed is given to the Intelligent and worthwhile stuff. A book like this can just bypass it. A side-point is that poetry cognoscenti are terrified of getting lost in a desert of brain-damaged banality, and may be very reluctant to read anything that does not come with wraps of metadata legitimating it.

Sean O'Brien's *The Deregulated Muse* (1998) harks back to poets of the 1950s who went through a process of rigorous self-examination to reach a moral standpoint and then wrote poems in which the world was seen as a process where actions had consequences of harm or benefit to other people and the poems trace the event lines of those consequences. This suggests that postmodernism was a grand error. O'Brien covers a thirty-year period which includes few debuts later than 1990. He genuinely isn't very interested by recent poetry, doesn't pursue it beyond the most conventional and High Street names, and doesn't share its values. The volume title suggests that poetry has become more diverse, but ambiguously could also be comparing modern poetry to a Thatcherite deregulated market, where the consequences for the majority of people are poverty and misery. O'Brien stands out for saying that morality, either religious or post-religious, is a component of art and that a poet with no standpoint is writing something so loose and slack that it is not worth reading. The topos of 'poetry becoming more diverse' is agreed on by most observers but the date tends to be movable, and assigned to where someone can claim credit for bringing it about. The evidence is that there was a huge growth in the number of poets in the 1960s, a boom, and that there was an explosion of diversity at that time, say 1965-74. The transition to hedonism and unconstrained experiment was in the second half of the 1960s, as in every other sphere of social activity. The idea that reading a poet involves taking on a version of goodness, evil, and harm, and that the process of imagining and judging that version is key to the process we call reading a poet, was prevalent in the 1950s and became much less fashionable in a wave of hedonism a few years later. O'Brien is unusual in wanting a roll-back to the 1950s. This is a neo-conservative thesis but he is not a broad-spectrum neo-conservative.

INDETERMINACY

Robert Sheppard has set out in *Far Language* (1999) and *The Poetry of Saying* (2005) views on indeterminacy as the key factor in modern poetry. The views were already expounded in his doctoral thesis (about Lee Harwood and Roy Fisher), accepted in 1987. The proposal is that indeterminacy is very good for poetry, and that the kind of poetry he favours is in fact very indeterminate, and is the most valuable sector in recent British poetry. By 'indeterminacy' we mean either language which has not had its meaning exactly determined (the root *termin* means 'boundary') by the use of qualifying words which say who, when, where how; or procedures which lead to results not set by the poet's conscious mind, and which can be exploited in the development of a project. It is essential to the notion of game, for example, that its outcome and course are indeterminate before the start. The more poetry is like a game, the greater a role indeterminacy has in its course.

The reach of this principle has to be limited by an opposite principle of precision. If Michael Roberts, in a famous description of Eliot (in the introduction to the 1936 *Faber Book of Modern Verse*), describes Eliot's extraordinary precision as a key to his poetic power, that suggests also that precision is one of the winning assets of modern poetry. Indeed, it would not be hard to make a collection of vague passages which fail because they are vague.

The theory is based on an element of formalist linguistic theory, as expounded by the Czech philosopher Jan Mukařovský for example. Those philosophers were examining how language means, and were interested in the precision of clear prose, for example an instruction which tells you exactly where to insert a screw in a machine assembly. This allowed the information value of messages to be measured. But they noticed also that aesthetic language was marked by indeterminacy and could not be given a particular information value in the same way. So they separated it out. This indeterminate quality was however a feature, for them, of all aesthetic language, and so could not also be a distinguishing feature of poetry, or of a particular kind of poetry.

For Sheppard, the indeterminacy of Allen Fisher's *Place*, where in the composition an apparently finished text is mutated and as it were crashed into another text, and whereby components can be run in two different orders, represents freedom and so virtue. (This principle was applied by Sheppard in his own work, dependent on Fisher.) Fisher's attitude within a long project, which *Place* was, was that he wanted to recover freedom and spontaneity by breaking the rules of the project. This related to enthusiasm for Situationism and for cherished spontaneity. *Place* was also full of abstruse design rules, so that the 37 parts of one book mirror the 37 parts of another book, but running in the opposite direction. 'Place' is the product of positive rules, and in this way was the product of determination, which indeterminacy was a modification of. It is based on variations which in one sense are clearly determinations.

I note that Sheppard wrote his thesis already in the early '80s (it was examined by Eric Mottram). This makes it less than wholly plausible that it can supply an explanation of what has happened in the last 25 years. Have we all been exploring concepts which had already been worked out by the time the seventies finished? Two of his main subjects were Roy Fisher and Lee Harwood – this would indicate, again, how important the basic concept is, since their poetry is surely very important and very widely respected now. However, they had certainly worked out their key artistic concepts by the time the sixties were over.

There is a jack-in-the-box effect that Sheppard wants this aesthetic principle also to prove the superiority of small-press poetry over other kinds. The trouble here is that he stands in a certain position on the spectrum, with particular allies and patrons. If an abstract and so to speak timeless aesthetic principle turns out, suddenly, to justify his own position, and to justify his closest associates, that is not only puzzling but also seems to be the reverse of indeterminacy: rather it sounds like propaganda, where the end result was calculated from the beginning. His use of a non-prescriptive principle is prescriptive; poets can only succeed by applying it in big quantities, and their success is based on that act of application. Thus his extensive book *Complete Twentieth Century Blues* is designed with several different running orders, as if connecting the parts in different ways produced new information or new reactions.

Tom Raworth (1939-) is an example of indeterminacy. His mature poetry contains very few definite statements and recedes into a negative linguistic space where fragments of social structure are suspended like objects in a glass case in a museum. Nothing is asserted or contradicted but the whole social structure, or the structure of social utterance, gradually emerges into clear sight. The lack of specific detail takes us to the level of principles, to the rules which generate structure. At one level this is satire, where the statements of powerful people are cut up and annihilated, but at another level it reaches the sublime, because of the level of abstraction, the exaltation. Glossing a linguistic creation so intense is risky, but it is clear that Raworth is manipulating indeterminacy and that this is key to his methods.

Lee Harwood (1939-2015) was Sheppard's first mentor and was one of the subjects of Sheppard's thesis. His early work resembles early Raworth, but they diverged afterwards. Both can be seen as radical developments from Pop poetry as it was around 1965. His work often depicts scraps of stories, from old films or adventure novels, products of the ego in a state of drift or reverie. The stories never complete; rather they are clouds exhaled by a state of mind where ego boundaries are very weak. The poet rejects coherence or willpower as a method for enforcing the self on the world; indeterminacy is a key to his poetic.

Roy Fisher (1930-) has explained that he uses Birmingham as an analogy, the thing he uses for thinking with. He writes about Birmingham but the details are not there as part of a realist programme but rather as starting-points for journeys into the unknown. He very often uses precise physical details ("salts work their way/ to the outside of a plant pot/ and dry white"), and his poems are evocative of Midland landscapes, but not as part of a documentary project. Rather his intention is to break out of a set of thought patterns which he identifies with 'bourgeois guardianship' and to develop a new set of analogies which would not bypass Birmingham and would permit a new set of radical political solutions. Artistically, he is at the very opposite pole to some project like 'collecting photographs of old Birmingham', and so this freedom from realist impulse, a recognition of the indeterminacy of social arrangements, is key to his project. More exploration of the theme of indeterminacy – or of withdrawal from realism – is given in Roy Fisher's exceptionally clear interviews (including one with Sheppard from 1982).

Glyn Maxwell (1962-) began publishing during the '80s poems which are ambiguous during their course and which turn out at the end to have no particular purpose. The core of his art is the phase of suggestion, the square of vagueness before we realise that nothing is going to happen and it doesn't matter. This was connected, by prestigious patrons, to early Auden, the Auden of the 1930s, who also wrote poems in which various traits suggested that something was about to happen, that something was about to fail and give way, but where we don't find out what it is or what the story is. Maxwell is not a poet Sheppard would approve of. However, I think that indeterminacy was a feature of mainstream poetry from about 1985 on, as showcased in the 1993 anthology *The New Poetry*. It related to a nervousness, a fear of asserting control in the poem.

Presumably, one of the key moments which Sheppard is rejecting is the stage of a conventional poem of the era where a description of a situation which is apparently developing outwards in freedom is cut off short and replaced with a conclusion, which not only ends the poem but gives the situation a prescriptive meaning, a moral. So it loses its power to generate analogies freely and is reduced to demonstrating a single truth, probably a platitude. Presumably it is a feature of all 'underground' poems that they do not finish off and fold themselves away like this.

Part of his argument is that there is a link between linguistic indeterminacy and an unpredisposed attitude towards the social order. That is, withdrawing to a space of 'before', where language is not yet an exact description of a situation, is also a withdrawal to a place where the social order is not yet fixed, so that oppressed groups could either advance to a better position, or we could at least observe the process by which access to power and wealth is arranged, so that we understand how it is governed. The indeterminate poem, by not reproducing the lineaments of the social order as it is, is creating a free space where another order can be imagined. It is implicitly an act of protest and of political speculation. The poet is seceding from a dominant discourse. He faces challenges by withdrawing: he does not give any account of what happened in history. Instead we are presented with incomplete statements, to be read as questions, to be read as critique. Critique is not information. Any solid text is liquefied. People are not inscribed into their social roles, instead the role itself is suspended, switched off. This is the argument, but we have to ask whether this is really the main reason why poets write in an indeterminate way. Or, if radical politics is really the dominant factor, whether girls and women need to be shown a stage before meaning, in order to distrust inherited institutions – or whether a conventional narrative showing a woman acting independently and carrying out actions A, B, C, which have a value which is then socially accepted, is more convincing and so more radical. It stretches credulity to assert that the indeterminacy is the artistic principle behind so many diverse works. It could be more that the audience is bound to react aggressively towards various positive assertions, and the poet removes the assertions to get into a space where the predictable political arguments are not going to get re-run. So this would be simply the preparation of the canvas, before any artistic moves have been made.

The notion connects to an older idea of the poem as something which described ideals rather than concrete situations. On the plane of ideals, we can look critically at real situations and engage in political speculation aimed at bringing the ideals about. The suggestive power of poetry, designed in this way, was the unfulfilled nature of the ideals, which could yet be fulfilled in a thousand different ways – a sign of indeterminacy. We can say that abstract thought is indeterminate with respect to direct perception and that its power to manipulate reality derives from that liberation from precision. If we compare 19th-century poetry with 20th-century poetry, the withdrawal from idealism is one of the striking differences. But within critique there may be lurking the 19th century ideas of the beautiful, the noble, the elevated, the harmonious.

It may be that linguistic tics like presenting sentences without tense or verbs are part of this wish for indeterminacy. The denial of specification is felt to signify 'openness'. So a fraction of the poets at work are not trying to describe concrete situations with accuracy, like clear photographs, but hold back from that because freedom dwells somewhere before the situation had become defined.

There is some relationship between language being evocative and its being indeterminate, but one of the frustrations of Sheppard's work is that he does not try to explore the limits of his big idea, he simply wants it to be big, to represent ownership of territory, and to consign his enemies to defeat at every point. Presumably a large amount of indeterminate poetic language has no evocative power at all and so no power to conduct a political critique. Meanwhile, some very precise and determinate language has great evocative power.

The notion of indeterminacy is essential to modern poetry and has apparently endless new facets to offer. If poets seem fascinated by archaeology, this is partly because of the notion of 'before' as 'undetermined': by going back to 1000 BC you can re-run the stories that lead up to the present day and make them reach different outcomes. Or at least, suggest that other outcomes were possible. The 'Before', of withdrawing to a place before things have happened, is a key square on the board of modern poetry and can be found built into the structures of a wide range of different poets. It is not a place at all, but poets go there and bring back poems from there.

The action of language in stating meaning seems to be equivalent to determining meaning: the wholly indeterminate thus stands before language. Thus silence may be infinite and speech imposes limits on it. This gives a privileged position to wordless art, in fact to concrete poetry and sound poetry. I understand that this is absolutely in line with Sheppard's position. Thus Bob Cobbing, a friend of Sheppard's, is seen as representing liberation, although he always seemed mediocre and out of date to me. His work, published in 600 pamphlets from Writers Forum (which coincidentally Cobbing owned), is almost wholly non-verbal. The theory of indeterminacy here seems to be predicting artistic results that are very remote from the common reaction of readers. Finally a blank is more vague than vagueness.

On a personal level, Robert writes mainly about a small group of poets he has been personally close to, in the past 30 years, who are well known to me also. While he has had a unique opportunity to get close to them psychologically, his published work is disappointing as history because the range of poetry it covers is so narrow. The indeterminacy theory does not seem well equipped to relate the parts of the poetic field to each other.

So What Just Happened?

To sum up, this leaves us with detailed work undone, and which a narrower survey such as the one I am writing is going to have to get on with while light allows. The critics I have drawn on find difficulty, as I do, in isolating anything around in the time 1990-2010 which was not already there in 1980.

The situation of the poet who says 'but I don't have to succeed by these criteria and you are saying I've failed because I didn't fulfil them' is something which needs to be photographed: this is exactly where so many poets are. It is what a thousand poets are grumbling about over the breakfast table. The melody of the period is poet saying 'you've just defined 50 ways in which I am not modern but I am still in print' and reader saying, 'I don't know what is contemporary but I can count 51 ways in which you aren't contemporary'.

The gap where we are vainly searching for generalisations about the modern period is there because so many people have an investment to lose by seeing what modernity consists of (which they haven't got) that they refuse to become conscious and try to prevent other people from becoming conscious.

Partially Named Terrain

These entries offer a few minimal details which may serve as orientation. Older poets have not been included so as to move the focus onto new and unexposed poets. This is not therefore a view of all poets publishing or being read. Evidently some books by poets born before 1940, for example Geoffrey Hill and Christopher Logue, were among the best of the period. In this list, asterisks signal the ninety significant books on a list of, in fact, 90 significant books. DSMT is short for *Don't Start Me Talking*, a book of interviews. LWC and SR are abbreviations for two earlier books of mine, *Legends of the Warring Clans* and *Fulfilling the Silent Rules*, in which longer treatments of these poets are already available.

New Poets

Tim Atkins (1962). Author of unfailingly ingenious and self-aware and pleasurable poems. Can be seen as a development of the New York School. **Folklore* (1996); complete edition 2011; *To Repel Ghosts* (1998); *Horace* (2007); *1,000 Sonnets* (2011). SR

Elisabeth Bletsoe (1960), comes from Dorset. Part of a group of writers in Cardiff in the 1990s who were interested in performance and in writing about landscape and myth. Early books collected in *Pharmacopoeia* (2010). Moved back to England and works in a museum. Expert in herbs. **Landscape from a Dream* (2008) collects her classic later work. SR, DSMT

Sean Bonney (1969) spent his early career in Manchester and Nottingham but benefited later from contact with the London scene around Writers Forum. Stands for the continuing strength and integrity of English radicalism, the surviving hopes for a better social order. **Blade Pitch Control Unit* (2006), is a definitive collection of his work to that point. *Document* (2009). Has benefited from the legacy both of Blake and of anarchism. *The Commons* (2011). Interview in DSMT, SR.

Andrea Brady was born in Philadelphia and came to England as a student. A scholar of Renaissance literature, she has been claimed as part of the Cambridge School, has also stated calmly and clearly that there is no such link. 'Avant-garde genealogy' can be seen as an invasive and colonising presence of ghosts. Edits avant-garde publisher

Barque, a leader in the field. *Vacation of a Lifetime* (Salt, 2001), *Cold Calling* (Barque, 2004), *Embrace* (Object Permanence, 2005), *Wildfire* (Krupskaya, 2010), *Cut from the Rushes* (2013) and most recently *Mutability: Scripts for Infancy* (2013).

ZOË BRIGLEY (1981) represents a 'second generation' of feminist writers as her mother was also a feminist writer and edited a very early anthology of Welsh women poets. *The Secret* (2007) was the most exciting Welsh debut for many years. *Conquest* (2012).

CHRISTOPHER BROWNSWORD (1981)'s *(in the field, the sunset)* was published online *circa* 2005, is intimate and has a kind of pastoral depressive sublime. *Icarus Was Right!* (2010) is confident and linguistically challenging. *Rhesus Distribution*, "a portal for black psychedelic word, art and sound" seems to stock further products.

> From there would
>
>   ebb by
>
> lighter..source, dense
>
>   fog grown
>
>   briskly over path soon
>
>   coiling outwards up
>
> gardenias left
>
>   fingering dry
>
>   scabs (yet)
>
>   hardly
>
>   teeth of gods kept
>
> safe beneath dull
>
> ash
>
> (from 'flakes of timber, drifting from the hollows of a dying fire')

EMILY CRITCHLEY – too early to judge but was a star on the Cambridge small-press scene shortly before *How to Make Millions* (pamphlet, 2005). Extravagant and intellectual. Exponent of avant-garde subjectivity. *Love/ all that / & OK* (2011).

IAN DUHIG, from Leeds. A poet with a deep affinity for punk and quite unabraded radical ideals whose command of sophistication and cultural erudition produced some astonishing poetry. *The Bradford Count* (1991) is his major work. *The Mersey Goldfish* followed (1995). His third book *The Lammas Hireling* showed a new admiration for folk styles. The wish to be Shane McGowan needed more restraint.

STEVE ELY debuted with *Oswald's Book of Hours* (2013). The jacket says, "A former Sunday League footballer, revolutionary socialist and secondary school headteacher, he's a Catholic in the tradition of John Ball, and he hunts with dogs". Oswald was a king of Northumbria and this is a kind of proletarian mythology of the North. Like that other Northern writer, Surtees, he writes frequently about hunting. The episodes range from the 7th century to the aftermath of the Falklands War.

MARK FORD (1962) – Clearly influenced by the New York School and works in a world which is generated by language more than generating it. His manner is assertive and forthright, which makes it different from other poets in this tradition. The poems are high concept but full of banal lines. It is not always clear why he is writing the poem. *Soft Sift* (2001)

GILES GOODLAND (1964) undertakes systematic poems which take on the underlying complexity of the universe, in a radically anti-personal way. Simultaneously exploits the complexity of data storage systems as 'givens' and the power of generating language arbitrarily. One of few poets to face up to the complexity of modern knowledge and not regress within the 'personality envelope'. "Towards the end I got broadband and found it easier to simply paste my research from various databases straight into the poem.": in campaigns like this, Goodland seems to be taking on the idea of the ego as a data editing agent, highly mobile and 'trapped' in a universe of data stores. Everyone sees something like this to be true but 'personal poetry' has usually not caught up. *Littoral* (1996), *A Spy in the House of Years* (2001), *Capital* (2006), *What the Things Sang* (2009). Interview at http://intercapillaryspace.blogspot.co.uk/2006/11/collage-capital-interview-with-giles.html

MARK GOODWIN – *Else* (2008) is the debut of a poet from North Leicestershire who lives on a narrowboat on the canal or the nearby River Soar. Is landscape poetry written with great care and ambition.

RODY GORMAN (1960) writes in both Irish and Scottish Gaelic. A mercurial poet, can be compared with Edwin Morgan. *Zonda? Khamsin?*

Sharaav? Camanchaca? (2006) has many translations from Chinese or Japanese nature poets, and Gorman resembles these rather than the Gaelic heritage. *Chernilo* (2006) is a large selected poems. 'Chernilo' means 'ink' – in Russian.

KHALED HAKIM mainly known for partly improvised performance pieces, his published work is not extensive. Moved from the Birmingham arts scene to work at the Film Makers' Co-Op in Camden, and his contribution to poetry was to re-introduce modern styles of narrative into it. As a performer, was provocative and specialised in exposing the audience's inhibitions and cultural investments. Not everyone found this funny but it was certainly exciting. Family came from Sylhet. Associated with the magazines *Equofinality* and *Angel Exhaust*.

GRAHAM HARTILL (1954?) – English poet who has lived in Wales for many years. Was part of the Cardiff offshoot of the English Intelligencer school of interest in geography, landscape, and mythology. An interest in Chinese poetry was a side-effect of this. *Ruan Ji's Island and (Tu Fu) in the Cities* (1993); **Cennau's Bell* (2005); *A Winged Head* (2007).

OLI HAZZARD (1986) aiming for the specific 'neurological space' of someone groping for a word for an unfamiliar concept. This space is transient and yet capable of renewing everything. To reach it the poem has to dissolve – the not yet conscious, the not yet language takes over. His poem which lists the definitions of interstitial or unknown words is, astonishingly, composed entirely of found material. **Between Two Windows* (2012)

W.N. HERBERT (1961). *Dundee Doldrums: an exorcism* (published 1991), was written entirely in the 'unfashionable' dialect of Dundee. This was ferocious satirical realism rooted in everyday experience in Dundee. Part of the Informationist group (with Crawford, Price, McCarey). Was probably at a peak in the early '90s. A widespread view is that the pressure of producing endless new work to fulfil the terms of grants and so on led to a dropping-off. He began writing entirely in English. He also decided he could write comic verse and that he had similarities to the gay, colloquial and brilliantly cultured, New York poet Frank O'Hara. Not everyone agreed with this and the books written in this direction are not widely admired. **Forked Tongue* (1994) shows his full vigour.

JEFF HILSON (1970?) Comic avant-garde poet who writes like a Shakes-pearean clown. **Stretchers* (2006). *In the Assarts* (2010). Has a unique flavour, both paradoxical and picturesque, and arguably no literal meaning at all. Thought of as founder of the Roehampton School (*freaklung*, Ninerrors, etc.). Is a friend of Sean Bonney and edited a political broadsheet with him at the time of the Second Iraq War. SR

PAUL HOLMAN – His poetry is indefinable but is laconic, occultist, and attached to the line of revolutionary and subversive yearnings. *The Memory of the Drift I-IV* (2007) is the beginning of a still continuing long term project. Book V, *Tara Morgana*, followed. SR

ANDY JORDAN – Editor of *10th Muse* and king of ambivalence and a longing for what he savages. Obligated to Jeremy Hooker and to postmodern critique of archaeology. *St Catherine's Buried Chapel* (1987), *The Invisible Children* (1991), *Mute Bride* (1998), *Ha Ha* (2007), *Hegemonick* (2012).

SARAH LAW – similar to Llewellyn-Williams but within a Christian framework. *Perihelion* (2006), *Ascension Notes* (2009). The language is highly coloured, too much so for some people. Gothic, even. Fulfils the main theme of the era, that secularism is too hard and 'theological' religion has to be personalised and fitted into the feelings and longings of the individual.

DANIEL LANE, pupil of John James and author of entrancing lyric poetry of the evanescent moment. *Stuff Culture* and **Wrecks in Ultra-Sound* both came out in 1995.

IRA LIGHTMAN was around 20 years ago as an absurdly prolific and stylistically learned poet on the underground scene. Evolved in maturity into a ludic poet, escaping the 'underground' due to a link with 'public art' – the managers tolerate modernity in visual art but not in poetry. Amazingly avoids the academic conventions of experimental poetry. Genuine surprise is achieved by genuinely being open to the new day. Taps the non-finite powers of linguistic variation. **Duetcetera* (2008) collects poems in double column, dual voices which refer back to all language being dialogic somehow. They abolish the conscious layer and create dual unconscious streams, raising questions about whether the self is only the most focussed area.

FRANCESCA LISETTE – poet working in the 'new lyric', section *In Thrall* shown in the shared volume *VierSome 2*.

RUPERT M LOYDELL (1960) has probably published more than anyone else his age. "His writing has appeared in hundreds of magazines", we read, and his books number over 30. Without any Loydell expert to consult, I have to conclude from limited exposure that he does not believe in the ego and relies on dissociation and drift. This may be enlightenment but is hard to recall afterwards. Being unpremeditated is not the same as being innovative. *A Conference of Voices* (2004).

CAROLA LUTHER – *Walking the Animals* (2004) striking poems about feelings which use conventional language. *Arguing with Malarchy* (2011) includes 'Moving House' which describes moving between two quiet farmhouses in an unspecified country:

> It began with the owl moving into the attic
> under the chimney where wind lived like an animal,
> then the mouse and its offspring bedding down
> in softnesses long forgotten in the cellar, then spiders,
> many of them, hanging their shadows in string bags
> beneath them, touching toes with themselves under lintel
> and eave, then flies dead or alive, lining up on the rims
> of windows, followed by the flurry of the neighbour

– a brilliant evocation of solitude and the vivid forces of decay.

HELEN MACDONALD (1970) Already a poetic prodigy as an undergraduate. Had a greater natural gift than anyone around her. A volume finally came out in 2001, *Shaler's Fish*. Interested professionally in ornithology, but apparently interested in everything. Has not shared the interests of her contemporaries and has appeared detached from the need to write poetry. SR

ROB MACKENZIE, a physicist by trade, of a Hebridean family and slightly resentful at being brought up English-speaking. Lived in Cambridge during the '90s and took part in the student poetry scene of the time. The poetry is advanced and hard to describe, the bilingual bits being the easiest to recognise. *Off Ardglas* (1997) is his only book.

PETER MANSON (1969) from Glasgow. More or less encompasses the Scottish avant-garde. Edited (with Robin Purves) *Object Permanence*, the only avant-garde Scottish magazine. Poetry is hard to define but is laconic, obscure, and attracted to Mallarmé (whom he has translated). *Birth Windows* (1999); *For the Good of Liars* (2006); *Between Cup and Lip* (2008). SR, DSMT

D.S. MARRIOTT (1963), from Gedling, on the edge of Nottingham; now lives in California. Family of West Indian origin, raised as a Catholic. Did a doctoral study on Prynne and began with work very deeply in the line of Prynne. Associated with the 'avant-garde neoclassicist' wave of the late 1980s, which went back to the highest points of the Cambridge School and dismissed what had come in between. This can be seen as an expression of belief in the decay of the avant-garde. More recent work, since the late '90s, has been more straightforward and more political and angry. *Incognegro* (2006) shows this later period. **Hoodoo Voodoo* (2008) collects early work. *The Bloods* (2011). SR, LWC

SOPHIE MAYER known for urbane and lyric poems. Published **Marsh Fear / Fen Tiger* (2002) as a debut (volume shared with Leo Mellor), then *Her Various Scalpels* (2009), which deals with film stars and exits from the personality. Originally published as Sophie Levy but then preferred to be known by her matronymic.

CHRIS McCABE (1977), from Liverpool. A radical and politicised working-class poet, one of many stirred into outrage by the Iraq war of 2003. ** The Hutton Inquiry* (2005). *Zeppelins* (2008). *The Restructure* (2012). Wrenches language into a direct response to a fragmented and violently unjust urban mosaic.

SL MENDOZA prolific author of pamphlets (*Junctions, Reckoning, Ninerrors, Die Fliege, *Frass Buik*) from 2009 on. Represents either a completely new artistic wave or (if you are going to be stuffy about it) a fourth generation of the Underground. Deploys a very free style in which disparate moments add up to a coherent whole. Edits *Freaklung* magazine and the Ninerrors pamphlet series.

MARIANNE MORRIS was a star on the Cambridge student scene circa 2004, associated with Bad Press. Has produced several pamphlets. Influenced by O'Hara and definitely in the 'avant-garde subjective' style where everything is in the first person and in the immediate present. *Gathered Tongue* (2003); *Fetish Poems* (2004); *A New Book From Barque Press, Which They Will Probably Not Print* (2006); **Commitment.* (2011).

ALICE OSWALD (1966) nature poet representing a revival of the mainstream during the 1990s. **Dart* (2002).

JEREMY OVER, from Cumbria. **A Little Bit of Bread and No Cheese* (2001) was a brilliant debut which seemed to herald a new ludic and soaring poetry akin to the New York School, comparable to David Herd and Robert Saxton. *Deceiving Wild Animals* (2009).

CRIS PAUL (1978) Welsh avant-garde poet who has participated deeply in the London School of concrete and sound poetry. *stenia cultus handbook* (2010) is his first book.

NICK POTAMITIS *N.* (2006) is a striking debut involving montage, and about Byron and Greek culture.

HEATHER PHILLIPSON – too new to call but an affinity with the '60s conceptual artist John Baldessari may be borne in mind. A conversation about the poem is mixed in with the poem, which has the freedom of speculation. *Instant-fLex 718* (2013) is flawless and very highly finished.

CLARE POLLARD (1978) plays an emblematic role as the hope of British poetry, uniting technical brilliance with emotional presence. Writes with more intimacy than most personal poets and more freedom of language than most mainstream poets. Edited an anthology of exceptionally young poets, *Six for the New Century*. Books so far are *The Heavy Petting Zoo* (1998), *Bedtime* (2002), *Look Clare! Look!* (2005). *Changeling* (2011). Interview at http://www.scribd.com/doc/91859393/Incorporating-Writing-Issue-Vol-1

KATE POTTS (1978) In *Pure Hustle* (2011) the realist subjects dissolve into figures of speech like nitrate flowing off film carrying the image with it – pouring out as a fuzz of glittering dots. The gestalt of the poems is destabilised by recondite and flourishing vocabulary, the primary line competing with a secondary structure of decoration. This can seem fidgety or an autonomous state.

> I twine in thicker hanks of flouncing
> – birded frittering, the wing's itch –
>
> tentative, sharp-winged into lifting, off-kilter pirouettes,
> hovers and flips.
>   (from 'Cloth Trick')

This is an extended metaphor about weaving, which is the 'pure hustle' (innocent strenuous activity?) of the title.

RICHARD PRICE (1966), member of Informationist school. *Perfume and Petrol Fumes* (1999).

NIALL QUINN, NICK MACIAS, and NIC LAIGHT, were the group represented in the astounding debut *However Introduced to the Soles* (1995);
wild and extreme avant-garde poets. They may not represent the Welsh
avant-garde, as Laight is English and Quinn Irish. Why were they in
Wales? Who knows. The form-up zone was probably Bridgend. LWC

NAT RAHA is a leading representative of either a new phenomenon
or, arguably, the 'fourth generation' of the Underground. Too early to
summarise the work, collected in *Octet* (2010) and *Countersonnets*
(2013), but it uses complex syntax and is politically serious. Has
collaborated with *Freaklung*.

> line on line-frame additive & the skirts of creature commodity
> limp before the declining temperature,
> before the jog of light scattering to field populous
> & sib in shown structure   nubile   dewed &
> few corner'd   on full anchor, dulled
> subscript sheaves in remnant light   paining minim –
>   sonata %brute by desire's famine, elected
> w/out Y's conception;
>   (from '(recumbent territorial)' from *Octet*)

The parts are not obscure in themselves but they stretch the conventional
frame and the accumulation of strange and rare words pushes the poem
into an exotic surface which is simultaneously the substance of its
distinctiveness and its allure.

DAVID REES – *The London* (1997) was a brilliantly creative trip through
the imaginary of London sites (mainly in the historic core) which owes
something to the author's interest in art history (he is an art dealer) and
in Iain Sinclair.

DERYN REES-JONES – noted dweller in the 'third zone' which is neither
mainstream nor avant-garde. Did a major 'recuperative' anthology of
women's poetry, *Modern Women Poets*. *The Memory Tray* (1994); *Signs
Around a Dead Body* (1998), *Quiver* (2004). SR

LUKE ROBERTS – *False Flags* (2011) is a brilliant debut. Hard to assess
at this point but he seems to be able to write fluently and clearly about
ideas, abolishing one of the barriers between poetry and a wider world.
Reminds me of Kevin Nolan.

JOHN ROBINSON – Yorkshire poet. * *The Cook's Wedding* (2001). Remarkable example of 'late Pop' work which has great charm and energy and never outstays its welcome. This is apparently his first book.

EURIG SALISBURY published **Llyfr Glas Eurig* in 2008, an astonishing combination of youth culture with classical Welsh metrics which made every map of the landscape appear deluded.

JAMES SHEARD published **Scattering Eva,* a first volume, in 2005. Enigmatic but sophisticated poet presenting passages of characters from some novel which is not actually available.

Shuddered (2009, 2nd edn. 2010). Containing some 272 pages of work by Piers Hugill, Aodán McCardle, and Stephen Mooney. The overall effect of this extension of 1970s full-on alienated experimentalism is like some rusting hulk of technology which has mysteriously stayed loyal to its toxins amid fifty annual waves of revisionism. Although it is hard to describe the result as aesthetically pleasing, or to see it winning any arguments with the cultural forces it is opposed to, it is authentic even if authentically retarded. An unmodulated linear push will cross boundaries even if it is moving slowly. The confrontation with everyday experience is rigorous to the extent that it never escapes into significance.

ROBERT SMITH. In the 1990s, I saw a lot of his poems in typescript and published quite a few in *Angel Exhaust*. No book has followed and I think he has left not only poetry but academic life. The poems ('sonnets'), each ten lines long, were quite exemplary, vivid and dream-like.

> SKYBLUE LYRE BLACK THROAT
> the box vibrates
> & earthquakes out
> into a wooden rose.
> The wreaths are set,
> wire twisted
> round a martyr
> head that hums
> from heavenly crack
> eyes slit upward.

SIMON SMITH (1961) part of the wave of 'avant-garde neoclassicism' impacted by the huge retrospectives of the English avant-garde put out by Allardyce, Barnett in the 1980s. Debuted with *Night Shift* (1991). Masterpiece is **13 Exits* (2001). Later work is more influenced by the New York School: *Reverdy Road* (2003); *Mercury* (2006); *London Bridge* (2010); *11781 W. Sunset Boulevard* (2014). Interview in DSMT. LWC

RHYS TRIMBLE poet of 'alternative' style who speaks Welsh but writes mostly in English. Published *keinc* (2010), descriptions of journeys. Edits CAD magazine online.

KARLIEN VAN DEN BEUKEL is the author so far of one brilliant book, **Pitch Lake* (1997).

> How I wept when it appeared
> I was unequipped
> to be an interpenetrative twin.
>
> Yes, I have nothing
> against the lamé underpantaloons of dawn
> thrown over the Backs
> whilst
> taking the matitudinal interpluvium
> in winsome
> losesomeness.

This seems to be a critique of the Cambridge school, the 'interpenetrative elite'. It argues some inside knowledge, we think. SR

VITTORIA VAUGHAN, ** The Mummery Preserver* (1996); intuitive Jungian poet whose only volume this is. LWC

SAMANTHA WALTON, poet working in the line between subjective and objective knowledge; shown in the section *TTAGGG* (a hash tag for a strand about genes) in the shared volume *VierSome 2*.

CAROL WATTS teaches at Birkbeck College and began publishing *circa* 2005. Seen as a continuation, maybe even a redemption, of the avant-garde line in London. *Wrack* (2007) is a collection of 'process' poems based on the shoreline. *This is Red* (2009), *Sundog* (2013).

MATTHEW WELTON (1969) is from Nottingham. Has published two books with Carcanet. Occupies a structural role as a poet using conceptual and 'process oriented' methods who is nonetheless accepted by the mainstream. Is fond of methods using systematic repetition and variation on preset texts. Gives away a personal voice in favour of the incalculable complexities of linguistic variation. Teaches at Nottingham. Has agreed with other Nottingham poets that there is no Nottingham School. *The Book of Matthew* (2003); *We Needed Coffee But...* (2009).

BORN IN THE 1950S

MONIZA ALVI debuted with *The Country at My Shoulder* (1993); *Carrying my Wife* (2000) collects earlier volumes. Drawing on 'magic realism' modes of dealing with exotic geography. Influenced by Jo Shapcott, adapting her surrealism to the 'double reality' of being of dual Pakistani and English culture. SR

MICHAEL AYRES (1958), prolific and advanced poet specialising in the impact of the visual-technological. *Poems 1987-92* (1994). Later work is too expansive in the tradition of extended dance mixes, luxuriating in variations (*a.m.*, 2003). *Only* (2010) is a return to form. SR

ALISON BRACKENBURY (1953) – *Dreams of Power and Other Poems* (1981), *Breaking Ground and other poems* (1984), *Christmas Roses and other Poems* (1988), *1829* (1995). *Bricks and Ballads* (2004). Impressive lyric poet of a conservative bent.

PAUL BROWN (circa 1950?), another star of the London School, began in the early 70s with graphic poetry but moved on to a verbal medium. *Meetings and Pursuits* (1978). *Masker* (1982). Believed to have stopped writing poetry in the early '90s – *A Cabin in the Mountains* was published in 2012 but credited to twenty years earlier. Little discussed in the 'living memory' partly because of a 'crowd-out' process of too many brilliant poets at the same time, partly because of a sophisticated and unshowy method.

ADRIAN CLARKE (1950?) – long-term presence in the London avant-garde scene. Involved in performance poetry. Edited *Angel Exhaust*, and until 2006 the Writers Forum series, and edits *AND*. *Ghost Measures* (1987), *Spectral Investments* (1991) and *Obscure Disasters* (1993) are parts of a trilogy called *Ghost Trio*, which consists throughout of lines of four words, with certain exceptions which are of eight words each. The preset line-model is a row of blanks, hence ghost measures, cf. also the spectre in 'spectral investments' (i.e. cultural or emotional investments). The effect of these insistent and asyntactic incisions in continuous verbal material is like a beatbox. His poetry is noticeable for its pace and can be described as dromoscopic (as described by Paul Virilio), to intensely exciting effect. It is somewhat in the manner of Raworth. Obliterating the rational tier of syntax allows a large-scale picture of contemporary politics and society to emerge in the fascinating emptiness. *Doing the Thing* (1997); *Possession, poems 1996-2006* (2007). SR

KELVIN CORCORAN (1956), major figure of the middle generation that followed Prynne and Fisher. Radically critical poet seeing paradoxes and self-betrayals in public life, informed by Adorno. *Lyric Lyric* (1993); *When Suzy Was* (1999); **New and Selected Poems* (2004); *Backward Turning Sea* (2008); *Hotel Shadow* (2010), *For the Greek Spring* (2013), *Sea Table* (2015). LWC; interview in DSMT.

ROBERT CRAWFORD (1959) Christian poet, part of Informationist group in 1980s, which largely meant followers of Morgan. **Sharawaggi* (1990, in collaboration with W.N. Herbert) is a classic of writing in Scots and of Informationism. Also functions as a literary manager not loved by all avant-garde poets in Scotland. Writes avant-garde poetry which escapes destructive attention from other managers because of his status as professor and Elder of the Kirk. *Scottish Assembly* (1990), *Talkies* (1992), *Masculinity* (1996), *Spirit Machines* (1999), *The Tip of My Tongue* (2003), *Full Volume* (2008). SR

DAVID DABYDEEN (1957) comes from the Indian ('East Indian') population group in Guyana but has lived here for many years. An academic specialising in the sociology of Caribbean writing who has published a significant body of poems: *Coolie Odyssey* (1988), **Turner* (1994). SR

MENNA ELFYN (1951) – pioneer of feminist poetry (and criticism) in Wales. Writes in Welsh but English translations are easily available. Writes personalised protest poetry in a style close to singer-songwriters: feminist, anti-capitalist, anti-war. Edited two key anthologies of women poets in Welsh. **Eucalyptus* (1995) is her selected poems from 1978 on. *Perffaith Nam / Perfect Blemish* (2007). SR

JOHN GOODBY (1958), from Birmingham. Early appearance in *Faber Poetry Introduction 8*, 1993. Generally seen as part of a school of Far Left/ satirically-oriented poets resident in Leeds, with Ian Duhig. Marginal politics led to a special view of history. Was one of the primary anti-Thatcherite poets. Moved towards the avant-garde. **Illennium* (2010) is probably his best work. Has lived in Ireland and Wales for long periods, and wrote a standard work on modern Irish poetry. Translated Heine's 'A Winter's Tale' and Pasolini's 'Gramsci's Ashes'. *A Birmingham Yank* (1998); *uncaged sea* (2008); *Wine Night White* (2010).

DAVID GREENSLADE (1953) – Welsh nationalist writing in English and occasionally in Welsh. *Burning Down the Dosbarth* was the only work in English published by the series of Y beirdd answyddogol. Inspired by conceptual art to work in projects where fixed rules generate unique outcomes. *Creosote* (1996); **Each Broken Object* (2000), *Zeus Amoeba* (2009), *Dark Fairground* (2009), *Lyrical Diagrams* (2012). LWC, DSMT

ROBERT HAMPSON (1950?), from Liverpool, associated with the London School of the 1970s, co-edited *Alembic*. Wrote during the 1980s the classic Objectivist/documentary history of the town, *Seaport* (latest edition 2008); **Assembled Fugitives* (2001) is a selected poems, 1973-98; *Explaining the Colours* (2010). interview at http://www. argotistonline.co.uk/Hampson%20interview.htm

RALPH HAWKINS (1953) Welsh poet and founder of the Essex School. Edited *Ochre* magazine in the '70s. Early on wrote hippy pastoral poetry embodying leisure and calm: *Word from the One, soft in the brain, more and more, But It May Be So.* Wrote off-brand Chinese poems like so many others. Pasted up concrete and collage assemblies with Cobbing (*Gloria, Pool*). Late work is indescribable but by far the best: *The Coiling Dragon, The Scarlet Bird, The White Tiger, A Blue & Misted Shroud* (1999), **The MOON, Chief Hairdresser (highlights)* (2004), *Gone to Marzipan* (2009), *It Looks Like an Island But Sails Away* (2015). SR

DAVID KENNEDY (1959) – A re-creation of '50s New York School poetry, so light-hearted, ludic, and following arbitrary rules to genre bizarre contexts. Lives in Sheffield and artistically resembles George Macbeth, who grew up in Sheffield. Equally ludic but without the range. *The President of Earth: new and selected poems* (2002).

FRANK KUPPNER (1951), labyrinthine and anti-realist poet from Glasgow. *A Bad Day for the Sung Dynasty* (1984) was one of the classics of the new playful and hedonistic poetry which emerged in the aftermath of over-politicisation in the early 1980s. *Everything is Strange* (1994), **Second Best Moments in Chinese History* (1997), *What? Again? Selected Poems* (2000), *A God's Breakfast* (2004); *Arioflotga* (2008), *The Same Life Twice* (2012). SR

TIM LIARDET (1959) – **The Storm House* (2011) is a moving account of the poet's brother's life and death. The attempt to deal with the depth of a long relationship by expanding the scale of the project is a pursuit of psychological realism. The individual poems are vivid like poetry but the overall structure aspires to the density of a novel.

HILARY LLEWELLYN-WILLIAMS, fond of deep subjectivity and New Age themes. The 1987 volume *The Tree Calendar* and the 1990 work *Book of Shadows*, which narrates scenes from the life of Giordano Bruno of Nola, are included in a collected volume, *Hummadruz* (2001). While the writing is unusually clear it is not intense; it is like a brocaded quilt, warm and rich and saturated – bright colours, rippling patterns, symmetry. SR

IWAN LLWYD (1957-2010) *Gwreichion* (Sparks) (1990) was a prize-winning realist sequence dealing with a contemporary Wales while thinking about ideal states.

TONY LOPEZ (1950?). Mainly a performance artist in the '70s. Wrote volumes in the process-oriented style – 'Change' was one of the major long poems of the '70s. Moved to a more discursive style, peaked with *Stress Management* (1994). *False Memory* (1996) shows either typical overuse of a rhythm over several volumes or else having the key to relating politics to domestic circumstance. *Only More So* (2012) is described in the text. *Devolution* (2000).

JAMIE McKENDRICK (1955), sophisticated and entertaining poet, a master of the affable spoken tone. *The Sirocco Room* (1991); *Kiosk on the Brink* (1993); *The Marble Fly* (2001); *Ink Stone* (2003); *Crocodiles & Obelisks* (2007); *Out There* (2012). *Sky Nail: Poems 1979-1997* (2000) is a selected poems. Interview at http://www.oxonianreview.org/wp/an-interview-with-jamie-mckendrick/

ROBERT MINHINNICK (1952) Most gifted poet of his generation within the Anglo-Welsh tradition. Edited *Poetry Wales* (1997-2008). Developed remarkably during the 1990s and left or re-invented that tradition. Moved roughly from 'communalist' to 'rustbelt poet' to 'magic realism' and thus became the heir to Dylan Thomas. Took off artistically after 1990, on realising he could be a world poet and not just the best Anglo-Welsh poet. *Selected Poems* (1999); *After the Hurricane* (2002); *King Driftwood* (2008).

JOHN MUCKLE *Fire Writing*, (2005) a searing set of social-realist poems which does not fit in with anything else and is neglected because it is so isolated. Muckle (b.1956?) was taught by Ralph Hawkins at Essex and met a number of poets later known as the Essex School. He was a writer of prose fiction until circa 2003 but was in touch with advanced poetry. He set up the 1988 anthology *the new british poetry* which was completed by Iain Sinclair.

KEVIN NOLAN (1953), prominent member of the Cambridge poetry world who began publishing poetry in the late '90s. *Loving Little Orlick* (2006) is his one full-length book, a lone development from 1960s Prynne and one of the most ambitious books of its time. SR

MAGGIE O'SULLIVAN (1951) star of the London avant-garde scene in the '80s. Writes ecstatic nature poetry in a radically primeval and non-discursive style. Evacuation of syntax makes for dense, pounding, stresses, in discontinuous, constant, peaks. Interested in concrete poetry and incantations. Influenced by Barrie MacSweeney (the *Odes* period). *Body of Work* (2006) collects pamphlets from the 1980s, *Alto. London Poems 1975-84* (2009) collects rather earlier work. Withdrew to Yorkshire and signed on at the same job centre as Michael Haslam. Seems to have written little since leaving London. *House of the Shaman* (1993). *Palace of Reptiles* (2003). LWC

JEREMY REED (1951) uncontrollably prolific poet whose first pamphlet came out in 1972. Represents the dominance of the 'intimacy' tradition in English poetry, permanently regarding small personal feelings as more real than anything else, and raising the feelings of bedrooms and small gigs to heroic dimensions. A pioneer in merging poetry with the world of popular culture and glossy magazines. Has published some 30 books, more than I could track down. It took four people to put his selected poems together. Masterpiece is presumably 'Stratton Elegy', from 1978 (included in *Black Russian. Outtakes from the Airmen's Club*).

LESLEY SAUNDERS (1946), author of *Cloud Camera* (2012), described in the text, and of the best ever poems about Chinese mitten crabs. Also co-author of *Christina the Astonishing* (1998). SR

ROBERT SAXTON (1952) from Nottingham. Poet with an awesome inventiveness of language. Seems to be preoccupied with puzzling ornate formal schemes. Has no preference for themes and seems willing to dissolve into language itself. Hard to compare to anyone else but verbal games are an ancient pastime of mankind. The poems are singular and varied. *The Promise Clinic* (1994); *Manganese* (2003); *Local Honey* (2007); *The China Shop Pictures* (2012).

JOHN SEED (1950), Marxist poet from Durham writing in a pristine neo-Objectivist style based on Oppen. *Interior in the Open Air* (1993); *Pictures from Mayhew: London 1850* (2005); *New and Collected Poems* (2005); *That Barrikins: Pictures from Mayhew 2* (2007), *Smoke Rising* (2015).

Jo SHAPCOTT (1953), writes vivid poems with a prudently exact deployment of fantasy and surrealism. Represents a new atmosphere in the 1980s, a decisive break with certain inhibitions in the mainstream of poetry. *Phrase Book* (1992); **Her Book: Poems 1988-98* (2000); *Of Mutability* (2011).

NIGEL WHEALE (1953) lives in Orkney. One of the Cambridge school, at a moment in the mid-70s when things were getting more politicised and less pastoral. Writes from a Left critique of the power order and with an interest in popular culture as something opposed to that. Has written about postmodernist culture and at one stage wrote high-tech postmodernist poems. **Raw Skies. New and Selected Poems* (2006). *Tracks and Flows* (2004) SR

CHRISTOPHER WHYTE (1952) Gaelic poet now resident in Budapest. A book of poetry is *Uirsgeul* (1991). Writes in a style presumably influenced by classical Italian art (he lived in Rome for seven years). Symmetry, finish and poise allow him to talk about deep and intimate feelings.

ALED JONES WILLIAMS (1956). Anglican clergyman who has published one book of poetry, *Y cylchoedd perffaith*. One of his main themes is his own alcoholism, and his principal work is writing realistic plays which ask people to come to terms with problems like his own. 'Awelon' (breezes), included in *Y Cylchoedd Perffaith* (perfect circles), uses experimental typography and stretches of blank paper to portray fading or intermittent consciousness in its depiction of a fatal cancer. This is hardly verse, but intense and surrealistic prose. It won the Pryddest prize at the 2002 Eisteddfod, which shows that the judges were not as conservative as Welsh guardians of culture are imagined to be. The reviewer in *Taliesin* remarks (issue 141, page 147) that a sort of apologia in the volume publication "is witness to the conservative and childish response which it obtained from some in Wales in 2002, almost a century after other countries accepting this experimental form of composition". This is a notably free era for Welsh poetry, and the liberals need to be counted as well as the conservatives crouched in their trenches.

BORN IN THE 1940S

JOHN ASH (1948) cannot be described without mentioning the New York School and the efficiency of his work has something to do with being a second generation. Unfailingly presents his peculiar character of wit, melancholy, and impressionability, which by now we could not bear to be without. *The Burnt Pages* (1991); *Selected Poems* (1996); *The Anatolikon and To the City* (2002); *In the Wake of the Day* (2010). SR

ANTHONY BARNETT (1941) has spent much of his life as a jazz musician, specifically a percussionist in the free improvisation area. His poetry narrates the texture of everyday life, as written by a musician. The tone is intensely personal, dealing with the evanescent and yet mysterious and poignant. The protagonist is sophisticated; he is leading life as opposed to wallowing in alienation. *Miscanthus* (2005) is a selected. *Carp and Rubato* (1995); *Poems* (2012) is a collected edition.

DAVID BARNETT (1942), Jungian poet who has lived in Wales for many years. Writes with a virtuosically quick flurry of monosyllables, describing myths and rituals of integration. *Fretwork* (n.d.); *All the Year Round* (1994). *There's Only the Dance* (2011). LWC

B. (BRIAN) CATLING (1948-), from London. Professor of sculpture. Possibly began being interested in poetry as a student of Iain Sinclair's at film school circa 1970. Inhabits the same zone of Gothic horror as Sinclair's early and middle periods. *Soundings* (accounts of performance acts), *The Stumbling Block, Its Index* (1990); *Written Rooms and Pencilled Crimes* (1992) was a retrospective. *Late Harping. Last Century Works* (2001) collects more installation scripts. Another selected poems is *A Court of Miracles* (2009).

DAVID CHALONER (1944-2010) leading exponent of the 'eternal present' style of the '60s. A designer by profession, was influenced by visual art and by the New York School. Reproduced the surface of daily life with hallucinatory vividness and with a poignant sense of unexplored possibilities. A combination of sophistication and immediacy. *The Edge*; *Collected Poems* (2005); *Beyond the Lines* (2007). SR

VICKI FEAVER (1943) from Nottingham. Slow-writing poet doing work of striking sensory intensity. Concerned with the violence locked up in myth and fairy tale and the feminist message of Judith and Holofernes. *Close Relatives* (1981); *The Handless Maiden* (1994); *The Book of Blood* (2006). SR

PETER FINCH (1947), can be seen as the equivalent in Wales of Edwin Morgan in Scotland: like him he has specialised in concrete poetry, sound poetry, and generative rules. Writes with astonishing energy, abiding at the tier of language before the personality, enjoying the boundless possibilities of the inchoate and the unbound. There is a *Selected Poems* (1987) but also a *Selected Later Poems* (2007). His books include *Make, Food, Useful, Poems For Ghosts* and *Antibodies. The Welsh Poems* appeared in 2006, and *Zen Cymru* in 2010. LWC

ALLEN FISHER (1944) Because of the complexity of the processes involved it is arguable that Prynne and Fisher together make up most of the informational complexity of modern British poetry. Allen Fisher did not get on with school; his earliest poetic endeavours were parodies or détournements of the texts they had to study in class, made to amuse his fellow pupils. There is a School of London of which Allen could be described as the leader. He spent a number of years in the Conceptual art world before publishing poetry. Because he was so bored by the visible ideology of society he had only a short distance to travel to become a conceptualist. Arguably, Fisher's movement into writing long books, capable of being named as classics many years later, represented a movement out of the conceptual thing. The writing of *Place* lasted from 1971 to about 1980. *Place* involves topographical information about Lambeth and adjacent districts. It is noticeably easier to assimilate than *Gravity*. It is not a simple topographical project; it is still conceptual art, and part of the conceptual programme involves crushing and 'cutting up' an original text by the writer himself, treated as a kind of raw material. The most basic act of *Place* was the wiping out of the existing meaning of the south bank of the Thames for a few miles west of Bank. Everyone knew what it meant, but Fisher's sovereign act was to erase that meaning and thus to found an immense pattern of data which was completely mysterious and silent. On this canvas he slowly built up the vast creation myth, experiment, or game of *Place*. From about 1982 Fisher was engaged in *Gravity as a Consequence of Shape*, which was completed in 2005. We now have it in three collected volumes, (volume one, *Gravity*), about 750 pages of mind-blowing complexity. In interview Fisher said, "I made almost categorical choices in the sense that I was reading through *Nature* and there were some elements of it that were more important to me than others. One of the areas was biotechnology and one of the areas was quantum mechanics. It was because of the discoveries being made in those two fields." He went on to mention "three or four" open problems which led the *Gravity* project, and one of the others was the issue of boundary in drawing and in perception generally. Allen has also since 1974 edited *Spanner*, the leading journal for poetic theory and for theoretically advanced poetry. Allen was wholeheartedly involved in the counter culture in this country, and knowledge of the ideas driving the counter culture gives a basis for imagining what the unifying pattern of his work is. An *Allen Fisher Reader* is in preparation. LWC

ULLI FREER (1948) represents the spirit of 1968. An anarchist writing anti-rational and intuitive poems with a lack of logical structures expressing beliefs about politics and emotional truth. Had Jeff Nuttall as an English teacher at school in Finchley, is associated with the London School founded by Nuttall and Cobbing. *Stepping Space* (1991); *Sand Poles* (1992); *Speakbright Leap Passwood* (2003).

DAVID HARSENT (1942), began as an associate of *The New Review*, and was a product of the '60s, operating on the borders of the tolerable in sexuality, brutality, delusion, the irrational. His early work is summed up in an important *Selected Poems* (1989). *Mister Punch* (1984) was a classic which took the polarisation introduced by radical feminism and brilliantly exploited it. It was also a rewrite of *Crow*. The Punch theme probably came from Harrison Birtwistle, who had previously commissioned a Punch work from another librettist. His acceptability to patrons in the world of opera and theatre has led to exciting commissions and celebrity but also to an inflation of style. *Mister Punch* was followed by *News from the Front* (1993) and *A Bird's Idea of Flight* (1998). A natural miniaturist, his efforts to write book-length projects (since *Mister Punch*) have gone badly (*Marriage*, in 2002, *Legion*, in 2005). He drew on the 'hare' imagery of the psychoanalyst J.H. Layard. He remains a gifted poet.

MICHAEL HASLAM (1947), from Bolton. Romantic and mythographic poet rising to sublime heights. *A Whole Bauble: Collected Poems 1977-94* states the case. There followed *The Music Laid her Songs in Language* (2001) *A Sinner Saved by Grace* (2005) and *Mid Life* (2007, a revised version of *A Whole Bauble*). Friends with most of the Cambridge School, took his early themes from the Prynnean interest in geography and myth, but is unfailingly impulsive and stricken by beauty where they are philosophical and critical. Interview in DSMT. LWC

ALEXANDER HUTCHISON (1942?), from Buchan in north-east Scotland. *Epitaph for a Butcher* (1997); *Scales' Dog* (2007). Virtuosic, laconic, and erudite poet using basically oral forms. Occasionally writes in Buchan dialect. Interview in DSMT. SR

JUDITH KAZANTZIS (1940), records that she began writing poetry (after adolescent production, lost) in 1973 after reading *The Colossus*. "It was painting, psychoanalysis and feminism that set off my poetry in the 1970s[.]" She belongs to what now seems a heroic generation, facing at the start the complete opposition and disbelief of a society. She reached insights for the first time which poets have been re-finding ever since. *Minefield* (1977) is the first product of this, about infantile states both as the basis for a greedy political system and as innocence, always the start of a possible new arrangement of public affairs. One of the most significant feminist poets in Britain, outstanding for political maturity and for her natural, persuasive, and light sound. *Selected Poems 1977-92* is a 'selected-collected'. *Swimming Through the Grand Hotel* (1997); *Sister Invention* (2014). SR

MIMI KHALVATI (1944) is British but from an Iranian family. Has been a frequent teacher at The Poetry School. A sensitive and artistically ambitious writer who became prominent during the 1990s. *In White Ink* (1991); *Entries on Light* (1997); *Selected Poems* (2000). SR

GRACE LAKE (a.k.a. Anna Mendelssohn, 1948-2010) from Stockport. Led a stormy life on the extreme wing of 1968 radicalism. In accordance with libertarian ideals, wrote in an irrational way. Her work is hard to interpret and much of it has not been published. *Bernache nonnette* (1995); *Parasol 1 Parasol 2 Parasol Avenue* (1996); *Tondo aquatique* (1997). There was a volume sometime in the 1970s which I have not seen. *Implacable Art* (2000) showed the weaknesses of complete spontaneity and nonconformism. LWC

ALAN LLWYD (1948) – writer in conservative forms on conservative themes, notable for his liberal and flexible outlook. Possibly the most eminent contemporary user of the historic forms of Welsh verse. Author of 13 books of verse up to 2005.

> They are still here, under the dust of the vague years,
> filling all the bags, toys, an attic full of them;
> toys of the two for their childhood under the idleness of the spider's
> web, layer after layer, though they are not children

any more, and the two have grown. All the same we have kept
all the toys with us, with the desire of parents
to keep back some traces of all the years,
preventing time from claiming every moment from the hour of our
    birth.
    (trans. of part of 'Clirio'r atig', in Bianchi's anthology)

His work is massively about memory and it would be difficult to reject
the things he is trying to keep in memory. As for pioneering, this is of
less concern to him.

TOM LOWENSTEIN (1942) was at a peak in the 1980s (*Filibustering
in Samsara*, 1987). Part of his work has been re-issued as *Ancestors
and Species. New and Selected Ethnographic Poetry* (2005). The most
intellectual of all Jungian poets and one of the most intellectual of any
poets. Notable for having a professional knowledge of anthropology as
well as a scholarly knowledge of Pāli and the Buddhist scriptures. Has
translated Eskimo poetry related to his fieldwork in Alaska, but his
reflections on what it means to be human are more valuable. SR

BARRY MACSWEENEY (1948-2000) began as a symbol of the new 'youth
culture' with a 1966 book, suffered when the High Street publisher
was not interested in his main work which was modernist and 'adult'.
Joined the Cambridge School, became a friend of Prynne, was a star
of the underground. Suffered with the collapse of the 'counter culture'
and the rise of Thatcherism. Was overtaken by alcoholism. Returned to
the scene around 1995 as part of trying to sober up, which gave him
terrible insomnia and caused a rush of poetic productivity. May be the
only important confessional poet from England. *The Book of Demons*
(1997). *Pearl* (1995). *Wolf Tongue* is a partial selected poems (1965-
2000). LWC

PETER PHILPOTT (1949). Part of the Underground scene of the 1970s
and edited *Great Works* magazine. Published *Some Action Upon the World*
and *Nine Men's Morris* at this time. After a break, related perhaps to the
political disarray of those in power and out of it, made a breakthrough
into major poetry after 2000. The long elegiac and narrative poems in
Textual Possessions (2003) and *Are We Not Drawn* (2009) are astonishingly ambitious and complete, incorporating debate about poetry with
contemplation of the sea and the mysteries of biology.

DENISE RILEY (1948) Idolised for combining emotional intensity with philosophical lucidity and socialist-feminist political commitment. More or less withdrew from the scene after *Mop Mop Georgette* (1993), but a new collection is due in 2016. Associated with the Cambridge School. Noted for lucidity whereas poetry favours the deluded. SR

PETER RILEY (1940) was an early participant in *The English Intelligencer* project and pupil of Prynne. Has resolved splits in the scene by becoming re-engulfed by the pastoral tradition. Likes to write about long walks, too long for some people. Can be seen as an outlet for Prynnean methods in conservative clothes. *Distant Points* (1995), later collected in *Excavations* (2004), carefully describes many Neolithic graves.

GAVIN SELERIE (1949), a prolific and enigmatic writer who has had almost no critical reception. He has been part of the London avant-garde scene for some 30 years without being accepted by the chief ideologues as forming a key part of that scene. His poetry is mainly in long forms organised around multiple interlocking themes and drawing on a vast range of research. *Azimuth* (1984) was a 400-page work of multiple themes sorted around a 'key' of orientation, navigation, and the eternal feminine. *Roxy* (1996) again explores the eternal feminine, apparently the modern thing of theology; *Days of '49* (1999), (with Alan Halsey) is a re-remembering of 1949, the year of their birth, a sort of avant-garde documentary. *Le Fanu's Ghost* (2006) is about 19th-century theatre and the history of horror. *Music's Duel* (2009) is a selected poems. SR

PENELOPE SHUTTLE (1947), author of poems in a 'magical realist', radically mythical style, based on Jung, folklore, and feminism. Arguably an early poet of the New Age movement. Can be seen as writing experiments in consciousness to help the feminist experiment in social arrangements. *The Orchard Upstairs* (1980); *Selected Poems 1980-1996* (1998). SR

IAIN SINCLAIR (1943) from Bridgend. Wanted to make B-movies but was forced into poetry by the tricks of fate. It is the one art-form that costs less than a B-movie. Wrote two works in the '70s, *Lud Heat* and *Suicide Bridge*, arguably not wholly 'poetry' but at the core of the Underground scene of the time. Like Edgar G. Ulmer, his camera remains steady even when his characters disintegrate. Has mainly been a novelist and psychogeographer since 1987 but has also returned to poetry, a frequent relapse. *Flesh Eggs and Scalp Metal* (1989) collected early poems (1970-87). *The Firewall* (2006) is a selected poems 1979-

2006. There is a volume-length interview with Sinclair (*The Verbals*). *Buried at Sea* (2006). His artistic ideas have been recycled by several hundred people by now. *RED EYE 1973* (2013) is a long poem recovered from 1973. SR

PAULINE STAINER (1941) began with Christian mysticism and developed this line through a range of miraculous imagery from other religions, science, and folklore; the impossibilism makes for poetic shock and awe. Books include *The Honeycomb* (1989); *Sighting the Slave-Ship* (1992); *The Ice-Pilot Speaks* (1994); *The Wound-dresser's Dream* (1996); * *The Lady and the Hare* (2003) is a new and selected poems; *Crossing the Snowline* (2008); *Tiger Facing the Mist* (2013).

ISOBEL THRILLING – **Spectrum Shift* (c. 1991); *The Chemistry of Angels* (2000); *The Language Creatures* (2007). Christian poet writing lyric poetry of cohesion and sensitivity. LWC

SUSAN WICKS (1947) – writes very short poems which achieve intensity through disorientation, like extreme close-ups which plunge you into the middle of an action. Dominated by sensuous detail and urgency. *Singing Underwater* (1992); *Open Diagnosis* (1994); *The Clever Daughter* (1996); **Night Toad: New & Selected Poems* (2003), *De-iced* (2007); *House of Tongues* (2011).

JOHN HARTLEY WILLIAMS (1942-2014), taught first in Yugoslavia and then at the Free University of Berlin. With *Hidden Identities* (1982) founded the new style of English postmodernism and the new 'ludic' poetry. An incomparable sequence of books followed: *Bright River Yonder* (1987); *Cornerless People* (1990); *Double* (1994); **Canada* (1997); *Spending Time with Walter* (2001); **Blues* (2004). Tumultuous, formally free, inventive; terms like 'magic realism' and 'folk surrealism' have been applied. *The Ship* (2007) is a re-issue of published and unpublished poems from the 1970s. *Ignoble Sentiments* (1995) gathers early poems and a memoir of his life up till 1970 or so. SR

FOUND FOOTAGE OF SELF-REGARD;
OR, PROBLEMS OF INDIVIDUALISM

If we look at the cultural field as a whole, it becomes clear that the proposition of using personal experience as the basis of poetry, as opposed to other sources of data and knowledge, other subjects, is something which structures the landscape. It follows that studying this issue helps us to follow the argument processes which poets have followed in reaching their style and the territory where their individual poems could be written. The goal here is not to define the correct answer and to define the winners, but make visible a decision process.

One of the things that happens to a poem is that people say it is a distortion of how things are – and that they know the higher truth which the poem is sadly missing. I can't see any basis for this. Maybe they're both wrong? They see the poem as ideology. If you live in a society you have to live with the rules that other people govern their lives by. That is not to say that they all use the same set of rules, just that the dividing line between ideology and a personal set of beliefs, wishes, experiences, game rules is not really there.

You could define ideology within poetry as the false reproduction of other people's feelings and thoughts. This could induce someone to exclude other people from their poetry. The poems become one-person units. They shrink in volume but exclude distortion – on the way to linguistic virtue. I think this line of reasoning is a mirage. The part of consciousness which represents the thoughts and feelings of other people is so overwhelmingly important that to represent consciousness while leaving it out is to offer something below the minimal – a scrap that needs to be scrapped.

The way to write poetry – this is my personal view – is to include in its course several people as they interact. It is to be persuasive and carry off the operation without breaking up. As for the reader, they were not part of the original event being described but the poem is *as a second event* to find a space for them and to carry them away. It relies on impetus and impulse and is like a game which takes on as many people as wish to play. It is also like a society – it offers participation. The content of that part-taking can also be called an ideology.

BANALITY/SOLIPSISM

The poetry regime of the last 50 years must be defined as a failure for lack of take-up. Its saturation of the cultural market is weak. It is amazing how many people are interested in modern culture but never go near poetry. Outside the poetry insiders, people readily accepted the idea of squatters in abandoned stately homes, the idea that the people who practice poetry now have lost the tradition of English poetry as it used to be (in the good old days, naturally), and have only an accidental relationship to Poetry Itself, in whose abandoned precincts they furtively lurk, emitting detuned noises. (A poem by Anthony Thwaite about barbarians from the hinterland issuing, in the early 5th century, to destroy the Roman civilisation of coastal, Mediterranean Libya, and the poet Synesius, could easily be quoted here.) A very interesting version of this was described in an article by Ross Cogan in *PN Review* (Sept-Oct 2007). He starts out with a recollection of an evening of poetry shared with a non-poetry-loving friend who found the whole experience ridiculously self-regarding, flat, and short of talent. He moves on to report a comment from the novelist A.S. Byatt describing how she had read 960 poems submitted for a prize award and how she didn't like any of them and had struggled to find six that she could short-list. He describes another large sample of 280 poems which someone else inspected and in which he reported finding an overwhelming proportion which were notably egoistic, merely describing personal experiences of the poet. It is important to note that this egoism is tightly coupled with a banality of language, and this is Cogan's real regret. Presumably it would be possible to write egocentric poetry which was also linguistically interesting and 'art poetry'. The thesis that this is rare, over thousands of poems, is key to this whole area. Underpinning that thesis is a regularity, i.e. that the egocentric poets describe only a narrow range of experiences which belongs to a basic human stock and repeats. We can wonder whether banality of language makes it impossible to say anything original, or whether the urge to be spontaneous and domestic makes development of language unattractive.

Cogan says, "By my reckoning, around 1,153 of our 1,240 poems or roughly 93%, can be fairly categorised as 'new solipsist'. And that's certainly in line with my experience." He says, "It is my contention then that there has been a turning inwards in British poetry over the last twenty or so years [date 2007!, AD] a focus on the personal subjective and introspective at the expense of the public and shared." As for the problems, he quotes Donald Hall: "At their common worst they are specialists in slack free verse, writing poems that are autobiographical, narcissistic, brief, short-lined and end-stopped, with no attention to sound or syntax, with all attention to image, detail, and SELF'." Hall is clearly thinking of American poets and this may not map neatly onto bad English poets. Cogan sums up the bad stuff as "autobiographical, self-obsessed, bereft of ideas, and with no feeling for language."

Cogan seems to have a background in classical music and its interest in technique, and he favours poetry which is more fascinated by the possibilities of language and exploration of unknown linguistic patterns, while moving away from banal language and repetitive egoistic thoughts. He does not mention in his article the whole sector of poetry (we suggest that this involves about 2000 poets, which of course is a minority) which already follows this prescription, and which takes on (sometimes even successfully) the other problems which inhabit that exploratory realm.

This analysis is too important to be dealt with quickly. It may seem superficial to get excited about a thesis put forth so briefly, in a magazine article. I trust I am able in what follows to expand the thesis without betraying its basic impulses.

We mentioned the absence of most cultured and intelligent people from the poetry audience. Information about this absence is, actually, absent. It is credible that the reasons for their absence are very numerous and diverse (and that any solution would only appeal to a fraction of them). I am not attempting to prove them wrong.

We can see three different sources of poetry scrapping its traditional means of adornment and expression and investing in something barer.

1. Disenchantment. Linked to the 1950s and The Movement. rejection of rhetoric and of 'ideology'. loss of belief in religion and distaste for anything else.

2. The singer-songwriter movement, and the assimilation of poetry to song lyrics coming out of the folk tradition which had an ethos of bareness. The bareness was originally associated with the lower classes, socialism, the rural and uneducated, with resistance to showbiz slickness and to elite, conservatoire, culture; and gradually

and unconsciously, egocentricity came to fill that bareness up. The political radicalism seeped out of the package, overtaken by privatisation and a preoccupation with lifestyle.

3. The wave of Critique and Theory which washed over literature and which made the traditional means unattractive. This is not within Cogan's criticism, it produces the sector of poetry which is not primarily egoistic and autobiographical. However its quality of starting from zero also produces an effect of bareness and monotony which has been unattractive to readers (and to other poets). Alongside an exploratory rule which constantly added new figures of language, there was an inherited rule of disillusioning the reader, part of liberating them from 'bourgeois illusion', which preferred bareness and sarcasm. The programme was 'sobering up', a cold bath.

Solipsism means 'the belief that only you are a person and other people are appearances or reflections'. It is not the most accurate word. If 1,000 poets are writing in one style, they are being conformist rather than solipsistic. Banality, equally, is not an intention. To get at the bad poetic thought process, we have to catch them thinking "if I record tedious details about myself that brings intimacy, and that may include curiosity and liking". Evidently you can only be intimate with a few people. The banal poet does not want to be the only person in the universe, but they do want you to feel close to them – restricting your movements. The phrase solipsistic banality does not describe the conscious intention of the writers, but an error. As they constructed their banal poem, they thought it was vivid because it was happening to them and would be vivid for you because of the pressure their attention and presence would bring to the verbal enactment, creating a moment of pure presence, a flash fusing space and time. It turned out as solipsistic banality. But that was afterwards. There is a quite fundamental concept of art as an invitation: the banal poets see themselves as personalizing the universe, as creating a moment of vividness as they invite the reader as a guest. The invitation to the bread and salt of life, viz. the intimate and banal moments, is seen as sacramental.

What I have to do to assemble this book is to make the case for the 'new solipsist' poetry, although I find Cogan's condemnation so convincing. This would start with shaving down the term, as the poets are not literally solipsist but instead write about themselves. We would say next that much conversation involves people talking about themselves, and this has at least a superficial appeal, even if we want to say that the domain of poetry is outside the realm of conversation. Further we would locate some good poems within this realm of 'spontaneous and autobiographical': poems by Clare Pollard for example.

If personal experience is so worthless why did Cogan start his piece with the account of a personal experience?

Realising an ideal

Imagine ten thousand poets writing in solipsistic banality. Each is creating a parcel of terrain which they own – the ownership is the guarantee of the validity of what they say. In parallel they believe in subjectivity – they deny other people the right to judge. They are what they say they are. Connoisseurship is at an end, literary debate is at an end. Nothing of what they say has any validity in the next cell, a few centimetres away.

All this sounds like the privatisation of a public utility. It sounds like the realisation on the symbolic plane of possessive individualism on the plane of economic organisation. Apolitical withdrawal is a way of embracing conformism in its extreme form.

LYRICISM AND INTELLIGENCE

Generalisation: poets are fed up after fifty years of being told that pop music is more hip and young poets in 2013 have worked out how to be as lean, as intimate, as sharp, as pop songs. They have also worked out that Depeche Mode have a role in popular music, alongside John Coltrane.

And part 2: poetry without music needs to be more intelligent (more data-rich, less painting-out ambiguities, more curious) than song *and* most poets fail because they aren't very bright.

And three: there are signs of being intelligent, as of a youth cult with distinctive clothes, slang, etc. Writing in an avant-garde style is one of these. The need to display these signs is mighty. They can be adopted without the artistic charge they point to. So in fact most poets who write in an avant-garde or Alternative style aren't very intelligent and don't have a cargo of ideas to transport.

The previous piece has already given the game away – that unreflective poetry seldom aspires to the intensity of being lyrical. Poetry survives in an ocean of popular music which is mainly about love and its perils. However, lyric poetry survives in an ocean of poems of the banal-solipsistic genre.

Twentieth-century British poetry has not been strong in the lyric dimension. Writers like Housman and Spender leave a warm memory because they were exceptional, they did what other people admired but could not do. The limit on emotionally direct poetry has presumably been education. Poets were more keen on discussing ideas – as status symbols, perhaps? – than on writing about love, loss, jealousy, longing, joy, courting, and the rest of it. Disenchantment, at a peak in the 1950s, was probably the peak of anti-lyrical writing; the whole course of history since then has been towards greater lyricism, and the influence of folk song and popular song has been the way poets have followed to reach this.

The most prestigious lyric poetry from the past is in the poems of Donne and the *Sonnets* of Shakespeare. The prestige is inseparable from the intelligence embodied in the poems. The combination of lyricism and intelligence is the most admired thing.

The advent of literary theory has made people more reflexive. Also, a lot of it attacked the primacy of feeling and degraded the status of subjectivity. There was a wave of people avoiding any personal statement at all in order to write critical poetry, poetry of ideas, attacking the system, etc. The counter-attack, that you can't write lyric poetry, was obvious, and inevitably there was a propaganda brouhaha about 'radical subjectivity', mainly incredibly bad writing, which illustrated a factional argument. But, over a forty-year period, some of the intellectuals have worked out how to deliver the *sugar rush*.

A lot of people want to think they can write about feelings but really can't. A lot of people want to think they are intelligent but they really aren't. All the same some of the poets who interest us are both intelligent and can write about feelings.

Intelligence does not show itself only in the modulation of the verbal message in the direction of complexity. It affects every aspect of the message, and shows up for example as delicacy, originality, brevity, allusiveness, and so on. It has to be admitted that most of our young poets just aren't very bright. At such moments, we think about Patsy Montana singing 'I want to be a cowboy's sweetheart.' Sigh. I quite like this record. Patsy didn't have to give interviews where she talked about "post-ironic irony" and "basically I'm interested in subverting form by not subverting it". And she had this very cute hat. So how do we differentiate the new simplicity from Patsy Montana? I am curious about the relationship between language as symbolic power and this new lyricism which is the opposite of power. If you are Simon Armitage, you no doubt argue that the distinction between his dullness of wit and the vacancy with which lyricism starts is simply social prejudice – the 'silent rules' which prestructure the emptiness. So experience and ignorance come to look like each other.

A lot follows from the decision that you aren't brainy. From getting out of the race to be intelligent. If you cease to be a threat, maybe you can be identified as a pet. "I'm such a fetching little nitwit." The new rules don't favour poets who aren't intellectuals. We may reflect that the nature of rock music, or country music, is cunningly to allow people without much musical expertise to please an audience. The tunes suit people who can grasp simple patterns and repeat them. So, what happens if such a musician tries to play jazz? This may feel like a breakthrough, but it's also a big embarrassment. So many English poets have spent their lives resisting abstract ideas, while grasping things like "this hat makes me look artistic", or which people in a room you have to please and which ones you can insult, because they have no power. They have restricted their ideas intake to what they can put into verse, and restricted the poem to the models handed down by a previous generation. So when they get the idea that "poetry must include Ideas", they go for appearance rather than process, they snatch the phantom of the envied object, and the result is truly unhygienic. This problem dates back to the 1960s (very sporadic sightings before that), but is by now a national crisis.

Two factions. One which dislikes ideas, which is irritated by them, made indignant because they don't want ideas to be part of the poem spoiling their pleasure, thinks things move faster without them, thinks the poet has simply made a mistake by including them. Another faction which dislikes feelings, dislikes identifying, wants situations to be anything except emotional, etc. It is hard for these factions to co-operate. If the goal is to write intelligent poetry about emotions, a phobia for intelligence guarantees you will fail.

The question of avant-garde legitimation is obvious to the insiders but much challenged on the outside. Supposedly an avant-garde work makes up its own legitimacy, and is otherwise "beyond the law" (in the words of that Deniz Tek song). Is Miles Champion's poetry more complicated than Glyn Maxwell's, or less? Is it really different in its appeal – selling "the awareness of virtuality", I suppose. Hey, this poem can go where we want it to. The act shown on camera is the gesture of pointing at the camera. Maxwell thinks he is an intelligent person, but then so does Miles. Maybe they're both right? Or both wrong? Vacuity is close to lucidity – once you throw out Subject Matter. The managers tend to judge poetry by its Asset Structure. Who you know decides whether your poem is "self-aware control" or "vacancy caught up in itself". Again, I don't want to lay down the law about "*this* is Real Intelligence and *this* is Assiduous Miming", just to point out that people estimate 'intelligence' in quite different ways. Is this why the audience is split? Yes, certainly, it's one of the reasons.

> GOLD LETTERS ROSE
> in coiled dust-gust
> flaps to the ear
> hair brushed aside,
> confidentially,
> precious truths
> circulate, unfold
> & fold in
> through the slit of silence.
>   (Robert Smith, a 'Sonnet', published in *Angel Exhaust* 15)

> In the cubicle of an early canto
> heliotrope those hot dry eyes
> snort lavender and silverpine
> do pistou with the John Canoos
> over those decorous ochres go
> to kick larks up sapphire skies
> & the water almond-white swim
> O, to be fauna-ing in avignon
>   (Karlien van den Beukel, from 'Bathing Suite')

Clearly, complexity is not the key stylistic value here. But also – this is very important poetry. And also – it's unacceptable to *Poetry Review* (although it isn't complex). Such poems are a return to the primary aesthetic world of textures and sensations, they are a new lyricism. This is the area which interests me most. This beautiful streamlined subjectivity. Lyric might mean songlike. Single-track. *al for a loue newe/ pat is so suete ant trew.* I don't want to draw up the battle lines, just to observe that the world of *Poetry Review* and Bloodaxe Books also involves things which are primary and simple. I adore the lyric quality of van den Beukel and Robert Smith and Simon Smith, and could wish there were an entire station broadcasting only this all day. A recent issue of *text + kritik* reprints a 1919 essay by someone called Hillel, where he talks about the forgetting which the poet has to undertake in order to write the poem. As he points out, this resembles philosophy, where the initial move is to act as if we know nothing, and no philosophical act has taken place unless we move from ignorance to knowledge. This has also been called kenosis, or emptying-out. Poetry seizes indeterminacy as architecture seizes space. What is inside the white cube is not, strictly, emptiness.

THE NOTION OF SIGNATURE; AFFECTIVE INDIVIDUALISM

The topic of distinctiveness deserves closer attention. Take these recent examples of English poetry:

> Each bubble considered the
> rest as it chose its place. Out
> in the morning everything
> settled, before I could look.
> Down centre is a tomb or
> shrine. The sun is shining on
> the corner of a panel
> set into its side. It's all
> paid on the nail. None of it
> is mine. Way off, and running
> strongly through the hazy, slate
> blue sky, that must be rosy
> Mercury, bent on a quest.
>> (R.F. Langley, from 'Still Life with Wineglass', from *The Face of It*, 2007)

he was certain of that
deliberately he sent his gaze
from one episode of hypnotic absorption
on a razed dais
to be authorised
into his library
at a particularly flat area
in the machine
a finger dramatically
formed it into a system
finding the thought that applied
needed no prolonged intercommunication
moment by moment
crinkled into a smile
            (Tom Raworth, from *Eternal Sections*)

    Still followed
            the question:
marked blown like immutable rockface.
Reflection mutual. In it
pre-lived experience afterthought,
driven to notice relationship more than its
prudence
    suddenly.

    That created original formula
spouting move insight.
The muscular character nerve type
played ending   was   proven to
valuable.
            (Emily Critchley, from 'Then there was [this] extension')

Each of these poets is highly distinctive. We may form the supposition
that in their work signature is prevalent over other considerations
(although intellectual exploration is obviously important). Forces like
individuation, personality, competition, and differentiation seem to be
at work here. It is not too much to say that something needs explaining
here, and that it is the distinctive feature of the era. It is as if British
poetry since 1960 had travelled out into territory which is completely

unfamiliar from the heritage of the eighth century through to the 1950s. The abundance of *maniera* is the main question that has to be answered about the era. (To say excess would be to close the books prematurely.)

There is a historical account of Mannerism which sees it as the origin of modern art (as in the title of Hungarian Marxist Arnold Hauser's book on the subject). The debate started with criticisms that Italian artists, in the early 16th century, were making pictures in which the personal '*maniera*' of the artist was pushing the holy subject of the work into the background. Hauser shows the artist's expression of their personality through style as expanding consistently over the intervening centuries. Although this would fit into a Marxist version in which this was a deviation (to be straightened out by Party-directed civic art in the second quarter of the 20th century), Hauser rather clearly does not present that argument and is compelled by the artistic merit of modern-style art.

This poetry would not exist unless it was fascinating to writers and readers, and this functional explanation also holds its ground. Actually if you read one highly stylised poem and like it then you already know the answer. I suspect that the discussion in works on Mannerism by Hauser and by Gustav-René Hocke already gives a satisfying explanation of what Mannerism is. Naturally the styles of individual poets need discussion on an individual basis. The style of the named poets is not simply due to a desire for distinctiveness. The signature is an effect of linguistic gestures made for artistic purposes, even if surprise and novelty are part of the concept. Distinctiveness is to start with an effect of the absence of banality. With Langley we can say that he is undertaking a philosophical project which starts from a rejection of received and general ideas, and that his poetry starts from this extensive empty space. Every line clashes with the context because the context was wiped out at the outset: this takes us to the rare and specialised mental state known as consciousness.

With Raworth the initial supposition is one of critique. The language of his poem is startling because he has erased the context: this implies that the ordinary language of the time incorporates a set of rules which are absurd but which only appear absurd when re-framed. In fact, his critique is the most radical on the whole scene. It may well be that everything in *Eternal Sections* is a quote from a found source: if this is true, the 'signature' is all in the framing, it is like the rhythm which a film editor imposes on film which they have in no case shot themselves.

This writing is in that sense the most impersonal of all – the claims of individualism are silently refuted as the poet is shown to be immersed in a society based on the arbitrary power of the few.

With Critchley the patterning of the language to become unexpected at every point achieves a surprise effect. The lack of context seems to be part of showing consciousness from second to second, with the uncertainty of the speaking subject reproduced in the poem. The uncertainty comes from a lack of defences – the tone is of high subjectivity and vulnerability.

The doctrine of individuality has an obvious flaw in accounting for the raw data. Most poetry is utterly unoriginal. In language, imagery, rhythm, ideas, etc., it is blindingly familiar. It is difficult – I will admit – to see conventionality as a proof of flourishing individualism. In the mainstream, everybody is more like everybody else than they are like themselves. I propose to ignore this area, on the basis that originality is valued by a consensus of all opinion, and with the proviso that banal poetry is a sign of incompetence at writing, rather than of a wish to conform. What we seem to find is that the most marginalised (and wilfully original) poetry is the most thorough fulfilment of the individualist core of Western society. This implies that underground poetry is an over-fulfilment of the possessive imperative – rather than a radical, Marxist, counter-cultural, break, as the poets might think. It implies, too, that the central literary institutions miserably fail the poetry which most fulfils our shared ideals. These implications are probably unacceptable to both sides. I am proposing that exceptionalism is the vital feature of modern poetry but at the same time I am privileging poets who are anomalous. There may be a circularity embedded in this. Further, sociologists may be able to find large-scale uniformity in the mass of poets – the ones who don't theorise and who don't write distinctively.

Obviously Langley, Raworth and Critchley are, each of them, important poets. The force of their work can hardly be separated from the level of stylisation in its fabric. The arresting quality of the poems derives from the originality of their design, including a complete lack of conventional lines or phrases. It is hard to look at conventional poetry and think that it is in any way superior to this highly developed and original poetry. Actually we have to ask why anyone would choose to write conventional poetry.

There may in fact be a sociological explanation for this *maniera*. My argument will rely on an initial datum that our society is highly individualistic, and that comparison with many other societies will show this as the distinctive feature, whatever other correlations or non-correlations crop up. If we read Lawrence Stone's work on the modern history of the family through Hauser's sociology of art, we can link the style of bourgeois subjectivity, in its various forms, with a style of child-rearing. The source of the kind of art we have is the affective individualist style, which involves small families with strong affective bonds between the parents, and between parents and children. This is the model which Rousseau elevated to ideal form, and Romanticism may be linked to fashions in child-rearing as well as to the emphasis on prolonged education in a more complicated economy.

In this ideal family regime, women are highly educated and spend much of their lives educating their children, who therefore spend much of their life in learning, and learn to please by talent. Teacher and child are locked in a mutual display of knowledge and manners. Where the female interest in the talents of children coincides with the power of the education system to redefine people's social status, the preoccupation with *maniera* really takes hold of art. The values which the education system tests for and rewards permeate the way people write poetry. But subjective art is also beneficially linked to the irresponsible play of childhood, with its high degree of subjective emotion, its disregard for convention, its wild inventiveness.

Affective individualism was linked to new features of domestic space, that emphasised comfort and intimacy. The military and display functions of the nobility shrink away in favour of a newly attractive domestic space. This privatisation has implications for the fate of a heroic and oratorical style of poetry. There was a halt called to the privatisation of art during the era of ideological confrontation, say 1933-56; over a further short period of time the economy was redirected away from heavy engineering (military, nuclear, etc.) and towards producing white goods and homes for a consumer market and the baby boom. (Western) art since that time has been an exploration of the privatised realm. Art has lost interest in the governance of the State and spends much more intellectual energy on dramatising debates of child-rearing and relations between men and women.

If you don't enjoy displays of talent, you really aren't going to enjoy modern poetry. It is a formal competition where the competitors have to overcome various obstacles and the spectators are fixated on the ability they display while overcoming them. The brouhaha about disadvantaged social groups was really just an attempt to adjust the rules of the game slightly, it did not have a specifically artistic purpose and in fact it followed a thorough acceptance of the interest in talent, visible display, and the triumph of talent. The correlation of this fine appreciation of innate talent with the education system, and with groups hoping to define their social status through that system, is obvious.

We could connect this back to a generational cycle in which parents transmit wealth to offspring in the form of education, in the form of dispositions to accept teaching and to pass tests, rather than land or money. This fits in with the 'meritocracy', where people take a job and their income level depends on their ability to fit into the job market, so notably on their qualifications. Free capital demands a pool of mobile labour, with skills and techniques, to realise its desires. The display of talent is the aversion of an anxiety about lack of talent, and this anxiety may have a social origin. The economy of measuring ability (but not output) connects to a society of the poem which dwells on talent rather than subject matter. This is not to say that those businesses do not have owners or that control of wealth is not of paramount importance. I am simply saying that poetry, even 'high art' in general, has been adapted to a meritocracy and to its anxieties. The visual arts have a connection with the rich, as clients, which corresponds to nothing in the poetry world. 'Meritocracy' is cogent for a subset of society, not for everyone.

The short range preserves subjective gestures, small-scale events which live in shared space but disappear with any distance. In it, the affective state of the other person is decisive (and entrains our own affective state). Intimate art is *either* distasteful *or* like falling in love with the artist. In the latter case, it is a glimpse of authentic being, something from which political ideals are a quote. Yet, we want to enter the perfect state with someone perfect, and we subject them to tests, and of course we include political ones. Withholding trust is an assertion of power at the expense of pleasure – and yet a form of pleasure. It may be a mistake to load poetry with demonstrations of integrity.

Raworth's radically personal style is based on an exclusion of the personal and may also be predominantly political rather than expressive in intent. His decontextualised montage of quotes, often from people he hates, perhaps acts to foreground the implicit and so force hegemony to reveal itself in the open. His Cézanne-like rigour of concentration, infinitely suggestive, forcing conjecture by withholding resolution, may bring about the return of the repressed – the power structure and the arbitrary nature of how attention is directed. Puzzlingly, there may be a very powerful Marxist element in the avant-garde, inspired by Herbert Marcuse's attacks on "affirmative culture" and seeking to transform the basic procedures of language and social knowledge. Perhaps – and I have never really got this straight – underground poetry is simply the direction that the cultural wing of Western Marxism went in after the end of the first Cold War.

Autobiographical, Instant, Direct

Clare Pollard made an impact at a very young age with *The Heavy Petting Zoo*, an account of adolescent sexual activity. A petting zoo is one with animals like sheep, rabbits, etc. where children can actually touch animals and get close up to them. 'Heavy petting' is a stage of courtship, American term. This was obviously first person experience: the naive teenager in the documentary was also the person behind the camera, directing. The content had a lot to do with observing other people: the scenes involved male lovers, or potential lovers, and satisfied a fundamental human wish to know what other people do and to think about what is going to succeed, to reach the realm of romance. It would be hard not to find this interesting. The set-up could be seen as feminist, since the male teenagers don't succeed brilliantly, but it is important that the female lead is involved in the situation, not sitting on a judge's seat of security and superior knowledge. If the work has the charm of genuine teenage pop, it is because both parties are hopeful about the outcome. We can say that the poetry works because of the frankness, honesty, and commitment of the writer – who does not claim to own the experience. When a poet is presenting experience that they own, into which the reader is being invited as if to a dinner party in a desirable home, the process of commodification involves all kinds of tricks, effectively status symbols, which drain all integrity from the poem.

I can't find any element of originality in Pollard's language, but it is extremely vivid all the same. The quality of 'first person, present tense' is basic to much of popular culture, and works for an incalculably large number of people there; we have to add another quality, that the experiences are intense and unpredictable and the 'first person' feels their wellbeing at stake all the time. Forties poets developed a theory that only individual consciousness at a particular moment made ideas significant. I suppose that when I first read her work (in 2010, in the anthology *Identity Parade*) I had a 'flash' on it, I thought that not only was this what I wanted to read but there would be a long supply of poems which had the same charge and I would go off and find them. That was perhaps the maximum moment; after research I think that Pollard has written a lot of poetry at that pitch, but I couldn't find anyone else who did. Even *IP* was full of poets who were writing about themselves but couldn't make it interesting. This was a disappointment but that just underlines how much I liked *Look, Clare! Look!*. This is mainly about a journey round the world (spending a literary grant) although the end of the journey with important family events back in England adds extra weight and adds deeper notes to the irresponsible and idyllic sounds of tourism.

> And yet hope exists, despite everything,
> in stilted shacks, amongst a fatherless people.
> We arrived to a night lit by sheets of electric,
> and acres of dust,
> and chicks and piebald pigs scrubbing round palms,
> and giddy girls balancing trays of locusts at loo-stops,
> eyes scrunched to the glare of our wealth.
>   (from 'The Journey', from *Look, Clare! Look!*)

The writing about politics in Vietnam and China is some of the most vivid in the book. The directness of apprehension of things seen, and of stories heard from people in those countries, revives ideas that may already be familiar and blunted. If we set it alongside work which is more abstract and more exploratory of what is not there, cannot be apprehended, it does not appear that Pollard's work is less stimulating and less radical. It is true that more abstract work is closer to the imagination of power, less attached to immediate and solid data. But in a universe where there are a billion billion possibilities, a concrete and immediate stimulus makes what you imagine focussed and coherent in a necessary way. The issues Pollard raises are so urgent that they make me think about political change – the limits on my area of reaction are given by me, not by the original stimulus. It is not proven that poetry which engages in a 'critique of representation' is more effective as political poetry than something immediate, personal, and committed like this.

PERSONAL EXPERIENCE

If 'first person present tense' makes for such vivid poetry, it is perverse to go back to generalisations which are inevitably 'third person, diffuse in tense'. However, I am here to do that. If this poetry is so excellent, we have to revisit Ross Cogan's strictures on poets who write about themselves. The situation is more that 'writing about your personal experiences is a good idea but if several thousand people have the same idea it can get so blurred that it encourages people to write badly'. This would be like *British War Films of the 1950s,* where the audience wanted to see war films so indiscriminately that people at a creative dead-end inevitably made war films – so, a good idea used by tired people. So in fact the extreme tedium of most mainstream poetry is not due to the deep cultural assumptions, but to something further upstream – fatigue, lack of inspiration, lack of creativity. Writing in an unoriginal way may be a symptom of apathy – of barely taking part in a creative process of any kind. So writing about personal experience, especially about relations between at least two people, and about feelings, may still be a good idea. It is possible, too, that the conventional magazine poem is too simple in relation to the complexity of experience, and that it is utterly superficial in comparison with films and TV drama. Effective autobiographical poetry needs much more information – a slowing down, collection of more observations, a longer rhythm. Building this extra weight in an autobiographical frame may look like narcissism – and also be the gateway to writing effective modern poetry.

To judge contemporary poetry it might be necessary to set it up against Depeche Mode and Tommy James and the Shondells, rather than Renaissance oratory.

The Falcon and the Gosling:
The Critique of Literary Imagination

Look at the plot of *The Maltese Falcon*. It has that terrific climax where Sam Spade explains to Brigid O'Shaughnessy (the Mary Astor character) that he has won at every level including being more in love than she is. "I'm going to send you over, baby. Twenty years in Tehachapi. I'll be around when you come out if you're still interested." Of course he is in the right and she is in the wrong. The law will uphold what he says. The scriptwriter speaks through Spade and the film validates what he says about it. Surely we must analyse the *Falcon* as a contest between a male heterosexual, a woman, and two gay men, in which the hetero male wins every point, and go back to a phase when they are all innocent and a fantasy process gave Astor the asset of being guilty (murdering Miles Archer) and the plot was unfolded to sustain a pre-existing need for victory. Three of the four lead characters lie throughout the story, while dominance is the quality throughout of the heterosexual male character, Sam Spade. But perhaps dominance means that his wishes become true.

The organisation of classical American cinema is such that identification picks the character who is going to win and, before we watch the other characters being humiliated for being the losers, we follow blunt and unambiguous signs telling us who is going to be the winner. One can imagine a different ordering of identification which would be less divisive, and which would correspond to a less capitalist and individualist ordering of the economy. In *The Maltese Falcon* the signs of gender such as the way muscle and bone are laid down, the size of bones, the line between gracile and craggy, are at once stylised and made the basis for events. Objects and decor are an extension of this displayed physical identity, and the events of the plot are further extensions of the décor – passive disclosing of truths already written into the body. Actors chosen for their exaggerated resemblance to pre-existing character archetypes inject a quality of unambiguity so that the plot recurs in clumsy proof of its presuppositions. A robust and archaic apparatus mills to persuade us that when Sam Spade shoots someone it is good and when O'Shaughnessy shoots someone it is *bad*. This is the primary zone, where creative work is apparently an endlessly repeating cycle of fantasies. This zone is where modern thinking about texts takes place – a new skill which we all practice. This zone is also where modern poets thrive, where real talent outdistances the pack.

Tehachapi is the California Correctional Institute, situated 35 miles from Bakersfield. This implies that O'Shaughnessy would not only be confined but also have to listen to country and western music. Modern taste involves not just watching *The Maltese Falcon* but rewriting it so that Brigid O'Shaughnessy is the central identification character and Sam Spade does all the bad things.

AFTER THEORY

A lot of the action in the academic English Literature world in the last 40 or 50 years has had to do with 'theory'. Thus David Scott Kastan entitled an entire book *Shakespeare After Theory*. It would follow, I think, that poetry now (2010) is 'poetry after theory', although that presupposes that academic life is decisive for new poetry. My perception is that there is a world of students, that this is where poetry is nurtured, but that as a leisure activity it has very little in common with formal and supervised study, the daytime world. It is hard to see how 'critical theory' affects the singer-songwriter albums which students buy in such big quantities, hard also to see how it affects the kind of poetry which they like to read. The question is not whether the political critique of literary judgement is part of the scene, but about its density. How many pounds of pressure per square inch does it impose on a poem? is it like the gravity of stars, theoretically measurable but rather weak in its influence on terrestrial objects? Or is it a fundamental force which accounts on its own for much of the shape of literary acts?

Recovering books from the mid-century and before reveals a 'holy knowledge' of writers which they built their texts out of and which was simply nationalism, the old Patriotic Insight. If you go back 100 years you find books of poems justifying the Empire, or about naval battles. In 1929, Robert Bridges, the poet laureate, published a book called *The Testament of Beauty*. It was one of the best-selling books of poetry of the century. Its thesis is among other things that Darwin was wrong because Bridges finds birdsong beautiful. We are supposed to believe this, despite the lack of scientific argument, because Bridges couches it in beautiful language – full of archaic and precious words. This is what places Bridges at the place of hidden truths – not an epiphany but somewhere resembling it. It seems to me that, first, poets since 1930 have gone to great lengths to purge this kind of statement from their work. The Big False Truths no longer feature in poetry. Secondly, the period when Britain was sliding from World Power Number One to Number Four produced a mixture of insecurity and grandiosity which encouraged overreaching poets purveying absurd Truths. Some of these poets have vanished from literary history. Marxism is one of the refuges which has preserved that kind of grandiosity for the use of poet-prophets.

It is hard to look back at the older literature and not see it as propaganda, or as recklessly exploiting available propaganda. Writers then wrote in such a way as to justify arrangements like the Empire, the war machine controlling or expanding the Empire, the inequality of wealth, the inequality of access to culture. This was a nightmare from which we have woken up. 'Theory' is based on the idea that recent literature is still equally oppressive and propagandistic. I suspect this isn't so. Things have changed. Social-critical reading of a poetry of 'national propaganda' is worthwhile. There are new sources of knowledge and modern writing contains the information which these afford. Theory is conservative, acting as if the Europe of the mid-century were still there, the colonial regimes still in place.

All artistic choices are subjective but that leaves untouched a question of validity. Because poems show behaviour with an implicit claim of truth, they can be subjected to tests of truth. Because we form an image of the poet while reading our experience also includes a claim of truth and can be affected by unconscious biases. The process of reading a poem is similar to that of 'reading' someone's character, which is generally admitted to be subject to variation. A classic feature of the modern period is the line of argument which rejects the judgement of male critics on texts written by women. Within this phase, we tend to argue through numbers. For example, we notice that Kenneth Allott, in his 'standard' anthology of the mid-century, selected 85 poets of whom 40.6% had studied at Oxford (and 7.05% were women). This line verges necessarily into the realm of numbers, where it seems to depart from artistic understanding altogether. If the principles on which existing selections were carried out are subverted, there is a phase when all texts seem to be equally valid. This is an impossible moment. It is like being pitched into the ocean because we don't like the ship we are on. The use of numbers is a sign of despair.

This line of argument is like a game you can play endlessly. For example, you can say that Allott's reading of poetry including the pleasure he felt is essentially like any other person's experience of poetry. There is no 'value free' appreciation of poetry. I mocked Allott's anthology because his commentary takes up almost as much space as the poetry, and he is so grim and negative. That whole 'close reading' style was an attempt to shore up the results of artistic tastes by claiming that close cross-examination supported them. The need to do this implies that the critique of artistic taste is already breathing down your neck. The inadequacy of close reading as an account for how poetry works presumably means that this war has been lost. Stepping up close reading by demanding scrutiny of the invisible presuppositions of a poet's work was even less successful.

Of course 'literary theory' involves other topics than the disqualification of artistic responses. However, this is a central topic. The theory which is about praising spontaneous reactions is less important because the default position is to believe in your own responses and the theory that this is good does not disrupt things. It is there simply to correct the Jacobin excesses of the anti-individualist wave.

The situation is made less clear by the preoccupation of poets with injustice as revealed by the failure of the world to make them famous. The idea that all critics/editors are inhuman and unjust is one of those 'unreasonable' notions which is held by a majority of people trying to get published, in fact then the majority of people on the scene. The idea of 'consensus' in the poetry world is exceptionally weak. The sources of this modern movement number in the hundreds and positing a single point source is necessarily misleading. It surely came from 'artistic speculation', but this zone of speculation may not even have overlapped with the areas of 'theory' which were being studied in academic libraries. There was a whole radical generation within which Marxist academics were part of the crowd. However, the relationship between radical poetry and 'theory' is important to understand. Does Alternative poetry come out of Theory? This question would take ten years to research. Basically the answer is No but there may be an element of coveting the institutional power of Theory.

A poet surrenders personal voice in order to switch off the preset narratives of social function and restraint. No doubt alternative poets believe that the way they write makes them innocent of the guilt which Theory pours onto writers. But every writer feels they are innocent.

THE IGNORANCE OF THE WRITER

We could hypothesize that the function of 'distantiation' is to get away from the deep enveloping banks of social ideology. Thus in *Separate Tables* (film, 1957) it is revealed that a character has a sexual failing. (The author, Terence Rattigan, intended this to be homosexuality, produced a version of the text as about homosexuality, but in the film it is not.) This comes as a revelation to the other guests in the private hotel he lives in. One of them, the snobbish one who wants to preserve boundaries, tries to get up a petition to the owner, which would mean he would lose his home, but the others accept him. They say that they do not understand his motivation but they will open their hearts and try to learn new sympathy. Thus there is an 'illusory consciousness' which reflects our conditioning and which we, as conscious adults, strive to transcend and to get away from. The idea is that the writer has to disrupt this false consciousness all the time in order to avoid reinforcing it. Thus we can interpret the 'distantiating' effect as a continuation of *Separate Tables*, disengaging projective ideas of motivation and social role. One would certainly question if this project is working if it is still going on after 53 years. Evidence is missing which would show that the 'alienated' writers are really animated by this motivation. Perhaps they are urged by something else, or perhaps they are copying writers who had this motivation and it is now part of the 'starter pack' for aspirant writers. Fairly obviously the character in *Separate Tables* wants warmth, sympathy, unquestioning acceptance, not anything cold and distantiated. We can question whether the distantiated style increases sympathy and understanding at all, and especially whether it does so better than stories based on character and identification.

Rattigan identified with Christian forces who hated homosexuals. You acquire ideology through the people you identify with. So you can liberate yourself through unplugging identifications. Rattigan's artistic nature related to a deep need for approval, enveloped by what unified wide swathes of public opinion and of the audiences who gave him payment and approval, that is tyrannical hatred directed at the way of life of Rattigan and people close to him. He abidingly wanted to give people what they wanted and to speak as someone they didn't want. The modern thing is an attempt to heal the splits.

Separate Tables was written in 1954, at around the time of the Wolfenden Committee, which investigated homosexuality and prostitution in relation with the legislation of the time. The brilliant and revisionist book about Wolfenden by Patrick Higgins is called *Heterosexual Dictatorship*. As Higgins discloses, the amazing thing about this committee is that it actually invited three homosexuals as witnesses. Almost all the other witnesses were concerned to abolish homosexuality, by punishment or treatment. His key observation is that none of these witnesses had any claim to knowledge of homosexuality (and there was no research basis for the opinions so roundly asserted as fact). This did not hold them back. The feeling about traditional English writers (among people born since 1945 or so) has been that they had the feeling of absolute knowledge of other people and right to decide for them. For the majority of them, this meant that they couldn't write about women and homosexuals, and actually didn't understand them even in the terms of daily intimacy. It would follow that the importance of a writer was or *is* their validation by status signs of belonging to the dominant group whose utterances are valid in this territorial domain, rather than their insight into other people.

Part of the push of criticism, going back to *la nouvelle critique* around 1965, is the criticism of the social judgment of writers. The writers can misjudge people face to face. Texts are made of information and this cellular substance of literature can be *wrong*. Writers may anyway be furnishing the material of fantasies rather than telling the truth of experience. These feelings about the substance of the 'information' of which literature was composed then are now shared by almost everyone.

Almost everything was known about the history of culture in 1990. My point is that the area of new development where intelligent people were working out new things was in this deep critique of the ego and its baroque defences. However, the prior stages of a literary work, as of a magazine, a film, a tabloid newspaper, etc., are not normally available, and the reconstruction is therefore not based on evidence. This line of analysis is authoritarian, intuitive, and hard to discuss, for lack of evidence. The critiques are not less based on intuition than the artistic texts. This does not reduce the fascination of the project. However, texts are produced by people. If someone is taking *my* poems and reducing them to some dripping and egocentric prior state, my rights are being breached. I do not have to accept this. Because the evidence is invented in the course of the speculation, most of the interpretations produced in this project are wrong, and there is no instance of such an interpretation being proved.

The story of theory is roughly this. The beginning is the Marxist movement, for which 'bourgeois literature' is something corrupt and false. As Marxism becomes more middle-class, the hostility becomes less class-conscious, more academic, and more lofty in tone. The theorist says that 'writers are mendacious and I am a writer and I am telling the truth'. After a point (which we can identify symbolically with the failure of the French Communist Party to seize the initiative in May 1968 and the subsequent migration of French intellectuals out of the PCF), the literary world gets the idea "if writers are all telling lies that includes the theorists because they are writers". They draw the conclusion that a creative writer talking about a few people close to the writer is more likely to know the truth than a theorist who generalises about thousands of books and millions and millions of people and draws their knowledge from 'solitary speculation'.

Modern poetry is based on empathy before all things. The counter-argument is that empathy is mostly wrong, and increasingly the people who resist this argument accept that it is true but that there is no alternative available.

THE IDEOLOGY OF EVERYDAY LIFE

If we imagine a newly born child, its prospects depend on the family it is born into. Those infants are headed for different parts of the social hierarchy, inequality is the goal of their stories of becoming, and the question is where it comes from. In the families, people acquire behavioural patterns and these suit the humans to positions of low status, whether via class or gender. By acquiring these patterns, or programmes, young humans come to reproduce society, including its inequality. As literature reproduces those behaviour patterns, it is given the blame either for unequal development paths or at least for failing to resist them. This is one of the themes of the critique of writing.

A widespread view of poetry is that the lyric is at the core of it and that what makes the lyric valuable is the regression to a state associated with childhood or adolescence where affective states predominate and affective urges govern behaviour. Poetry thus upsets an alienated and mediated adult personality structure and allows someone to recover innocence and subjectivity. Generalisation: the course of modern poetry is a constant series of clashes between lyricism and distantiation.

Modern-style poetry embraces both without language breaking up and within a single sentence.

The lyric-infantile justification of poetry is hard to combine with the radical view whereby childhood is where society reproduces its ideological structures, and where that reproduction takes place because the subject has no faculty of reason which could defend them, because they have a propensity to imitate, and because they are in a state of subjection to those stronger than they are. The attachment of poetry to the lyric, and to related pre-rational modes of myth and fantasy, is thus bound to make it clash with the approach to texts which sees them as *the genes of inequity*. The preset route of political commitment may simply take it towards an exit from art. The failure of the radical project associated mainly with the period 1968-75 may have been that it flowed ever more towards a reduction of art to identification with classificatory roles, to do with being working class, female, Black, Cypriot, Scottish, etc., which themselves were infantile, rooted in a period of early experience which was resistant to further learning and which proper reflexivity led people steadily away from. We will constantly revert to looking at the archaic, the irrational, etc., partly because this whole domain resists giving itself up to the examining intellect.

It is peculiarly difficult to use the irrational as the basis for claiming that the poems you write are true while also signing up to a rational project of reform and Enlightenment.

Perhaps the effectiveness of poems is more in their detailed linguistic organisation than in claims to truth which come from processes outside the poem.

The story of how someone reaches poverty as the culmination of their developmental course is the most interesting story. If it is the product of many steps, it is impossible to recover accurately. We have writers precisely because we want people able to recover parts of this story, even if they are fragmentary.

We can look away from the sphere of national politics as such, and the State. People learn how to behave in the situations which they are in. There is a line of 'domestic realism', of 'autobiographical narration', in recent poetry. As this reproduces the various situations of contemporary existence, it reproduces the processes by which people are socialised into their roles including the role of failure and subordination and service. It reproduces the patterned stimuli by which class society reproduces itself. Identification is presumably a key process within this acquisition of roles. One reason for writing poetry which is completely abstract and idealistic and blocked off from experience is that you believe that experience is oppressive.

It is also possible to hear the story of how individuals reach high status and win their fights. It is hardly a secret that some poetry of the past was a record of the high deeds, family alliances, and prized possessions of high status individuals. It is noticeable that 20th century poetry has abandoned this function – theory explains a decision which even anti-theoretical poets have committed to.

The Decline of Theory

Theory exists as a corporation, an interest or faction of a small number of concrete individuals and their assets. You can either be a member or not. This faction is ignored by the media and the book trade, but not by other academics. There is, in the same towns or faculty buildings, another corporation which they wanted to sink and run over. There may be other groups/agents in the field, for example the New Right. There is also the old Christian-Existentialist interest, strong in the 1950s, and specifically targeted by Theory as an ageing rival for institutional power and patronage.

Theory was compatible with hatred of the artist. It didn't always mean that but in a wide range of situations it did. It was suited to exploding the text, invalidating it. It worked for surges of rage against Fascism, conquering armies, dictatorships, colonial governments, factory owners. These emotions played a big role in 20th century Europe. In Britain, not a few people wanted to destroy bourgeois culture as a phase of destroying the bourgeoisie.

It may be that the popularity of the genre of singer-songwriter is as a protest against being dehumanised by measurement processes of which theory and the exam system are two notable examples. Students are treated as a commodity but their self-awareness does not coincide with this. While one line is trying to switch identification off, another is trying to enhance it, to defend it as the key moment in a soulless universe. Several generations of students have gone through university courses where 'theory' was something they had to master and reproduce, without 'theory' becoming the keystone of their attitude towards culture as consumers (or producers). They reached the conclusion that the self and the person are the most important things in the package.

Consider this sequence. High legitimation: defining who is to be rejected: imposing punishments on people: enacting many rules of conduct. The last step points irrevocably back to the first. The super-educated group could not have this high legitimacy without de-legitimating so many other people. The learned faction surrounds poetry, or indeed personal experience, with so many taboos and ways of doing it wrong that writing poetry is now like making a plea in a court of law. These taboos seem to me rather far removed from what constitutes artistic pleasure and success. I am simply pointing out that they are there.

I have a CD called *Weirdlore* on the Folk Police label. The reference is to a set of rules that old-style folkies apply to music as a test of whether it's 'proper folk'. If we imagine a 'poetry police' then the kind of thing they would be arresting you for is obviously failures to observe the rules of modernism. *No, you can't say that.* Because the artistic drive has slowed down so much since 1975, this is now a kind of interior design approach to language. *This* way of saying things is chic and *that* one isn't. Breaching these verbal manners could be a sign of spontaneity, but in other people arouses anxiety.

What is the restriction of the restricted? The answer changed after 1968. The mid-century saw the hegemony of the group of literary intellectuals who had, in their majority, gone on from public schools to Oxford or Cambridge universities, who were solid with the traditional upper middle class, and who are canonised in Kenneth Allott's *Mid-Century Poetry* (two editions in 1950 and 1960). Fairly obviously they were attacked by another group, who hoped to replace them, and who we can associate with the expansion of the universities in the 1960s, the New Left current which was so prevalent for ten years after 1968, and with 'literary theory'. People who cannot identify with either group are frequently admonished that they are living in the wrong country. The groups were the object of urges to assimilate and concomitantly had high self-esteem. Much of the discourse around poetry has to do with land-claims and status assertion in the rules of these two groups, and not with poetry. Poetry has presumably survived because both groups failed to understand it and so their colonising attempts were ill-focused – the poets escaped into the bush.

The academic world really took on modernism, and this was happening in the 1950s. It was a rallying cry which early on defined 'the happy few' and after decades came to define a restricted upper-middle-class in-group. Because the texts were difficult, they became a way in which the most academic kids, the scholarship winners, could shine. As this sank in, they became a display object in a middle-class status assembly. Meanwhile other kids were going to schools where the teachers couldn't understand modernism and wouldn't teach it. As the range of universities grew and grew, ways of differentiating their learning product grew too. The texts which are hard to understand, and this now means 'literary theory' even more than hard modernist literature, came to be studied at elite universities (and elite schools), and eventually to be signs of that lofty status. And people came to desire that status. And verbal patterns that broke with it came to be symbols of status anxiety. This is where your 'poetry police' come in. Modernism is now a status symbol, in the same way that listening to, or playing, classical music as opposed to jazz or dance music used to be. Its status as the land where great things happen is in question. The affluent have moved into the cold-water flats of the Artists' Quarter. Modernism has lost its radical impetus but become much more authoritative as cultural capital.

MALE AND FEMALE, EVEN FURTHER

I was trying to write a feminist analysis of some poetry. I liked those critics writing about Hitchcock – 'a closer look at scopophilia', what a great title. This didn't seem to work very well for poetry, so I will tell a story instead. In around 1982, I was working for a telecom manufacturer in the London suburb of New Southgate. My friend J, who worked for the mainframe division, Div 55, in Building 3, used to walk the security guard's dog at lunchtimes. When the occasion demanded it, I used to escort them both on this walk. J confided in me that the dog ignored women's voices and only reacted to orders delivered in a man's voice. The dog, sensitive to sound, had isolated a hierarchy, a chain of command, as a brilliant abstraction from the rambling turmoil of human signalling. Surely we are not going to accuse the dog of false consciousness? Devise a consciousness-raising group for the dog where it would read Sylvia Plath and come to terms with its own preconceptions? The dog was deploying notions of boundary, territory, intruder which very successfully represented how humans thought about these things. Property in land is something both dogs and humans understand. Possibly humans learnt it from dogs.

The possibility for being caught in a spiral of error is glaring. If you decide that someone is unimportant, then everything that happens to them is unimportant, even the fact that you may be misjudging them. A book of poems where you are offered information about their unimportant lives and theories could not heave itself up to importance. Even when you understood their feelings, they would not seem important. The volume on their voice would be turned down even while you were listening to them. How exactly could you escape from this logically connected spiral? Only experiences you believed were important could saturate and expand your senses and intellectual powers enough to become intense or memorable.

It is possible that a whole social structure with its scales of values is present in verbal art, which simply embodies it. So that to read poetry of grand scale simply recites the social order complete with its assignments of degradation, humility, and subjection, and rehearses it, smoothing off any awkward moments. How much people must want to change the social structure by changing the structure of the poem.

At this point I can imagine all my judgments being incorrect. Can I verify that my literary judgments, that my versions of what other people felt, that my conscious interpretation of my own feelings, are true and faithful? There is no objective evidence for this. This is a modern situation I suppose. When I read Nietzsche as a teenager, I couldn't visualise what he means by *the transvaluation of all values*. This is what you have to do if you reject the basis of your existing judgements. He doesn't explain what the rules are for generating new values once all the old values have been scrapped. How could they not have included the rules for generating values?

A critic of art can only discuss experiences they actually have. Without that burst of impulses going off in different directions, that heightening, which constitute an artistic reaction, there is nothing to say. I could easily derive a programme of relative values by reading poetry critics, or political theorists who were keen to lay down the values of people on some theoretical basis, and write about that. But this would be a blank pattern, producing blank prose, unless my own reactions came into line with it. This is intuition – it doesn't carry out the designs of preset schemas.

POWERS OF INTUITION

People who read poetry prefer the line of intuition, first person insight, creativity, personal symbols. This predisposition got them to the poetry section in the library, allowed them to be attracted by a book of poetry, and guides them into the meaning of the poem. People who do not share this preference chose a different path at each fork and did not end up inside the poem. Equity is for him who seeks to do equity; poetry has rewards for someone who regards its processes as rewarding.

It's not that intuition is sovereign. I am sure it is wrong a lot of the time. It's just that there is nothing to replace it with. Giving up ideology leaves us with a kind of glimmering darkness where we navigate by heat and by a dim mineral glow seeping out of living beings.

There is a classic moment in writers' workshops where you say that you like a certain style or texture, dislike another style, and the other people present reject that as a proposition. They would say that what is intuitive and before is not better than rationality but simply better defended. So anything you say is then just a ritual of defence of preset positions. A number of verbal jousts follow, in a preset order. I will say that the Underground want to prove that your intuitions are wrong and the mainstream don't. If you see poetry as a zone where intuitions prevail you don't see poetry as a zone where intuitions are there to be ground down and erased in the name of modernist reason. I believe that the quality of poetry is to turn up the volume of intuition. Some poetry rejects this precept.

Judgments about the relative value of different poems are especially subject to ejection from a merely rational process. The sociological approach accepts that archaic structures affect how people react to poetry but follows this up to say that these structures are self-aggrandising and that, for example, male critics cannot understand poetry by women (thus reducing the whole apparatus of artistic pleasure to ideology). The most noted effects of this line of thought are its discrediting of the emotional responses of readers to literature and its wiping out of the artistic intent of writers in favour of supposed, possibly imaginary, layers of unconscious meaning which are the utterances of social structures. Relating individual poems to these imaginary mass structures is like taking a patch of moonshine on Northern Europe and trying to identify which part of the Moon it came from.

This line demands proofs of what poets say about experience, and what critics say about poetry, beyond the subjective judgments of these individuals. Understandably, no such proofs are available. Readers seek authenticity, the relation of the poem to something outside it. But they only have the poem. So they seek tests of authenticity in features of the poem – not the primary assertions but the unconscious elements of style. It may be that living among the human race is adequate propaideutic for detecting deceptive intent in the utterances of other humans. Or it may be that what we take as valid signs are petrified, reduced to objects, conserved by piety.

My idea of poetry sees it as a zone where suggestibility, collusion, identification are enhanced and made effortless. Take Kenneth Allott. If he thought 40.6% of the significant British poets (1918 to 1960) were Oxford graduates, that shows he had taken collusion a long way. He was reading signs of authenticity but he defined them as signs of having been to Oxford – as he had. Prominently, he carried out repetitive acts of judgement and pleasure. What he sought was what he found and what he sought was what he already had. If we accept identification as the primary principle, we cannot avoid disasters like Allott's predilection for Oxonians. If we switch off identification we end up with no poetry. You can't go inside a work of art without becoming part of an in-group.

The primary phase of literary reaction is a source of pleasure. That is, what is happening in someone's mind as they read a poem; but also what was happening in the poet's mind as they processed other people's feelings or their own and wrote the poem. Writing and reading poetry have a point and the point is this. The accumulated knowledge of a wide range of poetry and of poetic pleasure finally becomes connoisseurship, as the piling-up and storing of journeys into a poem. Everything taking place under the label of theory acts to reduce the value of artistic connoisseurship and of individual taste. The only purpose of poetry is the first-person experience of someone inside the poem, where everything happening depends wholly and solely on individual judgements and acts of appreciation. So the only way to attack poetry is to degrade the value of this first person experience – whose appreciations are, at least, a million times more accurate than other, mass-scale, attempts to evaluate art. No-one has yet replaced first-person experience.

Chronicling the hostility of critics formed in the Marxist camp to artistic pleasure and to the acts of knowledge and identification involved in art has convinced me ever more that their aggressions are hysterical and unsustainable. This has been a long march whose goal never even existed.

Don't send a falcon to do a gosling's job

Three times in the *Falcon* Sam Spade refers to the Elisha Cook Jr. character as "a little gunsel". The director may have thought this meant 'gunman', but really it is the Yiddish word for 'gosling' and was used in gangster slang to mean the under-age male lover of some gay gangster. Gunsel is too appropriate to the naive and imitative Cook, who thinks he is tough but who is forced to be the weaker man in a succession of criminal couplings, to give up easily. Gunsel is an example of the unconsidered moment of betrayal. These moments play a large role in the staging of Theory, as overlooked because unimportant to the primary artist but given swollen importance because they give control to the Theorist and form a 'hidden switch' where the hidden layer of unconscious processing which the theorist proposes slides out into full view and buries the 'conscious' and 'rational' structures which the primary writer proposes. It is like one of several dozen moments in the *Falcon* where Sam Spade, grinning mirthlessly, reveals a flaw in the suspect's account of things and pulls out, with a conjurer's flourish, a whole narrative in which the witness actually committed the crime. Objectively, Dashiel Hammett may have known what 'gunsel' meant but it is quite likely that Bogart and Huston did not. Are these moments of self-betrayal ever genuine? Are they all just cleverly staged fakes? Show trials run by masters of dazzle?

The binary contrast between the falcon and the gosling is too tempting to say farewell to. One is covered with fat (schmalz?), one is covered with lead. Both substances are liable to melt at a moment of high emotion. Don't send a gosling to do a falcon's job. David Thomson describes Cairo and Gutman as "like Lear and the Fool at some queers' club" – the staging of the film clearly says they are queer (although this cannot be said), but anyway at the mythical level it is imperative that they should be, so as to be the helpless victims of Bogart's heterosexual dictatorship. Gutman bears a strong resemblance to Max Horkheimer and we can hardly do without an equation of Cairo, with his gardenia scent, with Theodor Adorno. Manifestly, 'Cairo gardenia' is an anagram of 'Theodor Adorno'. So is the film a coded allegory on the Institut für Sozialforschung? And is the Falcon a reference to the Siren in the relevant chapter of *Dialektik der Aufklärung*? After all the Falcon was lost on a galley in the Mediterranean. Are the victims of exploitation rowing to the song of the falcons?

There is a third bird in the film – the *Paloma* (Spanish for dove), the ship which carries the Falcon to San Francisco and which is set on fire in the harbour by Wilmer Cook. The Falcon, the gosling, and the dove. So what does this trinity of birds mean? is it just something like a dead leaf which blew in through a window while the camera was rolling and which no-one paid any attention to? Almost certainly. Is this the occult and logically coherent armature on which Hollywood's symbolic machines spin the coded luxurious shimmer of the filmic text? Actually, no.

EXERCISES

1.   Did György Lukács kill Miles Archer? Show your reasoning.
2.   Write a new version of the *Falcon* in which Brigid O'Shaughnessy is the virtuous heroine and comes out on top.
3.   Write the DA's speech indicting Sam Spade for framing Cairo and Gutman.
4.   How would you know if a poem is true or not?
5.   Does anyone understand you?
6.   Is there anyone you understand?

CUBE OF NOW, SHIP OF SHILLINGS

The forties poet Peter Yates writes about the Now, the constellation of a brain state which is more complex than anything outside it:

THE CUBE OF NOW

No bird of volted eye
Sky crashing grief
Will splinter this
Dead word of life,
No rocket of high fever
Ever bursting bars
Mounting out of this
Eye-socket shooting stars
Will journey out of this
Dense cube of now

The "cube of now" called for human beings to react now, jettisoning the luggage of acquired knowledge and ego defences, but it also subtracted the poet from the organised knowledge of the state and of cultural managers. It was a definition of authenticity valid for that time and place. It was a protest against the entanglement of poetry in long-term processes which had no salience at any point. Spender makes essentially the same point –

Tomorrow and yesterday are pictures
Remembered and foreseen, painted within
Man's two profiles facing Past and Future, pivoted
On the irreducible secret diamond
His Now. Past and Future, pictures only,
And all events and places distant from
The instant of perception in the brain,
Are memories and prophecies.
All distant times and places, all events
In other minds, all knowledge folded
In books, Pasts petrified in statues,
Spatial distance witnessed by telescopes,
Prehuman histories embossed on fossils,

Silent messages from star to star,
Exist only in the flash within the single flesh.
    (from 'Time in Our Time')

This idea of consciousness only existing in the immediate moment offers a way of exploring modern poetry, and a way of demarcating it from abiding knowledge – the domain of prose which poets take to be also the domain of loss of awareness, where both change and pattern disappear under grey data. The idea that the 'long time' of the fossil only exists at the instant that a human subject is aware of it is challenging, but also provides a conceptual peak for the single human being who is the poet to be at the top of.

By demarcating itself from the universal grey of sociological typicalness, poetry moves into the territory inhabited by the advertisements where a lyric impulse is also an impulse buy. Yet the protest against the understanding of the human as an 'object of administration' is one of the great achievements of modern poetry.

A notion we may find useful is that of the chreode (from roots meaning 'it is necessary' and 'way or passage'). This is not an electronic component and you can't buy them from Radio Shack. It is a concept developed by Allen Fisher to describe a constraint which it is necessary for a poet (also thinkers or artists generally) to pass through. It is a way of illuminating an individualist landscape; poets with very diverse verbal practices may be grouped by analysing what they rejected and what ideals they absorbed. This sheds light on the issue of time passing and 'being out of date', which has caused a lot of argument. Eric Mottram, in writings of fundamental importance, made it credible in the 1970s that there was a chreode, a multiple one, which British poets since 1960 had passed through in order to become modern. Conversely, the other poets, who hadn't found this chreode, had fallen by the wayside. It was a narrow tunnel into a vast and empty landscape. The chreode was not defined but corresponded, broadly, to 'American avant-garde poetry of the 1950s'. Although this overall map synthesized a vast number of disparate phenomena, it has become apparent (after thirty years) that this wasn't a chreode, or at least it was a facultative one: many poets had essentially bypassed it, and they were not tired and obsolete.

The historicism of the new avant-garde of the 1960s (and later decades) created a 'cube of now' by identifying a line of time which advanced ceaselessly and destroyed what belonged to the past. This allowed a signature for any personal style, held to be trapped in a moment as breach in the continuum of time. Just as the fossil dies once only but is preserved for millions of years, the 'signature style' is held to capture a moment of time and to be usable for a whole career. The poet remains in a crystal cube. The state of captivity and the uniqueness are aspects of the same thing. The coding of these styles was not equally obvious to all potential readers.

Dealing with the banality of political knowledge is a chreode for poets. If you deal with national politics, your knowledge base is patterns that involve millions of people. If you are dealing with irreversible social change, you are looking at processes which elapse over very long time periods. Poetry which takes on such processes has a problem with making itself bright and coloured, raising itself above the grey and sodden. Arguably, any unique experience has already failed to be typical and so to partake of this political knowledge. There are two likely outcomes for poets grappling with this, one of which is to emerge in the vicinity of a columnist and the other is to emerge in the territory of advertisements.

I am going to write about the second line, which deals with life as a succession of volatile instants, the cube of now. It does not eliminate the atypical. The problem is how to focus attention on one single individual. If the poet fails to attach the experience to themselves, the moment of brilliant focus does not start to shine. One way in which the poet achieves this lock-in is through the deployment of objects. In ways both complex and historically 'early', evoking feelings and processes through sensory data captures attention and reaches the 'attachment' effect. Objects weigh down the concrete moment and focus the sensory system. They provide a point of shared attention for two people. Memorable scenes often include objects as a key part. Poems notably often include objects or places. Types in literature are *colossi* (featureless stone steles marking graves and 'standing for' the dead person), *tekmerion*, (the object as evidence, where an example would be the shard of blade taken from a wound which matches the notch in Tristan's spear-blade and proves that he killed Morholt, Iseult's uncle); and *agalma* (a treasure which 'honours and decorates', often a gift or a sacrifice). The agalma has been discussed by Louis Gernet, noting how often stories use an agalma as a key functional element, as guarantees of the safety of the city, or as signs of recognition.

The interest of not a few poets in archaeology is connected to the perfectly developed symbolic code which old Europeans used for organising funerary objects in depositions. The absence of words, the mute nature of the statement, encouraged precision. Celan writes about stone boats:

Im Haus zum gedoppelten Wahn,
wo die Steinboote fliegen
überm
Weisskönigs-Pier, den Geheimnissen zu
wo das endlich
abgenabelte
Orlogs-Wort
kreuzt
  (from 'Frihed')

Are there boats of stone? Denmark is the place because the poem has a Danish word for title and another Danish word, the word for war (or possibly navy), appears in line 7. So the answer is yes, known as *stenskib,* they appear over a 2,000-year period, on the islands of Denmark and on Bornholm and Gotland. The monument clearly uses the shape of a boat but the analogy is made to be violated: there cannot be a boat of stone. Symbolic statements use series to point to things which are outside the series; that is the code can be used to mean things that don't exist. But the analogy may also be purposeful: if you are going to sail your boat through the underworld, through rock and darkness, stone may be the only material that would withstand those conditions, and the stone boat is there to point to the frightfulness of the voyage. Literally, the poem almost certainly refers to the rescue of Danish Jews, by boat to Sweden, before the Nazis could do something else with them. (As *Schiff* in German also means 'nave', Celan refers to them as *Boot* not *Schiff* – a stone nave is too likely.) Archaeologists generally assume that the deposition objects are making a statement about the status of the individual buried. This involves series again – the 'ship grave' at Jelling is 170 metres long, this in keeping with a royal burial. We find that objects often relate to a *person* and denote their *role*.

Poets too arrange clusters of objects. It is possible to study poetry by making collections of the objects which appear in it. For Pauline Stainer you would need an exquisite object-set:

hail drives
through the samphire
where the ammonites
show signs of healing

high-level
radioactive waste
is turned into molten glass
sealed in stainless steel

a pyx of white silver
is laid in a silken
compartment
in Christ's body

the limbs of mummies
crackle like chemical
glass-tubing
and give out great heat

(from 'Quanta', in *The Lady and the Hare*, 2003)

This poetry is dependent on its objects but reaches autonomy through the range and amplitude of objects, metaphorical or not, which it occupies.

The rest of this essay will deal with the acquisition and coding of these objects, which in our time points directly to the Commodity and its ancillary structures. I am claiming that (modern) poetry hews to the line of the subjective, the personal, and the fleeting moment, and that in doing so, it can hardly avoid migrating onto the territory of the advertisement. We must connect momentary acts of wilfulness with the advertisement. Advertisements could hardly be so brief without displaying the unique moment, to which access is given by consuming the commodity. To reach moments which make us glow with life and find enhanced exchanges with other people equally glowing – this is what you see in a high percentage of all advertisements. These ads narrate breaches in the continuum of time, rare and privileged moments in which emotional insights are grasped which are lost immediately afterwards. They show impossible things, caught in visual form by high technology, which seems to be outside the laws of physics. They do homage to Modernism and regard innovation as obligatory. They are fond of catachresis – trick perspectives which suddenly resolve with a click of perception. They produce the cube of now, singular moments lifted out of time in which disparate elements fuse together in a new pattern. This is the territory of poems.

The basis for purchase decisions, beyond necessities, is a disbelief in the permanence of social status as acquired early in life: status is no longer a binding condition but volatile, it is scattered over thousands of wilful acts whose validity is, in proportion, brief and evanescent. This is not completely alien from what Yates was saying. The burden there had to do with the possibility of choice, rejecting Marxist or other determinism, but this idea of freedom was remodelled, in the West, into an unrestricted series of consumption acts, amounting to choice and assent. If this choice is really there, the typical poem cannot be written. The subject has turned to smoke. There is no constancy to be fixed in a verbal icon. The atypical and momentary poem ceases to be sociological documentary but floats gradually closer to the artistic rule of the advertisement.

It's obvious that people in Britain spend a large part of their daily lives watching advertisements, and also that there is no clear dividing line between ads and other forms of narrative or image. Indeed it would be hard to name any device of modern art that has not been captured and imitated by admen at some stage. The documentary movement developed techniques for showing technology in film, such that industrial films like *Oil Review*, and *Desert Tractors* (for the Anglo-Iranian Oil Company) nourished techno-fiction like David Lean's *The Sound Barrier* but were recycled a thousand times for explaining how technology was making super products. This is where documentary went, and poetry which takes on science is likely to work like advertisements. I think critics should take on advertisements (and song lyrics, cigarette cards, transcribed utterances of disembodied spirits, anything really). It is no good objecting that ads show people as preoccupied with objects and with personal pleasure, because it seems likely that people really are inclined towards those things. We can either think that ads are Totally Corrupt or think they show the good life and there is no point being fussy and picky: if we could find it we would go there. This is already the case with propaganda: you think it shows what good government would be or else think that good government is too hard to imagine. Ideals are in any case similar to poetry.

A clutter of earth sieves, chest-ploughs, brass pots, rusting tines on rotting hafts, is supposed to make us thirsty. In the industrial belt north of the North Circular, pubs like to allude to a rural past, as if the objects thus heaped up had belonged to the fields now covered by remote suburbs. We can think of the Georgians as leaving this legacy of long country walks and decontextualised farming tools; *while for the scythes of his flight of mowers 'the best strickles are of proughy unseasoned oak'* and the like. The assemblage clearly goes back to poems by Edward Thomas in which the knowledge of the (landless) labourer of his tools is seen as pure knowledge, free from illusion, serving, restraining the self. Man, spade, and earth are seen as a cube of now. These tools are not dumb because they are coated by a coding which the Georgians laid on, and which speaks for them. The Georgians wrote so much about the rural poor. The point of the tools is that they are attributes of the worker, things which the land-owners never touched. This is an example of an *object complex,* which binds scenes together with an abstract meaning. Poets always want objects to prove something abstract. The objects never argue. They are happy to swing either way.

Archaeology has recovered the coding of objects over long time-scales, including the time before the wide extension of writing in society, although not long before it. They are rather alien to us but the link between objects and personal attributes such as status, prestige, prowess, has a long history. Although the Staffordshire Hoard was only recovered from the ground in 2009, Nicholas Brooks has already provided an analysis online which raises interesting questions about symbolism and contract. The hoard, dated to roughly AD 625-675 at present, is mainly a mass of gold 'fragments'. The majority of it consisted of war-gear, and "*Most of the gold and silver items appear to have been deliberately torn from the objects to which they were originally attached. We have over 80 gold and garnet pommel caps, and there also appear to be fittings from helmets.*" These have already been interpreted as 'plunder', wrenched from source objects (as the 'complete' site) seized in combat. Nicholas Brooks' view is rather that the fittings were intact but a stock ready to be hammered onto swords as needed for a ceremony in which a warrior was bound to a lord by the bestowal of a sword (or, other war-gear) which had been 'gold-plated' to make it precious, and where the decoration also, possibly, bore the brand of the lord, his recognition sign. A king (perhaps of Mercia) was thus travelling around with a 'hot shop' of luxury weapon parts, ready to equip whenever necessary a ritual which resembles the later winning of spurs, dubbing of a knight, or the heregeat or heriot. The hoard is like a stock of blank contracts. This king evidently had smiths travelling around with him, and this 'buying of loyalty' ceremonial took place wherever he was. Gold is very soft and lends itself easily to hammering onto harder objects, for example iron swords. Because, in leaf form, it can be cold hammered, it is like writing – it can record signs *quickly*. There is no word for 'scrap gold', but the word 'coin' covers some of the range. James Campbell had in an earlier paper ('The sale of land and the economics of power') analysed a passage from the possibly 7th century 'Widsith', (lines 90-96) which goes as follows, "*He gave me a collar in which there was six hundred coins worth of pure gold counted by shillings. This I gave to Eadgils, my lord and protector, to keep when I arrived home, a reward to the beloved man, because he, the lord of the Myrgingas, gave me land, the ancestral home of my father.*" Campbell describes this two-part transaction in which Widsith is given a treasure by Eormanric (Ermanaric), king of the Gothic realm in West Russia and Poland, for services as a minstrel, then comes home (to south Denmark, roughly) and gives the same piece of treasure to his 'hleodryhten', patron lord, Eadgils, in order to receive as grant the land which his father had previously held. Inheritance is here missing or at least incomplete. It is puzzling that although this is a bullion object, a treasure, we are also told its value in denomination, a scale which would seem to belong to a quite different phase of economy – to contract rather than status. 'Widsith' need not be contemporary with Ermanaric (died 375 AD) but the story predates England. The word is *scillingrime*, 'in count of shillings'; a simple soldier was feed by one shilling (the 'king's shilling', which as Campbell points out already appears in a capitulary of AD 813 as a *solidus*, in fact *soldier* derives from *solidus*) but Widsith is getting the equivalent of a star bonus from Goldman Sachs, and this is why he has a poem about him. A modern army does not travel with wagon-loads of loose sword hilts as 'piece parts', but possibly in the 7th century that was part of the order of march. To speak of plundering as a form of recycling would be anachronistic, I think, but we could call it *détournement*. Kristian Kristiansen has suggested that, in the Iron Age, the geographically vast spread of distinctive objects, mostly looking like war-gear but maybe 'too good for use', does not represent the colonies and conquests of a mobile warrior aristocracy, but the returns home of mercenaries, bearing 'golden handshakes' like Widsith. Where we see La Tène artefacts in Ireland, that is, we are not seeing a 'celticity' which reigns from Austria to Munster, but the end of completed terms of service. The power to raise such armies was connected with control of primary sources of wealth, like mines.

It is too soon for any interpretation of the hoard, which is unique, to be definitive, but this very striking account is offered as a model of signed objects which gives us a clue to how objects fit into poems and how signs acquire objects.

One of Christopher Logue's great poems of the 1950s describes recruits sailing out in some miserable imperialist campaign: "And nine white bellied porpoise led / Our ship of shillings through the sun", after taking the King's *solidus*. The campaign was in "an island in the sun / Where the Queen of Love was born", that is to say Cyprus. This was originally published in Autumn, 1957 (in E.P. Thompson's *The New Reasoner*, the New Left not yet conjoined with the poetic avant-garde, not yet in a failed marriage), and the first part of Logue's Homer translation followed, Aphrodite, East Med, shipborne phalanxes, etc., already in 1959. There is a certain embarrassment for the aficionado in finding how outstanding the later volumes are in the landscape of the past ten years, and how modern they seem. The 1950s theme of a Near Eastern invasion that displayed apparently boundless power and brought unwished-for and bloody results does not seem to have lost its force. This is a 'poem of action' dealing with combat, mostly, with the moment of supreme danger and ensuing death providing a perfect cube of now in which our attention is focussed. Logue writes like an advertisement, in describing these envy objects, bringing us brief narratives of rich people being killed by portable wealth. The objects are personalised; as weapons, body armour, chariots, they are adornments as well as implements. To paraphrase Alexander Kluge, they are constructed on a principle of 'pay and display with lethal outcome'.

> Achilles saw his armour in that instant,
> And its ominous radiance flooded his heart.
> Bright pads with toggles crossed behind the knees,
> Bodice of fitted tungsten, pliable straps;
> His shield as round and rich as moons in spring;
> His sword's haft parked between sheaves of grey obsidian,
> From which a lucid blade stood out, leaf-shaped, adorned
> With running spirals.
> And for his head a welded cortex; yes,

Though it is noon, the helmet screams against the light;
Scratches the eye; so violent it can be seen
Across three thousand years.
   (from 'Pax', in *War Music*, 1981)

This praise is barbed. The splendour of the objects bears out the critique of the poet: these are amazingly arrogant rich people, and their exit into the inanimate is intimately linked to their faith in their high-technology possessions. The link between a chariot and a fighter jet, in terms of arrogance and overdevelopment, is quite easy to make. Logue's description of objects is mesmerizing, but he is also writing off an entire ruling class.

The poem, as a customary act handed down from the Bronze Age, has notable analogies with the customs of prestige objects, also highly developed in the Bronze Age. Gifts and signs are both forms of exchange. The poems also proclaim prestige and also, in some cases, mark an exchange of social roles – marriage or death/succession. The earliest English words are recorded as runes on the surface of objects. These curving surfaces, of horns and bracteates, may prefigure the intricacy of Old English poems as written down later. The intricacy of the workmanship on prestige objects stands as an analogy, broad or close, to the verbal texture of poems. The aristocratic behaviour complex, around gifts signalling the status of giver and receiver, may have been shattered by a century of socialist thought, and that 'shatter dust' may have blown to a far larger number of people, to become their precious possessions – a 'pollen pulse' where the desirable thing bursts and flows to those who most desire it. The exit of the aristocracy has permitted the move of the artist and of *maniera* to the centre of art. Verbal assets are the product of excellence; art is a display of prowess as a suit for honour.

Not every poem is an agalma. There is also a line of *Gebrauchspoesie*, rigmaroles whose faith to a rhythm is not coupled with intricacy. There is a link between advertising jingles, skipping rhymes, and much older jingles, typically binary (eight syllable lines organised in couplets) and with an exact match of beat and word stress.

Pauline Stainer (b.1941) has written some of the most interesting and highly charged poetry of the past twenty years, work in which objects play a prominent role. 'Salt over Skara Brae' (1995) concatenates nine parts. The shared theme has something to do with flooding and recovery from the flood. Although this is not described in the poem,

Skara Brae is a Neolithic village site in Orkney, occupied during the first half of the third millennium BC. For long buried, it was uncovered by a sandstorm in 1850:

> under the heather
> the dead are spring-heeled,
> sand blown from the vertebrae
>
> there is spruce on the shore
> rafter of whale-rib,
> bedding of blue clay
>
> surf on the lintel
> hazelnut shells,
> elkskin and scapula
>
> stones heat the water,
> glistening lovers
> run to red ochre
>
> Queen of Peace –
> put the salt-white host
> on your tongue.
>
> (collected in *The Lady and the Hare*, 2003)

(This is part 1; surf because the site is also washing into the sea.) It was dug by Gordon Childe in 1928-30. Part 2 describes a woman carrying stones which eventually raise the floor of an inland loch so that an islet forms, and meadowsweet grows on it – to be reflected in the water. (Red-hot stones, that heat water to seethe meat in Neolithic cooking, are counterparts to 'floating stones' in the loch, and to the steps of tidal causeways.) Other parts describe other sunk ships, causeways that flood and float in the tidal cycle, the sailing of John Franklin's doomed expedition to North Canada. Stainer's power is to link marvellous events in higher scenarios – the bonds are strong and yet not immediately revealed. Salt appears throughout, perhaps as a sacramental substance – used to keep off evil? – as does the theme of devotion. These awesome processes fill the role of tekmerion, proof of the greatness of God. What is it – salt dissolves in water as the Host dissolves in us, yet burning resurrects the salt, crystalline? The salt prevents corruption and can be retrieved in pure form however dirty the water? Men are the fish that Saint Peter was to dredge up from the hidden places of the ocean. The objects, vertebrae, cyclopean lintels, elkskin, whalebones, meadowsweet, etc., are not central but moments of attention in the scenario of a ritual. Also in saints' lives, marvellous objects show breaches in the plane of the secular, and holy relics were kept as 'objects of devotion'.

This is radically different from mid-century Christian poetry and raises questions of its insertion in mundane time, as well as in divine time. It seems that while Christians were, throughout, a large share of the poetically active, there was a crisis in their ability to write poetry, which may have related to the loss of a sense that the community was Christian, and with an ebbing of the power and prestige of the Church. The great Christian poetry and prose of the past did not seem 'existentially valid'. Poets wanted to write about their sense of decline and desolation, even if they enjoined repentance in the last stanza. Stainer belongs to a phase in which this problem has been overcome. In her poetry, there is a noticeably happy marriage of stylistic frame and doctrinal assertion. She finds the marvellous in the present and in places she visits: the cube of now, reached through sacred geography. The rise of literate parishioners vis-à-vis the priest has brought a cultural voice which simultaneously allows for the decline of the congregation to be overlooked, for direction to be taken over by the unordained, and for new *but not heretical* forms to develop in poetry. The devotional life of Anglicans, that is, now bears certain resemblances to New Age spirituality, in that it is personal and individual and open to all kinds of exotic religious motifs – like someone buying CDs of 'world music'. In sum, if we wanted to take in the scene since the decline of the Underground from dominance, we would have to notice a revival of poets from Oxford and a revival of religious poetry.

B. Catling's *Soundings. A Tractate of Absence* contains prose descriptions of a number of performances (eleven, but one came in five parts) enacted by Catling between 1984 and 1991. The subtitle was a reference to the prehistory of Catling's work in the conceptual line (which abolished the object), also in the 'living sculpture' line where poses or actions of the sculptor replaced any object-effigy. This 'sculpture without objects' evolved, obviously, to performances. The transformation from carving and moulding external 'bearers' back to living bodies is an example of the 'cube of now': the fixed is being rejected in favour of the fluid and volatile. But objects do play a role in Catling's performances:

> *Nailed cones and rods scratch into the wave. Silked colours rent to white, they bleed tendrils that extend and wetly flutter into the arid bay. The dust mittens and parches their sinew, drawing whipped spoor faintly on the wood. They are blueprint roads to carry distortion across the planked waste, where the horizon is clouded in brick and signed against departure.*

> *In this shaft of light, the ink cupped from here is red, wood-hearted in a trunk of burning. It pumps its own light into a well where stars are: a parabolic night rafted in an iron sepulchre of day.*

This performance occupied a lighthouse at the confluence of the River Lea and the Thames, a relic of the 19th century stuck on the edge of a super-modern City.

'At the Lighthouse' redefined the already existing lighthouse, occupying in fact the whole swathe of riverine landscape which the shaft of light had played over. Objects played a rather large role in the conceptual movement in this country, if that is the right name for it. Leaving no pictures or objects, filling that 'absence', Catling is taking us back to the moment 'before coding'. This is the legacy of the conceptual movement, that it deleted the existing object codings and made it *blatantly apparent* that humans can invent their own codings and freely design rituals of object acquisition. These prose texts are arguably not poetry, but they are a significant parallel to it. They create blank objects, waiting for words to alight. But some of the poems we have include this 'object encoding' as one strand of their DNA. (From memory, the oil pump for the light was adapted to lift ink. 'Parabolic' refers to the parabolic reflector behind the light.)

There is an overlap, however at an edge of conceptual space, between Stainer and Catling. The overlap of imagery of the far North between Catling's Bergen action and Stainer's great poem 'The Ice-Pilot Speaks' goes less deep than a resemblance of structure; Stainer is designing performances even if these only exist as forms of words. She is recoding objects even if she has no past in the conceptual movement. (Catling has also published a body of great poetry, notably *Written Rooms and Pencilled Crimes*.)

> *In the far corner, at the back of the force lines is a vertical paper hood, sewn delicately along its edge, an identical lens extending from it to touch a misshapen mass on the floor. The scratched lines of influence here have bulged and distended their orbit in its presence. The mass is a dark gritty puddle of poured lead.*
>
> *The object was made at the Trollhaugen, a lake on the edge of the city: a place of significance and memory. It was deep winter, the lake locked solid, the dark ice steaming in the night. The lead was cast on the peak of the full moon, poured into its frozen reflection, the heat biting into the ice, the cold reforming: the exchange of heat and stability.*
>
> (from 'White Breath – Red Heart'; text in *Soundings*)

This Catling text could be the scenario of a Stainer poem. Stainer is a Christian poet committed to the 'box of beautiful things' but the range and freedom of her deployment of objects, and attributed meanings, make it possible that she has absorbed the new line of conceptual art – and conversely that performance art was modelled on ritual and has remodelled it to reach its new practice. It may be that there was a chreode in poetry in which the collapse of Christian symbolism and of other inherited fixed arrangements of symbols ran with and around the conceptual movement and its critique of the object, and that the outcome was a new treatment of objects in poetry. We would situate this chreode, crudely, in around 1963. It *may* stand in relation to the new excess of objects in the developing consumer culture.

CONCLUSION

The poets we have looked at have penetrated deep into the world of objects, comfortably exceeding the depth of advertisements and thus establishing superiority over them. They seem to have come out on the far side where they can invent and code ambitious scenarios. It is not clear how many other poets have a personalised set of objects, although the quality of their occupation and invention of objects might be an indicator of their autonomy. The Lighthouse 'installation' underlines the point that objects cannot be theorised as a separate tier, instead the 'cube of now' constantly involves other people, animals, substances, water, landscape. The appeal of the approach though objects is that it is compact – it is so much simpler than other issues. Insofar as objects are shared by human agency, they are not objective and offer no support for the truth of the symbolic statements they carry. They are merely sites where subjectivity makes itself visible, and those subjective states change because humans are free. The fact that objects change less rapidly than subjective consciousness makes them less full of meaning, not more.

I have not discussed where the acquisition of objects and moments fails. This is surely more typical of the period – stock footage of wonderful things is cheap and abundant, poets stuff themselves with it and the poems run off the surface of the 'spoils' leaving no trace.

Partially Coded Fields and Bastions of Exaggeration: Andrew Jordan and Nonism

Charles Mintern, known as "the Third Piltdown Man", originally emerged in the 1950s as the inventor of a hoax 'Jesuit palaeontologist' named Teilhard de Chardin. Although he has been described as "a pioneer adaptor of heideggerian philosophemes to the Dorset singer-songwriter tradition", I don't really like his poems. I remember him best for a sartorial resemblance to Captain Haddock. He said my poetry was "pretentious" and took the piss out of my accent. An illegal Provisional wing calling itself "the sons of the Nomintern" has issued a bulletin accusing Andy Jordan of "hookerite tendencies" and "crypto-authenticity". They report a rumour that a moderate nonist wing has emerged with a reformist platform calling for "more links to local businesses". Orthodox Nonist (Hillbillies) theory holds that there is no ancient subsoil, all objects found in the subsoil are recent artefacts and not "time soaked". Nonist field teams (the Field Poetry Club) have found many flat so-called "profile urns" in the subsoil of Hampshire. They believe that this is the original form, and that three-dimensional urns with cremated remains inside developed later, "in line with the development of illusionist perspective drawing at the Renaissance". Prominent hills are raised on artificial struts and embankments, regularly uncovered by nonists on their Sunday group rambles. Most of the English landscape was constructed by the Crown Film Unit, using conscientious objectors as labour, during the 1940s. The fact that the word 'exaggerate' includes the word for 'earthwork' (agger) implies that admen were originally landscapers creating artificial hills – the Pennines, for example. The past has been lost and so there is no 'root of title' by which lawyers can trace ownership, legitimation, stylistic sequence, or records of observations. Q-landscapes are easy to find near your home, but are more common in some parts of the country than others – hence writing authentic poems depends on where you live. The breakaway Moderate Nonists (for example, Beddington, the nonist Consultancy Agency) say that there is a past and that they can provide access to it, and to ways of influencing it, in return for money. This so-called Weymouth Fraction is led by 'avant-garde neoclassicist' Petroc Nondelson, a restaurateur and former follower of Jordan's – who now accuses Jordan and Mintern of "proletarian idealism" and "French tastes". His position is that "nonism can only be true to its own past by denying that that past exists" and he calls for "broadband access for West Dorset". He and Ned Benbow argue that more stress should be put on the moment of appearance of cultural artefacts, prestiges, and stylemes. The disappearance of authenticity from poems by Andrew Motion and Tony Harrison is in direct relation with the appearance of authenticity in poems by David Barnett and N.S. Macias. These are in fact the same object: being transferred like a Greek vase being looted from an Apulian tomb and turning up at Sotheby's. *This is also believed to happen underground.* Less stress should be put on primary (de-) production and more on retailing – the deliverables side. According to Finoola Minterbrot, head of the Wessex Country Record Office in Bridport, their new GIS shows that the Dorset shoreline is "an artefact" – "an incomplete Bronze Age contractual situation" related to a public-private partnership among the Dumnoriges. "The fingerprints of data compression techniques" are all over Lyme Bay, according to her recent posting on the Wessex Online website. The constant appearance of new fossils is "an artefact of the first release of perspective geometry", and known as "the bends".

While writing that in 2001, I found Andy Jordan's letter where he explains that "My landscapes are not directly related to religious or ritual man-made fields. I am interested in any false landscape and in any theories related to that notion. I have read *The New View Over Atlantis* (the 1980s re-edit of the original) and I did subscribe to *The Ley Hunter* magazine for a while but that stuff was not the source of my idea nor of my attraction to it. My use of falseness is much more philosophical and pathological than that. It is allegorical/ metaphorical/ linguistic/ psychological (in particular, it relates to the workings of 'simile'). It relates to difficulties of belief (ideology) and trust inversions (affective dissonance, ouch). Working out how to respond to the falseness of 'things' is both an occult and an artistic endeavour, as well as a necessity within the realm of interpersonal relationships. The issues are to do with myths of authenticity, authorship, boundaries, identity, and responsibility. The absence of effective agency in relation to these things – which is a sort of given in my world – is a conundrum which I have to sort (whilst being happy, oh yes). If I do not sort these issues I remain disconnected from the world and from meaningful intimacy.

I am then an economic cipher, a consumer, a foiled poet and little more. As the EPA slogan, *Realisation Now!*, suggests, I'm just looking for something that's real." More of this in his magazine, *10th Muse* (33, Hartington Road, Southampton, SO14 0EW). The EPA is the 'Equi-Phallic Alliance', perhaps a reference to chalk figures of horses on hills in Wiltshire. "The EPA – the 'military wing' of the Poetry Field Club – occasionally destroys picturesque landscape features as these are used to construct a consuming ideal (nationalism)." For nonism see the site nonism.org.

Hegemonick is a volume of poetry which Jordan published in 2012 and which may date back to 2005 as a composition. The cover photo, a startling lyrical and rural image from 1932, resembles the cover photo on Matless's book and indeed the group on the cover of *Electric Eden*, which, excitingly, we will encounter in a later chapter. Landscape photography has been written about as a mass art where ordinary people got their vision into visible form. This was a genre where many amateurs captured the kind of sublime vision of the land which Jordan is trying to disrupt. These photos have the peculiar quality of capturing an ideal, something which should not show up in a mechanical image at all. I should point out that Charles Mintern is a fantasy figure written by Andrew Jordan. This chapter begins with a gossip column on nonism ghosted by me. Nonism believes that landscape is an illusion composed of projective fantasies and designed to produce social coherence in which the few have the greatest share of power. Mintern began inside *10th Muse*, Jordan's poetry magazine, a total environment of sarcastic commentary which is strangely more in the voice of Mintern, of whom Jordan is consciously an opponent, than of nonism, a system of disbelief in which Jordan believes.

> This bulletin is produced as a response to the projection of place upon placelessness, to the fabrication of a 'Southern regional poetic', to cultural fascism in general and the imposition of destructive and picturesque aesthetics, a false cultural particularism, onto landscape, poetic and imagined (post-national) community in particular.
> [...]
> Dr Mintern's excavations within the virtual Wessex proved, to him at least, that not only were all of the archaeological remains synthetically made, and placed, but that the chalk underneath

the archaeology was also made, that it too is synthetic. If that is the case then all Wessex history is myth, right down to its version of the class struggle (that aspect in particular being cheesy in the extreme). He discovered the theory of the underchalk (and was the first person to postulate that caves are suspended in a wider void). Together with Barny, he proved that places are on stilts, that machineries exist which can raise and lower the elevation of place, as required, according to social conditions, in order to pacify the dispossessed, to quieten those who still suffer enclosure. Now we must finish his work.

[...]

The poetry of the south and south west sometimes seems to be synonymous with 'the poetry of place' (although this too is an illusion). The 'Blandford elite' (Ha Ha) have attempted to possess and enclose this 'poetic ground' in order to exploit it, but – as such – they have become entrapped within their (mystified) experience of place.

(from the *EPA Bulletin*, issue 1, [1997?])

Hegemonick is a kind of documentary about the symbolism of a landscape on Portsdown, a hill overlooking Portsea, an island in Hampshire (on which much of Portsmouth is built). It gives us a tour of a set of solid structures and symbolic networks which are completely invented. Here Jordan sounds like a cultural historian narrating a TV documentary in front of shots of prehistoric monuments:

Modernity assessing itself.
Modernity, the victim in all this –
like a child – abused
and demonised,
or made into an ideal;
always the same.
In the Pleistocene, at Leucomagus,
Carnac, even Rome. Modernity,
telling it as it is.
The true word they hate you for.
Stonehenge, an amended form
of the Brutalism
first practised at Avebury – the ugliest

stone circle in England, too modern –
loathed in Neolithic times
and eventually pulled down.
Now a rough facsimile,
faked for the tourists,
is improperly presented as
Romance and the blueprint
for St Paul's and the Reichstag.
The lyric of a work.
          ('News of the World')

The cover says the book is "a 'free history' of the war against children, something unearthed". I don't find a 'war against children' in it – the reference to 'Modernity, the victim in all this – / like a child' seems to be something different. 'Free history' seems to mean roughly 'data-free history'.

The impetus for nonism was a satire of writers who talked about a Wessex regional identity, who were some of the poets who wrote about 'archaeology and landscape'. First came Thatcherism, then a panic among the cultural managers at realising that neo-conservatism was a losing cause and that they could go down with it. The fix was to find some Northern poets who could be wrapped up as innocent authenticity due to their victim status. This required exceptionally stupid and shallow people, to preserve the victim status in its pristine condition. They could have found real poets from the North but in their squirrel-like frenzy they didn't take the time. So there was a lot of discourse about intact northern anti-bourgeois roots. This really irritated people in the south-west. Port cities there were especially hard hit in the 1990s by the end of the Cold War and the closing of the Cold War industrial base. Conservatism was big in the south-east, the dominant region with 17 million people and much higher average income. The south-west was irritated at being lumped together with the south-east, against gigantic economic gradients. This was the basis for the Wessex thing, which was not a big fuss. They did have a certain amount of resentment for the North, actually for talentless northern poets being paraded by cynical cultural managers in London. His work is mainly double coded, being a reaction to a source text and then a new statement made out of the objects in the source. It is, in architectural terms, not a portfolio of buildings but a series of designs by other architects which someone has re-drawn and annotated in an original way. Jordan in *10th Muse* is reacting to a large amount of cultural discourse, prominently editors in the south-west such as Tilla Brading, David Caddy, Brian Hinton, Tim Allen, Rupert Loydell, Norman Jope. Their 'discourse territories' in the magazines (*Tears in the Fence* and so on) were the main competitors of *10th Muse* and his immediate frame of reference.

Portsmouth and Plymouth were both large port cities on the south coast with a long tradition of naval service and defence industries. (This history goes back some way. N.A.M. Rodgers' history of the navy describes an artificial improvement to the harbour at Portsmouth, a work in stone. This was in the year 1212.) Plymouth is larger and this is where a poetry scene really got going. I hear little about activity in Southampton – apart from Jordan and *10th Muse*. Jeremy Hooker lived in Wales for many years and is one of the classic commentators on Welsh poetry in English. After a while, he was writing Anglo-Welsh poetry about Southampton. This in many ways is where Jordan started from. *10th Muse* criticises everyone except Hooker – who writes about archaeology, the landscape, feelings of continuity in front of landscape and the deep past, working-class history and his own family. The Plymouth guys were really into the social or mythical divisions of their city, it was a shared metaphor. In this, Sinclair's mythical and topographic vision of London may have been decisive. Jordan's 'psychogeographic' writing about Southampton is partly a kindred line to what was happening in Plymouth – in the '90s, essentially – and partly a parody of it. When Jordan writes about 'Wessex' it is important to recognise that he is probably excluding Southampton from that territory – although over centuries the boundaries of Wessex shifted a lot and certainly included Southampton (in Settlement times supposedly Jutish) for a long period. (It may be true that there is a cultural affinity between south-west England and Wales.) Jordan was reading magazines from the 'classic south-west' all the time but wasn't really part of it.

The most striking aspect of nonism was that Jordan was parodying the kind of poetry he himself wanted to write. Hooker was very close to the poetic archaeology that Jordan was satirising. This ambivalence has stuck to the nonist project, and its ability to capture forces of discontent, withdrawal, and rage, usually excluded from the uttered part of the poetry scene, has been more impressive than its ability to create a voice. The authenticity which was so offended at the outset is unable to return because the ambivalence is too pervasive.

Hegemonick is his most impressive poetic work. It has a homogeneous high finish, like a building made entirely from a single material. In this thoroughness of fabrication is the full realisation of themes he has been working with for twenty years. It comes integrally out of its own world and is freestanding from literary models or personal experiences – even from the people he is satirising. Yet it is not as mordant and subversive as the nonist prose, cast entirely as a parodic recoding of something he hates. The final validity of the critique is less impressive than the voltage of the intellectual process which takes place along the way. Here Jordan writes his 'cultural history' about the objects of the modern defence industry, on the Hampshire coast, as if they were megalithic masterpieces:

I was due north of the research facility now called QinetiQ.

> The fort on Old Winchester Hill forms a high abutment overlooking
> the Meon Valley, a once Jutish buffer state between the
> West and South Saxons. Even then it was redundant,
> adrift amongst the chalk hills like an abandoned raft.

> The view from the summit seems immense
> and the hill appears to be much higher than it does
> when looking up from below.
> Copses, farmsteads and the homes of rich settlers,
> the landscape around in perpetual motion,
> tossed on the waves, – and there is the curvature
> of the earth and the shifting of shadows as the sun moves.

> I sat on a burial mound beside the triangulation pillar.
> I ate my sandwich. I drank my orange squash.
> (from 'A Walk in Hegemony')

Jordan explains what the firm-name means: "According to QinetiQ the name can be broken down into three component parts: *Qi* represents the firm's energy, *net* its networking ability, and *iq* its intellect." However, it seems unlikely that potential purchasers of kinetic solutions have those notions in mind when looking at the QinetiQ product portfolio. According to David Kilcullen, a leading contemporary practitioner and theorist of counterinsurgency and counterterrorism, "Kinetic operations are about killing the enemy and breaking their stuff…" *Kinetic* seems to be like *ballistic* but extended to include the high-velocity qualities of the vehicles that move the launchers of projectiles and the flexibility of the intelligence that guides the obedient weapons. A ship carries a plane which carries a missile. It may also imply the projection of power – something else which covers vast distances and reacts at great speed. *Qi* is a Chinese word meaning 'breath' (hence oxygen, oxygenated bloodstream, energy, animating force), which in an older transcription came out as *ch'i* (as in Tai Ch'i).

"Even then it was redundant" is a reference to Hampshire naval bases and dockyards closing after the end of the Cold War. Jordan says: "There is a long history of weapons research on Portsdown Hill. It is a tradition continued to this day in compounds first enclosed during the Neolithic period. Many new or experimental weapons are based on prehistoric originals unearthed, it is said, from the very barrows upon which today's research facilities are located. What was once considered 'magical' is now merely 'state of the art'." The name Mintern comes from Patrick Wright's *The Village that Died for England*, an evocation of a particular part of Dorset built around the evacuation of the area in 1943 to serve as a tank exercise ground for rehearsing the invasion of north-west Europe, the storming of 'Festung Europa'. This was basic for Jordan but the linking of the military and the picturesque is pervasively present in earthworks like Maiden Castle and in castles – which for 19th and 20th century onlookers have a kind of visual beauty. To uncover the history of domination in these ancient features of the landscape justifies a version in which the undoing of power would liberate the great majority of individuals – a breakdown of something old, venerable, resistant and malign. This is almost a hippie philosophy. Jordan's sarcasm disguises hippie attitudes.

Start by deciding that the narratives of archaeology up to 1950 were largely the projections of the egos of the scholars putting the narratives together. It would follow that the central activity of archaeologists in the modern era is to uncover and critique the projective part of these narratives. It follows that the study of the ego and its narrative anatomy is a key activity of critical archaeologists. This is the founding assumption of Jordan's poetry, which simultaneously narrates and decomposes the fantasy projections. The poetry is bizarre in flavour but is continuous with a normal activity of most professional archaeologists, taking apart the emotional investments of older excavators in order to clean up and extract the retrievable parts of their write-ups:

The psyche exists within affective walls.
It has a single ditch and bank enclosing
a rectangular precinct surrounding a circular
timber structure which may have been roofed.
The latter appeared to him in a dream
as a series of three concentric V-shaped gullies,
the innermost containing post holes. Two
large post holes flanked an entrance
on the eastern side. This is where the self lurks,
holy mutant, craver, administerer of small things,
an addict swayed by sentiments, stupidly
vain host to thoughts, this dark interior.

> The central area contained post holes and
> a pit in the middle, perhaps used for libations.
>   ('Theory: the Self')

With these fake narratives, Jordan is further into the 'post-modern' thing than most poets, is in fact completely captured by it. He wrote movingly in defence of the Tricorn Centre, which "was a Brutalist shopping, nightclub and car park complex in Portsmouth, Hampshire", sometimes regarded as the ugliest building in Europe. It was demolished in 2004. (Portsmouth is on the same near-landlocked body of water as Southampton but is the naval base.) He was defending working-class culture even including alienation, failed modernist authority fantasies, crassness and monotony. He has a sort of headless loyalty to the imposed culture. He wants to preserve the memory of alienation. The memory of wanting to be somewhere else. This is the shared past. Its memory can produce reflexive knowledge even in the dialectic form of a plan for preventing it from ever happening again.

(When Jordan refers to Stonehenge as 'brutalist' the word means undecorated concrete as a visual feature of buildings, held also to symbolise 'the look of modernity' in around 1964. It was first written down in 1952.) *Beton brut* is 'unpolished concrete' (left as rough-cast, without the casting seams being polished down) and 'brutalism' was a witty reference to that. People are even more infuriated by authoritarian claims that taste is arbitrary than by ugly concrete high-rises taking over their cities. "Taste is a matter of conditioning" means "I am going to ignore your wishes". What else could it mean? The comparison between the rugged and undecorated stone of Stonehenge and brutalist buildings has been made by other people than Jordan. The photograph of the Tricorn in Wikipedia shows a tower feature capped by a cube, which actually looks like one of the trilithons of Stonehenge. The Tricorn was called 'the Casbah' by its creators, after the old citadel of Algiers. (The Wikipedia article cites Andrew Jordan as one of its sources.)

In this emotional complex, he is unable to develop 'working class utterance' as a counterpoise to the bourgeois ideology of owning the past which he hates so much. Besotted by grievance, he is nonetheless expert at insulting people and giving them grievances. There is a paradox, in the land downstream of Berger, that you define any creation of symbols and impressive artistic objects as the projection of power and so as alienating. But because you define everything impressive and grand as oppressive, you cannot take on any culture at all. Only something wretched and inconsistent and meagre could possibly be 'authentic'. The gap between being prosperous and being evil has been elided. Economic success has been redefined as theft and artistic success has been redefined as propaganda for theft. How then can you engage in economic activity or in art? There is no way out and the more impressive *Hegemonick* becomes as a work of verbal art the more it falls prey to the ballistic weapons of nonist critique. Inside his project is a deep attraction to the patriotic and sentimental archaeology which at a conscious level he rejects.

Around the time I read *Hegemonick* I read in *Fortean Times* about the 'popular conspiracy symbology' of someone named Rik Clay. He was a conspiracist/musician who produced a whole theory of alien conspiracy in reaction to the announcement of the London Olympics in 2008, analysing the Olympic logo as a complete figuration of an alien plot – a sinister message lurking beneath the surface of something cuddly and commercial. He also visited Central America:

> >>So to conclude, a company using eye and pyramid symbolism, control and run these tall red masts which permeate the Yucatan Peninsula, the Mayan Riviera and maybe the whole of Mexico. A monopoly for sure. Without any doubt in my mind forces both terrestrial, extra-terrestrial and godly are at work. Time is drawing closer to the day when the capstone of the Great Pyramid will be laid and a grand plan, centuries in the making, will commence.<<

Clay saw a pattern in street names on the edges of the Olympics site in Stratford:

>>Temples Mills Lane. Temple Mills were water mills belonging to the Knights Templar – 'The Poor Fellow-Soldiers of Christ and of the Temple of Solomon'.<<

>>The Olympics 2012 site is situated between Leyton and Leytonestone. The 'Ley' found in their names originates from the term 'Ley lines'.<<

People found a hidden message in the 2007 design for the Olympic 2012 logo, involving a picture card in a card game, *Illuminatus: World Order*, and an episode of *The Simpsons*. This may not have been Clay. His style overlaps with Jordan's:

>>The bender site, and the old yew tree in it, were the short-lived heart of Leytonstonia, decorated with a kerb-henge, a replica of Stonehenge made with kerbstones. (Some talked of the significance of the names Leyton and Leytonstone, of their relation to ley lines more generally, as though this might explain the energy of the protest sites. A brickhenge was made at Clarement Road, halfway between Leyton and Leytonstone.) The Olympics site lies in an area synonymous with mystical – metaphysical – earth energy.<<

(This energy would be called Qi.) (Leytonstonia was the 'free republic' of road-building protesters in the area in 1994. It was Claremont not Clarement.) Rik Clay took his life in 2008 and he took all his web stuff down in the weeks before that – possibly a loss of faith was connected to his collapse. (See also http://www.rikclayfoundation.org/rik-clay.html, published by his friends.) This project is extremely close to *Hegemonick*, whose process is close to a core of paranoia, damage, apocalyptic resentment, which is a genuine tendency in modern society. It records something outside itself – it is the myth of a real structure (a delusional one). It is genuinely populist. The part of the book which devises a part of the landscape as a 'realisation' of Mary Millington, a porn star of the 1970s ('Come Play With Me'), portrayed as a fertility symbol and avatar of 'the Mother Goddess' is equally populist. The loss of negativity in the realm of the rejecting? Paranoia is not exotic but at this stage in history it is populist. Conspiracy theory has no standing in academic institutions, it is not registered among their modules of knowledge which are legitimate and which confer legitimacy. Dan Brown and *The X Files* are not just super-popular but completely assimilated, ragged memories of them fuel a million websites. The paranoia weakens the text because it is unattractive, its relation to gnosis and to enlightenment is distinctly a mirror projection – every value inverted even if every point is present in both patterns.

Jordan approaches Iain Sinclair, even, in channelling the desolate, the destitute, the illuminated. But the closer it gets the more desolate it gets and the stronger feelings of terror and simply disbelief grow in the reader.

Shape and analogy are the basis of magic (at least Western magic and its East Mediterranean sources) and both Clay and Jordan are preoccupied with unseen shapes detected in buildings or whole landscapes. The spelling Hegemonick can be related either to Magick or to 17th-century radical tracts with the *-ick* spelling. The book credits it to a paragraph in a popularising work on vocabulary which quotes "aegemonie and sufferaintie". Magical practices are that other populist genre. Some regions of the websphere by now include a heady mix of radical post-Marxism, for example Situationism, and the occult. *Hegemon* in Greek means 'leader' or 'guide'. Mount Igumen, near Sarajevo, means 'Abbot's hill'. In political geography, hegemony over a territory implies authority over it, but not monopolistic and permanent sovereignty. The title refers in fact to a Marxist theory of hegemony (associated with Antonio Gramsci). This is the unspoken agreed and the rules which define the unspoken which is rejected (and which must not be spoken). It takes us to the heart of 'subjectless action'. Law puts rules into words but there is another class of rules which is never verbalised and which it is very difficult to bring into consciousness. Hegemony defines the domain of propositions which people will not even react to but simply act as if you hadn't said them. The action of writers might be to push the silent into consciousness. (This is a modern view of writing.)

It is a political notion but it must surely be applied to art as well – to the weave of shared symbolism which is the basis of art and which allows strangers to understand your personal creation. The weave is frayed and distressed by recent cultural processes. To speak seriously of 'hegemony' challenges the warm identification between writer and reader which is the attraction of poetry for so many readers. It launches a critique of participation.

The unspoken is above all beneficent and warm and the peaks of art occur where that warmth and togetherness reach a peak. Coldness is being outside the human weave, the light that pours out of human beings. The music of human behaviour has a boundary. Anywhere on the outside is cold and if you have ambivalence then you are always outside the music. Becoming something that light and warmth just bounce off. There is a geological power of resentment that shows in its landscape, the fall of its hills and rivers.

A point of departure for all of Jordan's work is John Berger and his 1967 TV series (later a book) *Ways of Seeing*. This redefines all art which shows beautiful places, things or people as display, and display as a behaviour of the bourgeois, and the bourgeoisie as inherently bad and dissimilar from everyone else. For Berger art is the projection of power, and of pleasure which he is happy to write off. Identification is something he feels no need to do. Even if the way he writes is quite unlike the way Berger writes, Berger's distrust of art is a stratum underlying the whole Jordan thing. For Jordan too the cold metallic feel of power spoils virtually all art and the association of art with power means that he rejects history. He is expert in the anatomy of egoism, how projection creates the meaning of symbols and the scenario of symbolic experiences. On every page he punctures these projections. It becomes very difficult for him to project values of his own. Berger too is someone whom light and warmth just bounce off. (The interaction between the critique of nationalist archaeology and this critique of non-Stalinist art is significant.)

If you accept that symbols are not solid objects and that projection is a basic human psychological act – basic at least for contented and vigorous human beings – then the critique both acquires universal validity and loses all validity. Why should the bourgeoisie not project their wishes into the symbolic realm? How can power be bad if powerlessness is so close to despair and destitution? Is any symbolic order free from ego projections? These are fundamental questions but it is arguable that Jordan has resolved them in too fundamental a way and has not allowed an organic quality to ripen in his work.

Jordan talking over Stonehenge is a kind of parody of the designed landscape, a soft flow of talk lapping over the silent objects. Imagine a BBC voice murmuring that Stonehenge offended a lot of people because it was too modern and its surfaces were rough and brutal. It is as if the surface of English life were a kind of guided tour, a series of views. We give ourselves to consumerist wandering, unable to pull out of this flow that soaks and leaks everywhere. Somehow the material environment, something which we originally can know by the senses alone, is covered with a facing of words and these words are basic to our consciousness. They are the English mythology, like the elaborate verbal structures of some tribe in Melanesia or Brazil. They are the organs of the collective.

Hegemony decides that 'to write in the terms of conspiracy theory is to acquire low prestige'. No individual decided this. It is not the outcome of a reasoned and controlled process. It is simply there, pervading every street and every room. (I should clarify that Jordan is not advancing a conspiracy theory in *Hegemonick* but devising a fictional one that he does not believe in.) If universally accepted, hegemonic values are not a conspiracy – but if you reject them, they become one. Both the dissident opinions repressed by the system, and the act of silencing, are silenced – this is the conspiratorial secret. Some widespread opinions are, I presume, correct.

The symbolic content of the best underground work is a feeling of a successful group – intelligence, knowledge, idealism, feelings of freedom and an achievement about to be reached. This feeling was rather well founded, and is the reality on which the attraction of the high-flying language is based. As Jordan's position brings to light, the poets of the underground abandoned the radical critique of form, actually form/power relations, in order to write underground poetry which was beautiful, autonomous; which created warm feelings about each other, gave a sight of a life being led. They *abandoned* the critique which had originally led them into the wilderness and so their work is a ripe subject for a new stage of that critique. A prolonged education has become a form of wealth and defined them as a new bourgeoisie. In this context of prosperity, there are anomalous individuals without prosperity, and they own the original critique more thoroughly than the others. Their forward dynamic is unimpaired – at the same time that their feelings of ambivalence and resentment permeate their work. At this point it would seem that unhappiness is authenticity – but when turned into verbal art it is not attractive and so its dynamic energies, its ability to mobilise masses of people, are restricted.

People did not drop out in order to be unhappy. The status of the Underground as an 'imagined village' where everybody knows each other has brought about stability – and compromised the forward dynamic written into its charter. This describes, at least vaguely, the role of the malcontent. No-one is more malcontent than Jordan. And it describes also the feelings evoked by *Hegemonick*. The 'affective dissonance' is unpleasant. I am unwilling to describe Jordan's poetry as good. It doesn't take you anywhere. I had qualms about publishing it and I have qualms about putting it over as major poetry in a book. It is full of bad feelings. But genuine malcontentment.

Greyness and High Glare:
The Critique of Individualism

At the British Council show of English Art 1960-76 at Milan in the year 1976, a film by Chris Welsby was shown. *Seven Days* (1974) shows frames photographed at a small stream in south-west Wales. "One frame was taken every ten seconds throughout the film": choice was eliminated. "The camera was mounted on an equatorial stand, which is a piece of equipment used by astronomers to track the stars [...] the mounting is aligned with the earth's axis and rotates about its own axis[.]" This reduces choice, but there was a further programmed instruction, so that the camera was pointed at its own shadow when cloud covered the sun (and filmed towards the sun only when the sun was covered by cloud). Sound was recorded in much the same way to add a soundtrack. The result can be seen as a nature poem about the sun and a small landscape; but also as a critique of the subject in perception, exposing every point where the subject dwells on a sight, walks closer to it, focuses the eyes on a sight, injects emphasis into the recording, edits the results, etc. In a media-soaked society where you are immersed in the effluent of other people's subjectivity all the time, this could also be the dream of an exit into silence where we glimpse a completely different social order that we could live in.

Maybe this impulse has got weaker since 1974, but there is an abiding longing for a stream of representation from which subjectivity has been eliminated: an exit from the massified era noise of individualism. Welsby's preset gaze program defines the activity of the self: the self is both the source of *artistic value*, by imposing choice on the mindless flow of events, and the source of *ideological distortion*, as the cluster of self-interest and fantasies which imposes its wishes on the pristine flow of events. Every line of ideology is the deposit of *someone's* wishes.

If you write a poem about your personal experience, the basis on which the elements are chosen and assigned emphasis is their relationship to you. That is, the poem is constructed on an egocentric principle. If the reader consumes the poem with their identification with the poet as the central drive, that means the relationship of the process to them is basic. Again, this is an egocentric principle. The processing of poetry in these terms is a dual narcissism. Confining the poetry you write to personal experience, with moments significant to your autobiography as the most intensely lit moments, may be the decision which attracts the *most* objection and criticism. A central aspect of the theory of poetry in our time is the attempt to construct a counter principle to correct this egoism. It wishes to eliminate the vividness of personal experience because the glare of the highlights prevents every other part of the scene from coming into view.

In certain rooms the company will react to words like *expressivity, personal, intuition, emotion, identification, enthusiasm* with scorn. Rather than work through, immediately, the arguments around this, I suggest we take it on and try to see it from the inside. It is a big part of the landscape.

Imagine a book about an English village. In it, the naive position would be the first-person account of one person who lives there and is a poet – let's say, a man who lives by writing. The 'grey array' would include all the male persons in the village, all the female persons, the children, the very old, those without property, those without letters, the alcoholics, the nonconformists, the whole lot. What is not clear is in what verbal form this 'grey array' could be recorded. A vision haunting the art of the past 40 years has been that of experience which covers the entire spectrum. This is less like white light than like grey light. Everything which belongs to one spectrum band has been destroyed. Only what is present over the whole spectrum is retained. This featureless diffuse glimmer is supposed to be transcendent and ultimate knowledge. While we cannot point to any poetry which is possessed of this knowledge, the vision flits over the landscape and, from time to time, drives people to obscure actions.

We spoke of politicised individuals trying to intervene in texts and correct them. This was a fundamental process in the cultural activity of the 1970s. Art presented an analogy with events in people's lives, and people defined their lives as their property and then defined the art as their property as well, on the basis of this analogy. The philosophical problems with this were very serious. However, the invasion could be seen as adding extra information, adding another point of view, and so moving towards a more complete apprehension of the whole of a social totality that we can barely imagine. If a given text or picture could acquire a second owner, it could acquire a third, fourth, or fifth, and presumably there is no end to how many times this process could take place. The question is more what is the terminal point of this development, and the answer is the 'featureless glimmer'.

This problem is a narrow passage that every poet must go through, and whose exits lead in fundamentally different directions. Responses to the 'spectrum segment/ whole field' problem might be:

1. Reassertion of egoism, assuming that the subjective perception of the I-figure adds value and their personality is generous and attractive. A buoyant personality is offered as the precondition of poetry. Withdrawal 'past' the problem to a point where it is not acknowledged. The poems offer a series of bright, focal areas, but all around is greyness. This makes the unspoken assertion that "this experience is important because I had it". The self justifies the poem but what justifies the self?

2. Reduction of the poetry to what the self of the poet perceives, but without the reliance on subjectivity to create meaning. The poetry is 'empirical', refusing everything which is outside the tiny perimeter of the senses of the poet-I. The basis is that only personal experience is certain. What is omitted 'cannot be vouched for' and its omission is branded as a virtue.

3. Writing of banal opinions and experiences under the pretence that their banality makes them significant and shared by millions of people and literally captures the 'grey array'. Writing at a level of excessive generality, like proverbs.

4. The surgical removal of egocentricity to produce a kind of writing which deals with experience before it is shaped by a personality. Possibly withdrawal from 'felt experience' to write something which is critical but does not assert anything. Privileging of the process of critical recovery of information possibly becoming 'conceptual'. Poetry without a central personality corresponds to art which does not produce objects – the end of painting.

5. Withdrawal into myth as a tenor of poetry which is felt to be 'collective'. Removal of action to a point in the deep past where the actors are 'everyone's ancestors' and the opposition between 'me' and 'you', between 'my experience' and 'your experience', is washed away. However, in the secular era of the late 20th / early 21st Cs these tend to be 'personal myths' and only hesitantly collective ones.

6. Writing poetry which has several strong central voices rather than just one. So not trying to reach 'spectral neutrality' but putting the

poem on a basis which is more stable than the 'one-legged' support of the ego.

There is possibly a seventh response. This involves a theory that the Imagist notion of capturing singular and intense moments is basic to the whole range of contemporary poetry. Poetry no longer writes narrative or dramas partly for this reason. The scale of contemporary poetry thus only includes snapshots, snatches of minimal duration. The light flares and dies almost immediately. Poets writing in flickers thus bypass the question of giving an account of events, as they omit the events. The intensity of the momentary experience explains why the poem stops short before a second moment. (This is the theory, even when the poem lacks intensity.) This is still egocentric and perhaps just a variant of type 1.

CONNOISSEURSHIP AND THE SHARED GAME

It is to David Lewis' work (David Lewis, *Science and Archaeology*) that we go to recover an opposition which has been of importance for poetry. Writing in 1974, he describes the application of science, of objective findings and quantified arguments, to prehistory, and the utter horror of some 'humanist' archaeologists, for whom Jacquetta Hawkes is the spokesman in his book, at the prospect of having to do hard work and to subject their beautiful theories to such rigorous tests. Thus we have an opposition between people with technical knowledge, the bearers of a new civilisation, and people whose claim to superior knowledge relies on emotional intuition, on aesthetic experiences faced with the past, and finally on egocentricity – the feeling that their feelings are so important as to be right.

Lewis's book is about what is still called The New Archaeology, although it was new in the 1960s, as laid down by thinkers like Lew Binford and David Clarke. It offered an intoxicating trip, that of being someone who had mastered mathematics and technology, and who could make the material remains speak with their own voice, sweeping aside the ideological overlay of mediaeval historians and of 19th and 20th Century scholars.

The immediate background event was the arrival of Carbon-14 dating, which in the 1950s put chronology on an objective footing. Its findings were flatly resisted by a number of established archaeologists, because they disagreed with the dates accepted by the profession. On deeper investigation it turned out that these dates had no better basis than the assent of professional experts to the intuitions of their peers, based on 'series' of artefacts where similarities, and so transfers and progress in time, were based on the intuitions of experts gazing at the objects, in close communion. This whole framework was based on subjective evaluations and being legitimated by institutions. The collusion of scholars seemed solid but in fact was not. Rather, the value given to certain judgments corresponded to the social power of certain individuals. One professor validated another, they wrote the textbooks and ran the museums, students who disagreed failed their exams, a sub-world of crackpots wrote hundreds of 'unauthorised' books, but the whole structure was resting on thin air. The knowledge of ancient artefacts which pre-carbon archaeologists claimed was related to the knowledge of fine and expensive things which was a component of the lifestyle of the gentry. As the bourgeoisie acquired wealth, they took over the lifestyle, including vital parts like knowledge of the fine objects, to be applied when purchasing them. The price of the objects was related to their provenance and the makers' marks, and dating them was a significant part of shopping. After purchase, they became status objects. This kind of appreciation did not necessarily mean an interest in the technology by which such things were made, or in other aspects significant to dating ancient objects. The Carbon-14 laboratory dates destroyed, over a generation, a whole edifice of scholarship. It came to look more like a collusion – an elaborate and respectful set of imitations. (It is important to remember that there were errors in early Carbon-14 datings which were removed, over decades, by 'recalibrations'. Also, that the chronology used by 'pre-carbon' scholars was correlated by means of artefacts with dates in written Egyptian records, which were correct; this was valuable for areas close to Egypt and having Egyptian artefacts as trade goods, but was very weak when it came to remote areas such as Western Europe, which is where the errors were just wild.)

Lewis puts in conveniently terse form an opposition that was surfacing in literary studies also, from around 1960, where the bearers of a new method which claimed not to rely on identifying with the author were trying to overwhelm and remove an older kind of scholarship, based primarily on egocentric identification and on the experience of pleasure. The march of anti-identificatory approaches to literature was a kind of generational war, an expression of youth culture. The French scholars who established the boldest positions found the authoritative attitude with which the weak intuitions of older scholars were preached as truths, the investiture of their antiquated literary tastes, often strongly marked by nationalism or Catholicism, as exam knowledge, quite unbearable. It was a hostile and noisy confrontation of a kind not unusual in French culture. Its outcome is not that we give up artistic pleasure or that we treat our intuitions with scorn.

To get back to the web of connoisseurship which David Lewis was critical of. We can describe it schematically like this.

I am right because of the power of my intuition
I am right because I am supported by my peers
By virtue of being right I can judge whose support is valid
I invalidate people who disagree with me and put them in a new
    category of the unqualified
I offer support to my peers and together we form a power structure.
We hold office and ascribe values to things (perhaps to people?) by
    virtue of this investiture

Of course this entanglement which props itself up is akin to the poetic 'epiphany' as the basis for the information in poetry. I suppose that the environment is one of many opinions clashing over a few assets, and what is at stake is the syntax of invalidation. By growing up in a milieu of books and education, you unconsciously acquire the skill of invalidating what other people say. Everything acts to develop this skill, which yet may be something which in the end is unattractive and perhaps worth unlearning. The intellectual is someone who is supremely skilled at invalidating what other people say or believe. The connoisseur is also good at it.

This structure may be familiar to people who read feminist works, a possible starting point for feminist thought being the perception that the powerful are locked into a web of alliance and self-aggrandizement which has no deeper justification and from which objective knowledge can only with great difficulty be disentangled. If it is people who are being judged, then they also have to disentangle themselves from the value system in order to be free.

The critique of the subjective scholar extended to criticise the privileged moment or the preferred individual in a wider sense. Archaeologists could prefer the evidence of house remains or bones to written sources because they recorded the long run rather than moments. Historians could prefer the history of structures to the experience of individuals. They could find individual consciousness to be misled – well-informed on the egocentric and transient.

Naturally, somewhere in the background was Marxism (trying to exclude all 'bourgeois consciousness', especially pleasure, as a hindrance to revolutionary commitment) and a number of working-class scholars, with a greater attachment to technology, as the product of the world of engineering, than to the cultural products of the bourgeoisie and aristocracy. The study of work processes was inherently more working-class. Probably the 'structuralist' approach to literature in the 1960s has connections to Marxist campaigns, in the 1930s, which simply assumed that bourgeois literature was bad. There was no solid band of error in literary scholarship answering to the 'subjective dating scandal' which was exposed by Carbon-14 labs. Mathematics and technology have almost nothing to offer, even if you master them. Subjectivity just can't be removed from literary study. Lev Kopelev, the Russian writer who lived in West Germany for a very long time, was a major in the Red Army while its troops were devastating East Prussia early in 1945. He saved some of the locals from death, and was sent to a concentration camp for ten years: his crime was 'propagating bourgeois humanism'. We find also some scholars in the West who rejected 'humanism'.

THE HORIZON OF THE TEXT

Brecht wrote a famous poem, 'Questions of a Worker who Reads' (1935), in which he sarcastically quotes "Caesar conquered Gaul" and then adds, "Didn't he even have a cook with him?" Modern people generally agree with Brecht that there is something outside the text and that the significance of what the author did not allow within the precinct of the text can be high. To take one concrete example, during the reign of Elizabeth I an intensification of the colonial regime in Ireland led to the seizure and re-allocation (to English adventurers) of most of the landed property in Munster, and to a series of wars during which, in the 1580s, perhaps a third of the civilian population of the province died as a result of famine assisted by 'economic warfare'. The existing, Gaelic and aristocratic, society of Ireland was destroyed, its laws made invalid. Can you write about the glories of Elizabethan literature and leave this out? Edmund Spenser lived in Ireland as one of the Munster land-takers and wrote a *View of the Present State of Ireland*. Can you leave this fact out of consideration of 'The Faerie Queene', which is after all a glorification of the Queen and so of her government and its policies? The problem with the 'empirical' approach is that it only offers a tiny strip of light, so, if what is outside the lit area crucially affects the significance of what we are seeing, then the narrow focus prevents understanding. Brecht's poem starts "Who built Thebes of the seven gates?/ We hear the names of kings". Thebes is in Greece, and the verse drama 'Seven against Thebes' (5thC BC) has one hero to attack each gate of the city. It is true we don't hear who built the walls and the gates.

This is a glaring example and the situation for 20th C poetry is much less clear-cut. Poets write about private affairs and eschew epics about how great the government is. But the sheer complexity of modern history is something corrosive, it threatens to make modern poetry unreal. Or, the ambition of some poets to transcend the personal, thus out-competing 'merely personal' poets, is one of the basic gestures of poetic politics not always carried out in good faith.

The question of 'horizon line' is fraught. By this I mean the boundary defining what is visible from any point. I mentioned a village just now, but that is well defined and presumably atypical of modern society. Should a poem about two or three people be extended to describe the whole town they are living in? the whole country? the other countries which carry out trade with this country? the other possibilities which the initial 3 people are ignoring as they live under capitalism? Brecht draws the Gaulish War on stage; how do you write about Caesar's entire army? and should the poem include the armies of the Gauls? and the other members of the Gaulish tribes, if they were being conquered and so were the real subject of the war? Is there anywhere you can draw a satisfactory and enclosing horizon for any poem?

The contrast between the diffuse greyness of thinking of the possibly 10,000 poets writing and the strong bright focus of reading the poems of a single poet already brings on stage the possibility that one can get away from individual consciousness and capture a wider awareness. If a social process involves many individuals, then it is arguable that one gets closer to reality by bringing into view more and more of the individuals. This is what one might call the sociological heresy in poetry. If the Paladin anthology wheels on 85 poets, you can trump it by wheeling on 850 poets.

The problem is that collectives do not have a voice. A voice belongs to a person, a self, a brain with its complement of nervous system and body, to a moment and the consciousness of that moment. But, if you ignore this problem, then reading can be a path to 'social knowledge', and seek by preference a wide spectrum of sources. The literary process of choosing the most articulate voices, who also tend to be very well educated and to come from relatively well-educated families, can be put into reverse, and poets can be chosen at random or on the sociological basis of what kind of family they come from or what gender they are. There is a current in cultural management of people who cannot tell good poetry from bad, do not believe in this distinction, and who therefore think that the history of poetry can be written in terms of the sociology of the people who write it. This is not unlike writing the history of a literature when all the texts have been destroyed.

It is not clear how we can stitch different subjective accounts into each other. It is not clear that the textual invasions of the 1970s were able, ever, to produce an improved text, rather than an abiding disarray, denial, interference in the message.

TELEOLOGY

The task for this section is to understand implicit teleology and preconceptions in texts, and how poetry cracks out those elements and produces 'purged' texts to work with. The one I wanted to use was *The Character of England* (1950, but the introduction is dated "1947"). I would have liked to analyse this text from Vita Sackville-West about the owners of large landed estates (not the feudal super-estates of the nobility):

> Mixed in with the village life are 'the gentry', whose activities also embrace a wider range, taking in all interests which affect the county. […] I fancy that not the most extreme member of the Labour party would deny the respect in which they are rustically held; and although the accusation of snobbery has often been brought against the English, I submit that respect is based less on the any snobbish regard for birth or wealth than upon confidence in their reliability, probity, and unselfishness. In accordance with the old topographical plan 'the big house'

usually stands at a little distance from the village. It may not be a big home at all, and the bigger it is the more likely it is to be impoverished; but its size does not affect the matter: it is the home of the local squire and his lady.

Maybe this was too soft a target. Doesn't "respect" mean 'the way you behave towards people who have wealth'? It's obvious that English people writing patriotically about England write in a mendacious and sentimental way. If you look at that high-calorie political junk food you realise how much of the project of the last 60 years has been to push it away and then to ask "what is England really like" and gather information which then appears in texts. Maybe people haven't been consistent enough with that one.

There are copyright problems with modern English texts. I didn't want to do the write-up and then find I couldn't get permissions. If you use text from around 1950 the problem is that publishers and writers are untraceable – somebody still owns the rights but if you can't find out who they are you can't get clearance for your dissection of the thing. This is a 'nonplus', you can't proceed. No single possibility is satisfying, but we will make do with Ammianus Marcellinus, writing around 390 AD. I am concerned about the effect of choice. The scope of this exercise is limited because Ammianus is such a good writer. He was born in Antioch and lived from about 330 to after 391. He describes himself as "a former soldier and a Greek". This means he spoke Greek, although he wrote a great book in Latin. Almost seven hundred years after the conquests of Alexander and the arrival of the Greeks, a high proportion of people in Syria and Mesopotamia spoke Greek. We don't know whether he, or people of his social group, would have spoken a Semitic language, a dialect of Aramaic in fact, in domestic surroundings. The evidence on this is difficult. Was he a Syrian? This looks like just a modern hang-up.

The 'culture area' of Aramaic, the 'fertile crescent', was divided between Rome and the Parthian empire (later the Sasanians). Whether that international border (the Euphrates, some of the time) was a divider for culture and 'mentality' is an interesting question. The Parthians came from an area of east Iranian speech, related to dialects we would hear in Afghanistan or Tadjikistan today. They did not interfere with local societies, apart from favouring Zoroastrianism. Ammianus never talks about "east versus west" and I think the division was not of significance at the time. Of course barbarian Europe was different from the Mediterranean, people recognised that. Oswald Spengler promoted ideas about unbridgeable contrasts between different cultures which are literary rather than good history. He creates a 'collective subject' which most historians regard as quite fictitious. 19th-century historians wanted Syria to be much unlike Rome, as part of Europe, and there is a line of poems about the Syrian (from Emesa) emperor Heliogabalus which illustrates that idea – but it was probably a complete fantasy. Geoffrey Hill wrote such a poem in *Canaan*, based on Stefan George. The idea of 'eastern tyranny' and 'western freedom plus individualism' is not there for Ammianus. It didn't apply until 1800 AD, we may suspect. Anyway tyranny has been quite a feature of modern Europe. So this is a form of modern teleology which Ammianus tends to subvert. I chose two texts from volume 3 of the Loeb edition, with J.C. Rolfe's 1937 translation. We will address these as sources for possible poems, with a particular interest in how to wash teleology out of them.

One passage is a description of the character of the emperor Valentinian, who ruled from 367 to 383 AD. The first heading is "of his cruelty, greed, jealousy and cowardice". But he had virtues too:

> If he had regulated the rest of his conduct in accordance with these, his career would have been that of a Trajan or a Marcus. He was very indulgent towards the provincials and everywhere lightened the burden of their tributes; he was always timely in founding towns and establishing frontier defences. [...] The result of this was turmoil in Britain, disaster in Africa, and the devastation of Illyricum. In every observance of chastity he was pure at home and abroad [...] In council he was a fore-sighted persuader of what was right and a dissuader of wrong, most strict in examining all ranks of the military service. He wrote a neat hand, was an elegant painter and modeller, and an inventor of new kinds of arms. His memory was lively; so was his speech (although he spoke seldom), and he was vigorous therein, almost to the point of eloquence. He loved neatness, and enjoyed banquets that were choice but not extravagant.
> [...]
> His strong and muscular body, the gleam of his hair, his brilliant complexion, his grey eyes, with a gaze that was always sidelong and stern, his fine stature, and his regular features completed a figure of regal charm and majesty.

A 'teleology-free' poem from this might be:

Carving in wax or resin models
of unheard-of designs of arms
the imagined technological edge
breathing life into the taking of life
dragging the agent of mutilation
into hard external form

he hated the well dressed, the learned
the rich and the high-born

after one last call to the dead, he
was interred among the remains of the deified rulers
the tombs confining the gods

This is now an avant-garde text of the kind I dislike reading. The detail of Ammianus' description of Valentinian is almost embarrassing, because it is so rich. Ammianus is critical of Valentinian's behaviour. I don't know how his text was circulated but evidently he wasn't worried about criticising emperors, dead ones anyway. Among the surviving writings of the time there are panegyrics (i.e. soaring praise of those in authority) but the text we have got is not anything like them. Ammianus speaks of his book as *opus veritate professum*, a work which speaks the truth. It is all about senior Roman generals, with emperors as the most featured, but it is not a panegyric of great men.

The point to challenge is the role. Valentinian was an emperor and could not have been if the role did not exist. Why is there an emperor at all? this is the non-discussable basis for the whole passage. We may be dealing with unconscious preconceptions beside deliberate teleology. The text is completely restricted by this. It does not even have a sentence or a heading saying "Valentinian was emperor" because that is *too* fundamental. I counted 39 sentences about the character of Valentinian. Evidently there is a possibility of changing direction at the start of this character which decreases at the end of every sentence.

The key here would be to write a text which showed the role as excessive and asked the reader to depart from reality and imagine a different way of distributing power. Once you throw out the designation of 'emperor' from your text, you have the problem that the whole narrative becomes incomprehensible. We get 6 pages of description of Valentinian because he was emperor. If you suppress that fact the poem becomes bewildering. This is a clue to why a range of avant-garde texts are motiveless, bewildering, savagely incomplete.

The modern critique of texts does not start by accepting the roles in which people find themselves, as the constituent parts of the social fabric. Rejecting the roles makes the text disintegrate and makes the process of events impossible to follow. But, after all, the real social fabric does not involve agreement on all sides about what roles someone 'belongs' in. Much of the social process consists, it would seem, of the struggle between people to decide what role each one is obliged to occupy – which could only emerge as the *outcome* of struggles. It is possible for people to carry out the tasks of a given role, and to have the standard of living associated with it, and yet to resist that ascription and to wish for something completely different. So if a text just records the norms it may be quite misleading. Ammianus is not recording the norms, instead the theme of his writing is universally the process of wars in which rather prominently two or more sides disagree about the control of wealth and territory. Because Ammianus privileges conflict and works all the time to dramatise and describe it, we must say that he sees conflict as the proper subject of historians. So we can hardly say that literature cannot deal with conflict.

The principal function of the emperor in the 4th century was to conduct wars against Rome's external enemies. Again it is difficult to 'estrange' this rule without destroying the meaning of the text. But there is a line of argument here, which starts by asking what would concretely happen if the barbarians won a war, and would go on to discuss how wealth and privileges were distributed between different people living within the Empire. One move would be to take Ammianus' excellent descriptions of battles and rewrite them so that you couldn't make out who won. This would be very frustrating.

One thing we could do is to add lots of material about other people, so that Valentinian is no longer the dominant subject. We would then have him sidelined in the poem – the dominance would be at an end. But this would effectively reverse a process of purification and con-centration which produced the brilliant focus on Valentinian. We would end up with a dispersed text. This is similar to other processes of disintegration – if you take a fine poem and strip out all the rhetoric, you end up with something bleaker and less persuasive than the original.

Indeed we get the impression with many modern texts that the process of stripping down has been fascinating in itself, and that the lack of sense in the finished product is not a consideration.

A rewrite of the source in Ammianus might read:

> wax and clay
> reshaping the instrument for reshaping limbs
>
> stylus in the clay of the tablets
> recording the movements of war
> a spreading archive the simulacrum
> of marches and campaigns
>
> out of a million dice
> only one has a face
> the signs of the others
> slur valueless blur
> a die that carves itself
> imagine a reign dissolved
> count dice as rain
> again dissolved

This eliminates human subjects in favour of process. It doesn't say very much. The opposition of two models, the 'weapon toys' and the writing tablets, is formalistic, which is what tends to come out if you get rid of human subjects. There is a way of writing poetry in which everything gratifying to individual wishes is rejected. The poem now says that Valentinian was just one person in a million – the Empire may have counted 50 million people at the time – and there was a chance process deciding who was in the ruling class, which is not anywhere in the text, but the stage before the text began to be written.

It is fairly obvious that if you go back 1,500 years from Ammianus you already have incredibly detailed written descriptions of the actions of a monarch, Pharaoh. These primal texts describe the ritual aspect of the monarch's day, every act the realisation of benign and luck-bringing analogies. By the time you get to Roman times, you have officials (their title *a commentariis*) writing a description of the orders of a general, and incidents affecting his army, for every day of a campaign, and these official day-books were the basis for the very good-quality histories of writers such as Ammianus. These 'log-books' did not ever exist for generals such as Attila, the Alans, or the Moorish leaders whom Theodosius fought against in book 28. Ammianus is not consciously ignoring them, they just never existed. The ones which existed did supply the raw material for the advance of detailed description of character in literature.

The transition from ritual texts about the ceremonial acts of kingship to business is interesting. Presumably the daily campaign diary of a general in the field was a form of accountability – it was going to come back to the Court or the Senate to be scrutinised, especially if he lost. The general was a servant of the State. So the text had to answer questions, and was a legal document. The close focus on individual behaviour in Ammianus, relying on the campaign diaries, is not simply egoism but rather a form of accountability; it catches also the failures of the central figure. The *acta diurna* of the emperor followed this pattern because it was prevalent. I suppose that this kind of diary originated with the Hellenistic kingdoms, perhaps specifically with Alexander, and was the raw material for historians like Polybius, in whom we already see traits of modernity. Ammianus constantly measures his senior generals by their ability to succeed in military operations – it is critical. The interest must be connected to making decisions about who to promote. He describes events as tests of the character of the generals or prefects commanding armies or provinces; the notion of character which provides the substance of modern European literature seems to owe something, genetically, to the management techniques of the Roman State.

Ermenrichus, a king of the Goths who appears committing suicide after the Huns and Alans invade his lands, does not get a character description. Perhaps seizing character is only possible in literate societies, which generate documentary accounts of State processes. Ermanaric appears also in 'Widsith', a tale set in the 4th century without real historical memory of the time, being instead magical and heroic. Widsith is a barbarian subject happy in barbarian courts. Widsith played at the court of Ermanaric but as a 'court official' he is not comparable to Ammianus as an officer of the Praetorian Guard, even if both were members of a royal household and both were writers. The Goths had a history but did not know, outside living memory, what that history was. There is no line of historical self-awareness on the other side which could give us a wider view of the Roman-barbarian wars of the 4th century. Once you have biography, you can have autobiographical poetry.

The other passage is about five pages later, in book 31. It is an ethnographical one about the Alans, living on what we would see as the lands around the Don and the Volga:

> Thus the Halani [...] are divided between the two parts of the earth [Asia and Europe] [...] all are called Halani because of the similarity in their customs, their savage mode of life, and their weapons. For they have no huts and care nothing for using the ploughshare, but they live upon flesh and an abundance of milk, and dwell in wagons, which they cover with rounded canopies of bark and drive over the boundless wastes. [...] In that land the fields are always green, and here and there are places set thick with fruit trees.
>
> Moreover, almost all the Halani are tall and handsome, their hair inclines to blond, by the ferocity of their glance they inspire dread, subdued though it is. They are light and active in the use of arms. [...] Just as quiet and peaceful men find pleasure in rest, so the Halani delight in danger and warfare. [...] there is nothing in which they take more pride than in killing any man whatever: as glorious spoils of the slain they tear off their heads, then strip off their skins and hang them on their war-horses as trappings. [...] No temple or sacred place is to be seen in their country, not even a hut thatched with straw can be discerned anywhere, but [...] a naked sword is fixed in the ground and they reverently worship it as their god of war[.] They do not know the meaning of slavery, since all are born of noble blood [.]

The optic of this text does not see the Alans as individuals. They even look the same. Only the Roman gets a character. Burning out the individuality of the artist as Berger recommends destroys the value of individual moves. It yields a kind of statistical flatness, with variation razed away. This erasure of the ego and its assets is *also* how the avant artist wants to see artists. Stripping individuality away. As you remove identification, you delete the interest in individual character. The possession of it becomes irrelevant to the direction of the artistic text. One problem with the Alans all having the same personality is that

Ammianus also describes the Alans as having conquered and absorbed numerous other peoples: the Nervi, the Vidini, the Geloni, the Melanchlaeni. We would usually see facial expression as varying from second to second to reflect inner states, but here we see (all) the Alans having one ferocious glance. If you write out powerful individuals, the question is what you replace them with. The answer might be subjectless action or a 'collective subject'. But does this subject carry out any actions? describing English politics in 'collective' terms may raise the same inaccuracies as this description of the Alans galloping up and down the Volga. I tried to turn this into a poem:

> *from frost to forge from crystal to cycle*
> The droplets of the sun freeze out as gold
> in crystal earth bound in a strange apathy.
> The loose arrows of heat release the strings,
> an army lighter than their projectile flight
> hisses off empty land as steam, like the permafrost
> slackening grip to clear the pastureland.
> From frost to flood, from Asia to Danube,
> to the marshes where the birds go in winter.
> Draw lines across the sun to represent empire.
>
> Over meadows of hemp, ephedrine and wormwood
> the path curves back to its beginning
> mimicking the action of the stars
> from frost to metal. from line to curve
> *from ray to ring from thaw to reign.*

This has the problem of being 'ethnographical forgery' – there are no individuals.

Modern poetry follows a course strangely parallel to that of Roman historians, building the text around the *res gestae* of one individual. The biography is a downwardly mobile literary form – it starts with supreme rulers but disseminates to the lower ranks. We can see three different kinds of modern poem. In one, the acquisition of objects as assets by a personality is the key, the poet's individuality is the subject matter. In another, pre-existing religious patterns are the theme, and human individuals are shown as enacting them. In a third, the poet is against the idea of the Individual and is designing the text to make individual wishes and perceptions seem less important.

Does having a detailed description of someone's mental processes mean that they are complex and that a barbarian, who is not observed closely by any literate person, has only simple processes? The Halani (*alt.* Alani) may have had rigid social customs and turned to these customs as a guide to behaviour. Does this argue that their decision processes or self-awareness were undeveloped? This hardly seems persuasive. The idea of the West as being uniquely dominated by individual autonomy and wealth (basic to the position of modern Marxists, including Berger) could either lay bare a form of political economy or be an artefact of unequally precise means of recording and storing data. Evidently the emergence into view of individual differences coincides with closer observation and better recording. Could it just be better data storage media? Once you have buildings, you can store information. So perhaps society could appear to be more individualist when the changing factor is actually the dissemination of cameras, writing, documentary records, and so forth. If a poet around 2010 writes in great detail about themselves and a few people close to them, this may not be a sign of a collapse of belief in the public sphere. It may be a function of the way they write being of very precise registration – with more dots per inch, so to speak. This would be in parallel with better and better registration in other media, such as digital music recording, photographs, computer screens, which are some of the sources of information used by poets. An autobiographical poem which has more detail could also be a more convincing and richer portrait.

Individual focus also comes from discarding large-scale or artificial constructions. If you exclude 'important people' like Valentinian you must end up with small-scale poems in which an individual occupies a lot of the space. Maybe you could write a poem which eliminated both important and unimportant people and showed a depersonalised subject. This is an interesting exercise.

How to engulf prose texts inside the poem is a major modern issue. A critic has to know how to recognise destroyed prose texts inside poems. Enough has been said to show that a considerable part of avant-garde activity consists of engulfing prose texts and changing their metabolism at cell level. The belief in their own powers of possession and mutation is basic to the avant-garde ideology. It is not so often shared by other factions. You will never hear within the avant-garde the idea that an artist could take on a source and fail to give a convincing account of it, producing something feeble and arbitrary and weaker than the original.

The idea that every act of symbolic subversion of what exists must be effective is a fixed axiom, never discussed. A generalisation would be that the Underground has a critical attitude, turning source texts inside out, while the mainstream is happy with their source texts, seeing them as objects of pride and cultural wealth, like a curator being proud of objects owned by the museum they run. Large-scale poetry is unlikely to happen without source texts of one kind or another. The Thirties Cantos are the origin of this line. Pound got everything wrong. It was not an auspicious start.

GEOGRAPHY OF INDIVIDUALISM

A key section of the *Cantos* presents the Italian Renaissance, in the guise of a tyrant and leader of mercenaries, as the apex of culture, the secret to be uncovered. Ever since the 16th century, English writers had identified the classical lands of the Renaissance with tyranny and amorality, in fact unrestrained and calculating individualism. In around 2010 the newspapers were full of ominous stories about Italy, Greece, and Spain, the so-called Southern Tier, as threatened with government defaults due to the well-off faking accounts, hiding their incomes, and avoiding paying taxes. This pattern of ignoring the law and the community to protect personal wealth is clearly individualism. It has been called amoral familism and is of a different type from the individualism which has so often been praised as the source of success in areas like England, France, and the Netherlands. So there may be two different types of individualism in Europe. The process by which the forms of Renaissance culture, with its preoccupation with individual glory, originated in the Mediterranean and were copied in the north-west, may have been influenced by this. During the Cold War, we heard so much about individualism being the key to economic progress that it is enlightening to realise that individualism may be the key to economic stagnation – as some families do well and the majority get nowhere. The teleology of Cold War discourse needs to be unravelled to recover the real history of individualism – and the truth of modern history.

CUBE OF NOW

We saw earlier on a line of opinion which saw the poem as necessarily happening to one person and in one moment, in the cube of now. Every part of the aesthetic intensity and cohesion of the poem came from that existence at a single point. The contrast could hardly be stronger with poets who want to abolish personal experience and intuition and make poetic truth the record of something always smeared along a spectrum, with every bright colour faded to grey. Already in the 1930s poets were reacting against a perceived demand to make poetry subservient to politics and documentary, and to make economic issues paramount. I want to note the courage of the faction which went in for 'spectral dimness', because the disadvantages of the linguistic method they were adopting could not be more obvious. The motives for attacking the voice of intuition and inspiration were uneven, but the importance of the personality was one of the founding dogmas of European art, and abolishing it was a way into fundamentally new territory.

EXERCISES

Brecht's poem is criticising historians, not just poets. Given that poems are normally short, is there a basic incompatibility between writing poetry and being as inclusive as Brecht demands? Is it possible to write an authentic poem without writing at book length?

We do not hear who built "seven-gated Thebes". Is there any poem that gives the names of the workers who built a city? Can you think of any poems that would be improved by naming some builders or road-layers?

Why would you want to know about the productivity of the fields as well as about sculptures, vases, and paintings? Or instead of knowing about these things?

Is there anywhere you can draw a satisfactory and enclosing horizon for any poem?

Why write short poems?

The Gothic Counterpane:
Preservationism in Poetry

It's obvious that the 'alternative' line in British poetry has been mostly followed by male poets. The question of whether the 'neo-modernism' of the 'alternative' British poetry is ever going to reach legitimation in the way that the Tate Modern legitimates anti-pictorial art seems now to depend on whether the new audience will swallow the fact of male domination in the 'society of the poem'.

One thread in this rather damaged textile is the question of being modernist, and we are directed to this by Andrea Brady's comment (on-line):

>>I would guess (though I haven't been around long enough to know for sure) that the first problem is a historical one. Following the unbearably macho legacy of modernism, and the drear post-war period, something happened in the 1970s and 1980s which dissuaded women from entering into, or staying in, the poetry scene. It sounds like a Gilbert and Gubar cliché, I know, but it's a fact that of the few women who did, several later withdrew (e.g. Denise Riley), died, or went mad.<<
(*Jacket* magazine, October 2007; http://jacketmagazine.com/34/wagner-forum.shtml)

This was a remark in a whole forum, and the "scene" referred to is the Underground, the innovative world. Obviously women joined the mainstream scene in huge numbers. "Overwhelmingly macho" is a difficult phrase which may simply mean that few modernists were female. This also allows us to consider why so many creative artists did not want to be modernists, and what values they preferred over that. The elision in making "the poetry scene" refer only to the innovative sector (whose innovations would be denied or ridiculed by those outside it) makes us look away from the fact that women, not during the Seventies but starting in the Eighties and on a mass scale in the Nineties, did expand their share and move towards majority status in the official or mainstream poetry sector. In fact, an elementary count suggests that one of the gross differences between 'mainstream' and 'alternative' is that women poets are far less numerous in the latter.

(Actually, saying 'innovative' is another elision. Based on the ALP – Association of Little Presses – catalogues, some 2,000 individuals had published a volume in the alternative poetry sector by 1990. They, and however many hundreds have swum up since, form a nebula rather than a category. Sandra M Gilbert and Susan Gubar wrote *The Madwoman in the Attic*, 1979, subtitle *The Woman Writer and the Nineteenth-Century Literary Imagination*. Elaine Showalter wrote *The Female Malady*, 1987, which observes that in the 19th century the majority of patients of the psychiatry industry were female. The conclusion, that society was designed around male needs and that women were 'sick' by the norms of male doctors, is not utterly certain but is unrefuted.)

I can't interpret "something happened in the '70s and '80s", since documentary records do not show that women poets had been more dominant in the period 1940-70, or 1930-70, or really any 'baseline date' you choose. That does not weaken the basic point – that there is something wrong with the 'silent rules' of the Alternative world. I want to add, in case people are rejecting this whole line of discussion, that Brady has an original critique here and the founding act of the whole scene was critique. We can't ignore a new and coherent critique. In fact, my proposal is that the cognitive process of understanding, modelling, and testing these critiques is basic to the metabolism of the avant-garde. It is a form of pleasure, and a close and intense way of experiencing the cultural acts of the poems themselves. It would be perverse to enjoy the process of anti-capitalist critique and not enjoy the process of feminist critique even if directed at the avant-garde itself. My intuition is that we may find flaws in the critique at say stage ten of modelling its real-world implications, but that we should enjoy the process of developing and filling out the critique at (say) stages one to nine.

BUILDING FOR NUCLEAR CONFRONTATION

Why did women who were going to put major amounts of life energy into poetry not get into Modernism? I described in *Council of Heresy* the miasma by which aesthetic decisions are taken, profound rejections rapid and unlimited by reason. Modernism is tainted by just such a miasma. Obviously, its implication, that anyone using modernist techniques is a Marxist and rejects democracy in favour of a feverish élite of the Illuminated driven by a will to defy History, is 'miasmatic' and wrong. Thinking by miasma and identification is rapid but desperately inaccurate. What styles 'mean' seems obvious but is something people endlessly disagree on. They could freely choose the meaning but were forced to make an act of choice. We might take it as a goal to imagine the artistic landscape with miasma neutralised and removed.

The concept involves a 'chreode' where poets mandatorily fall into the Modernist camp or the Gothic camp. Because this is a fundamental division in British culture, it is also covered over by mile-deep layers of dulled responses, and I wanted to approach it here in a new way.

I don't think the Modernist camp have any understanding of why people don't want to be Modernists. They are trapped inside a building with no windows. Critics from within this camp have difficulty understanding why most 20th century poets did not want to be modernists. One by-product of this is an industry dedicated to redefining conservative poets as modernists, a patient labour of self-deception. Perhaps the reasons for the resistance, in England, evidently also in Wales and Scotland, to the modernist onsurge are of more interest than faking the evidence. The drama of mid century may shed light on poetic taste in the period we are living in. So the theme of this essay is why poets *don't* want to be modernists.

In simple terms, the ideology of women in mid-century was femininity and feminism at its advent was devised to replace this, and was faced with early opposition which said, roughly, that the feminists were failing by the aesthetic standards of femininity and were unattractive. Femininity was an ideology which took the form of an aesthetic, and art by women was prominently influenced by its rules. Features of 'the feminine' would include:

– preference for affirmative culture, (to use Marcuse's phrase), viz. a vision of the human situation which is uncritical, which avoids conflict and an interest in politics, which accentuates the positive and has a longing for harmony

– love of nature, esp. small birds and flowers; preference for smallness and neatness as qualities of admired objects and of poems

– preservation of inhibitions, avoidance of aggression; affection for institutions of social control which subdue the aggressive

– wish to be approved of; being 'other directed' and unwilling to be assertive or to take risks

– sensitivity to delicate stimuli and towards the feelings of others
– assuming responsibility for creating comfortable situations for others to enjoy
– interest in adornment and lack of interest in competitive games (as variants of 'frivolity').

The Alternative scene is populated by people who were not other-directed and so ignored the clear signals from responsible officials and stewards that they should stop. Before the impact of feminism this type was more prevalent among men.

To the extent that feminism did in fact enact femininity out of existence, to define this quality is to define what changed in the years 1980 to 2010. I acquired a copy of the *Collected Poetry* of Sylvia Lynd, as part of researching the mid-century. The jacket says Lynd's poetry: "is marked by an appreciation of the delights and subtle charms of the English countryside. The verses in this collection fall under such headings as Night and Silence, Pastoral, Personal, Birds, Children, Epistles, and Fairy-tales." (This book came out in 1945.) This is conservative, not revolutionary; aestheticised, not existential. The project of redefining it as tough and modernist, to suit the book of a small faction of scholars, is doomed.

That mid-century culture knew a category of people who believed in the force of pure ideas and wanted to overthrow the given state of affairs. This applied as much to the rules of verse as to town planning, ownership of the economy, the Empire, the design of buildings, what have you. They were arrogant but exciting. Modernism is all locked up with the fate of those ideals, of that self-declared ruling group. The problem here is that the radical and demanding and rebellious writers we know about were mostly not women. They chose modernism as their line of expression and they weren't writing neat, rhymed, stanzaic poetry. They occupy almost the whole horizon of our optics for looking backwards, and there is a real problem in buying optics that would let one revalue Pitter and Raine, never mind Nott, Bowes-Lyon, *et aliae*. The poetry of these women falls into a category which does not even overlap with that. It was not revolutionary. It was neat and proper. They were happy to have inhibitions in place which restrained the arrogant. They were not much on smashing inhibitions or overthrowing the social order. They were certainly reading *Poetry Review*, not Ezra Pound. Few people were reading Pound between about 1930 and 1960.

Imagery to do with delicate and fragile things is common in these majority poets – thus flowers and birds for Lynd. This quality noticeably resembles the poems themselves, delicate and inviting sensitivity. I would suggest that this predilection is involved with a kind of politics, one where small units are to be autonomous and massive redevelopment programs are not to be pushed through by alliances of the powerful. This is anti-capitalist as much as anti-government. Modernist poems are fond of things like trains, cars, Metro trains, aeroplanes, tanks, escalators. Speed, long distances, metal, power. Even the intellectual thrust is based on power, on great spatial and temporal perspectives. So I suspect that there are political beliefs inscribed into the 'small is beautiful' attitude, a preservationist position. I am going to discuss this inclination, or opposition, in terms of nuclear war. In the world whose 'present time' began in August 1945, the fear of being bombed into annihilation has taken two forms: either of building a nuclear state which intimidates potential enemies by its visible success at the business of nuclear arms, or of a 'small solution' which reduces the risk by redesigning human society into units which do not have violent designs on each other and which do not have the ability to sustain nuclear armaments. The rivalry would thus be brought to an end by cutting down the pretensions of both sides; the bipolar world would be replaced by one in which hundreds of calm and peaceful entities faced each other. Naturally there are other factions, but the opposition between those two is of peculiar importance to poetry.

I went to an exhibition of sculpture by Helen Chadwick, one of the really gifted artists of my generation. All of it was extraordinary, but one group of works sticks in my mind. It was a series of bits of furniture. The theme was development through life, and each piece was roughly the size of Chadwick herself at a specific stage of life. So it was an autobiography without words. Suppose we think of Sylvia Lynd in terms of size. Adjectives like delicate, slender, exquisite come to mind. So if we take the poems in terms of body size we can consider that most women wanted to have smaller bodies and then speculate that Lynd wanted to write small poems for a similar reason. The preference for birds and flowers is not random – these are small and delicate organisms.

Writing small-scale verse could be the expression of a belief that autonomy means everyone living on a small scale and that creating large-scale units is connected to power-mad individuals seizing control of them, so that many other people forfeit autonomy. David Matless' book *Landscape and Englishness* describes the line of spatial planning and town planning, which was in fact where Theory and university graduates came up against the old landowners and the old society, also where 'crime' comes up often as a metaphor. Part of slum clearance was to develop new towns, and these were not built from scratch, but added to existing nuclei, which had a certain amount of infrastructure. When in 1946 Stevenage was chosen to be one of these New Towns, to have several thousand families from London moved to, the local upper class put up quite a fight. East End families did not fit into the pastoral vision. The minister in charge was Lewis Silkin, and the reactionaries referred to the planned town as "Silkingrad", a covert reference to Silkin's family history in eastern Europe. There is no doubt that the development changed the character of Stevenage. Anyway, public opinion was keenly aware of the possibilities of excessive use of transformatory power, as seen in England, although Soviet Russia and Germany were used as metaphors. My point is that these formally conservative mid-century poets were quite aware of the possibilities of revolution, that their vote was to restrict the powers of any group holding sovereign authority, and that their anti-revolutionary verse form expressed this social-political belief. There is a latent theory of political virtue waiting inside their poetry, but it is not revolutionary. The belief that the quality of inhibitions is all-important applies just as much to the legislative powers of the State and to the speculative intellect as to personal relations and to verse form. The hypothesis that X or Y wanted to dominate can be replaced at this point: if you don't want anyone to dominate then you don't want to dominate yourself.

This theory – if it is accepted – would correlate with a sense of a diminished share of power, and with being other-directed. All the criticism of conservatism misses the point of why writers found it attractive. Presumably it was low-risk – the primary wave of reaction would find the method unexceptionable and so would neither criticise it nor give it a fanfare. This is an important 'submerged' dimension of modernism, if you like – why between 1920 and 1960 so few writers exploited it in any way, once the method had been taken to such heights by 1914. Conservative writing was simply comfort writing, it was low-risk. One correlative of it was a diminished ability to develop a personal style – old styles cannot be personal to any great extent, they are 'previously enjoyed'. So the fear of sticking out too much could be due to social timidity, a sense of cultural weakness and inability to defend enviable and desirable positions.

I am tempted to compare the bird theme with the birds of Ted Hughes. The contrast suggests that what poets see in animals is almost purely subjective – the organisms are merely coherent projections of volatile subjectivity. Birds are devices that eat, compete, and transform, as well as ones that twitter and fly. Hughes' poems are in one aspect a form of literary criticism – taking on poems like Lynd's and rebutting them. What we should be seeing here is ourselves as organisms onto which people project radically incompatible imaginings of human beings and their nature. The debate about the use of space and terrain is a debate about what humans, as the dwellers in that terrain, are like.

Lynd does not stick to strict metres:

> A bird of urbane
> Elegance is the flycatcher, straight-backed, self-possessed, slim.
> He watches and marks his prey and neatly outflies him –
> A peregrine in miniature. The midges are conspicuously
> Fewer for his hunting.
> Good luck, it is said, attends the dwelling that he makes his own.
> Certain it is, when he is gone, Summer is gone
> (from 'The Flycatcher')

With syllable counts of (13, 12, 16, 6, 15, 12), by my telling this is free verse, quite a departure for a poet like this. There is a rhyme scheme although it is irregular. The poet is perhaps thinking of D.H. Lawrence.

Cold War: Building for Nuclear Confrontation 1945-89, by Wayne C. Cocroft and Roger J.C. Thomas (English Heritage, 2003), is about the 'built environment' of the Cold War in Britain. What it says explains the New Town Story in more depth. The people moved there in around 1950 had jobs as well as housing and this was because the new Aerospace-Communications-Electronics industries were being set up in those towns. This was a sort of anti-bombardment defence – as well as putting facilities in bunkers you put them 50 miles away from any other factory so that they don't get hit as an 'overspill'. So it is Day Ten after a nuclear strike. London has Gone. There is no London. Your radar and plane bases want spares and new items of hardware. Because the factory is in Stevenage it is still there, it can fill the orders and maybe you can stave off Wave Two of the Soviet bombers. This is what Cocroft and Thomas' book explains. The radar gear is above ground rotating and listening. There is a limit to how much you can harden it. The migration of those firms out of military applications and into consumer electronics is a story of great importance. This book is published by English Heritage, which is a government department, so what it says is probably not an X-File or some kind of hippy divination. The Cocroft/Thomas book lists the firms involved and shows photographs of their works. Lewis Silkin's vision of Ten Days After doesn't really slot into some squire's belief that Stevenage cannot change from what it was in 1910, your 'pastoral poem'. But they were both thinking of the same few acres around Stevenage. This is the kind of argument town planning throws up. In the arguments people imagine the land and those images recur in poems and the poems take place inside those images.

Matless does not cover this but recovers the planning row over the new Stevenage in a very compelling way. Matless' book shows everything inserted into 3D space as emerging into about 97 different planes. Planning the New Towns was like three-dimensional chess, every move had simultaneous implications in all those planes. I think inserting poetry into 3D space is a key to understanding it. Maybe you have to look at the whole town to understand the poem written in it. Sound keeps bumping into objects, it is articulated by those obstructions or reverberations. Poetry takes place in imaginary space but it is often a space imagined by people other than the poets.

Whatever pitch it had reached during the world war, the contrast between 'great space' and 'personal space' became much more intense after 1945. East Britain in the 1950s was being laid out like one giant fortification, drawn with a view to bombardment from above, designed for blast containment. Recovering this is 'landscape archaeology' of a rational and impressive kind. The West was the 'rear echelon' and Norway was the gatehouse. Forget about archaeo-astronomy, we have to map NW Europe through the eyes of radar batteries. All this development is before the advent of the ICBM and even before the advent of the supersonic bomber – it is a defence against subsonic nuclear bombers flying from bases on the western or north-western rim of the Warsaw Pact area. The New Towns were like the towns in Wales that grew around Norman castles.

The debate about the International Modern Style in architecture can shed light on formal splits within poetry. Fairly obviously the 'postmodernist' thing was picked up by the powerful forces in the cultural world which had never accepted modernism in the first place. Charles Jencks was aware of this direction and has been rather clear about dissociating himself from it. The analogue in poetry is 'language derived from theory' rather than from intimate and lived experience, imitating the voice and thoughts of someone embedded in a social landscape and little interested in moving on. Invented language is 'inorganic' and stands in analogy to living space derived from geometrical theorising (imagination?) of an impassioned architect, not idiomatic, vernacular, or regional. The idea is that rooms within a Corbusian tower block feel alienating because they are just cells in someone's overweening fantasy and not reproductions of what was previously successful and comfortable. Rather obviously, someone who objects to those 'imperfectly imagined' dwelling spaces also thinks that the cells of a Marxist society, or in general a society built from the theory of ideologues, are cold and inhuman in the same way. Thus pure architectural invention is compared with law-making by a slow process based on precedent, debate between many individuals, property rights, and conservatism. By this point we seem to have got some grasp of why English people said no to modernism. I say "seem" because in a century of asking this question no two people have given the same answer.

E.H. Kossmann's history of *The Low Countries 1780-1940* includes a classic description of Belgium's old order as a "Gothic constitution". For Kossmann, Leopold I, in the 1780s, swept this away as an Enlightenment monarch – the enlightened despot, to use the phrase of the time. He produced something efficient, consistent, flat – and there was an armed rebellion. The good people of Belgium did not want the Enlightenment. They missed the elaborate and tiny privileges which they had before they were given equality. Perhaps they did not want other Belgians to have so much equality. Leopold was forced to give them their old constitution back – the one which Kossmann refers to as "Gothic" because it was old, irrational, and full of irregularities. (The term Belgium was not in use at that time, state documents spoke of the Austrian Netherlands.) I think the key to this resistance is that the irrational system prevented individuals from acquiring too much power, the power to change the rules. The danger of this power was blocked at every step by territorial boundaries and by the blocking power of councils and consistories who could veto reforms which affected their, usually tiny, territories. The 'gothic' system was thus one dedicated to preventing anyone from making radical changes. The traditional boundaries limited the power of mighty individuals. Perhaps Belgium is culturally more similar to England than conventional wisdom would have it. At the same time the small amounts of power vested in *bourgmestres, échevins* and so on, in petty public offices, gave great satisfaction to these individuals, and culture was often looked after by clubs in which individuals could, again, hold formal office and make speeches, without wielding power. Surely one component of modernist affect is the sensation of power, of partaking in processes which defy limits to operate on a vast spatial scale and at a high velocity. Old and small-scale features are razed to allow speculation to unfold without having its momentum broken. I want to deploy this private definition of *Gothic* because there is no other word for what I mean, and yet Gothic evokes so much about the English notion of beauty, preservation, and innovation. Some writer on the Gothic style (I forget who) remarks that the Gothic style never disappeared in England – the need to mend and maintain the large number of Gothic buildings meant that there was an uninterrupted line of craft knowledge. The Gothic Revival of roughly the 1830s could draw on this craft knowledge of building trades in the cathedral towns.

The history of the 'empirical' line in English intellectual history is hard to write. All the same it is a major feature in the discourse around poetry, and has been at least since the 1950s, probably since the 1930s. Because it is the aesthetic aspect which we are now considering, I will be allowed some latitude in explaining the artistic meaning of this mostly political tendency. The preservationist line in English culture had an idea of beauty which never really coincided with what England looked like, or what it had looked like, but which was visible to those who wrote about it. For poetics, it implies that everyone wants to create an ideal world at the outset of their adult lives. The primary quality of these imagined worlds is perfection; the secondary one is monotony, because the world is not imagined in detail, and most of it is blank repetitions of simple modules left in a primitive and schematic state. As artists mature, what they imagine becomes ever smaller in dimensions and ever richer in detail. The richness of detail usually implies a loss of perfection: the results are vivid and reminiscent of real events, people and places, if by that removed from fantasised perfection. The worlds composed of pure imagination are autocratic by nature, whereas the effect of democracy is to produce differentiated images which do not reflect the wish of any individual with fidelity. This compromise also affects self-idealisation and reduces it, adding reality to make it a character study as opposed to sheer beauty. The empirical attitude holds that idealised art is anti-democratic, a threat to individual rights. In the 1950s, this was concretely a resistance to communism – if also to fascism and, at least part of the time, to versions of art and society based on theology. At this point we have come back to what we have defined as Gothic: the purpose of the empirical bent is to block the power of individuals, and a system of inhibitions and closely spaced boundaries is the means of bringing this about. The empirical attitude is allied, in Britain, to the love of the past which is embodied in the Gothic sensibility; it is preservationist because what is already there can be perceived. The result of switching off the whole modernist thing is to reveal in intact form the Gothic landscape compounded of many strata of the past, an order whose parts are not intact but already broken, damaged on many planes of existence by the remorseless processes of time. The argument against small elites defined by superior knowledge and group cohesion is based, usually, on a belief that the inherited compound is effective – and that something which lacks system is the most robust. The empirical approach is not opposed to change but insists that the change should be gradual and qualified by measuring its effects, and that a range of interest groups should be engaged in it and be able to qualify it.

The blocking of exciting ideas about politics, the self, and artistic form, removes most of the intense sources of appeal in art, and may in fact yield a kind of art which is extremely short of surface appeal. It is cautious and unimpressive. The artist plays a very subdued role in it and the idea of the artist gathering around him or her a gang of close allies afire with glamorous ideas which other people don't know about, is excluded from the start. Perfection, even formal cohesion, is abandoned in favour of the representation of character, which contains a massive dose of imperfections and compromises. Familiarity is a very large part of the appeal, old artistic ideas and old artists are imbued with the same respect as old laws and constitutional restraints. Intelligence is not respected because it leads to ideas and dangerous innovations. However, these qualities are quite typical of English art, and could stand as a description of Englishness – in art and in the period since roughly 1930. I think it is very difficult for young poets to admire this set of attainments. The system finds it hard to recruit – as well as finding it easy to crush or block innovations. It is not a set-up where the young admire the old. It creates frustrations which magically create modernists and cultural rebels in every year that anybody hits 18. This is a flaw scored into the basic cell structure of the ideology of respecting old laws and institutions. I can't wish this contrast away, all I can do is describe the ill-effects. The problem of respecting the past is that new people are born every day and they are destined to be virtually incapable of preserving the older social order. Cultural transmission is a process filled with noise. Since you can't expect wisdom from young people, depriving them of the right to innovate is a step too far.

Matless explores a certain sensibility whose ideal we can describe as "Gothic counterpane". I have mentioned 'miasma theory' as a way of explaining the most subjective and pre-rational aesthetic reactions, proposed as the structural factors which decided why the poetic landscape became the way it is. I will say now that people in Britain make the equation 'Modernism = Town Planning' and that by this piece of logic the refined and schematic features of modern art are defined as bleakness, and the heroic capacity of great artists to create something new in many dimensions at once is viewed as the next worst thing to autocracy. People are quite well aware that tower blocks are an expression in some way of the ideas of Le Corbusier, and to a great extent their wish not to live in a tower block translates into a wish not to read modernist literature or to spend an afternoon looking at modernist paintings. There is in fact a chreode which divides people into two channels, the *other* of which has decided that anything which is not modernist is tedious and oppressive – a miasma field of extraordinary virulence and penetration.

What *is* the Gothic counterpane? The counterpane is a view of the land as seen from the crest of a hill, in some unnamed county, where the woods and fields are seen laid out like the squares of a counterpane, in colours which change in every square and yet harmonise. That is a visual image, but it is mainly about social relations and the visible form is an allusion to other planes of existence. Like the Imagined Village, the Counterpane is a totalising imaginative version of the island, in which everything is on the small scale and boundaries are very close to each other, so that nothing is large and no one is powerful. The landscape is designed so that there are no views, the horizon is always close at hand and there are no buildings higher than three stories. This clustering of boundary lines is partly because nothing in the landscape has ever been destroyed, so that the principle is really one of complete clutter.

There is no room for anything large or for long views. In this Gothic world, every building is old, irregular, full of picturesque detail. Every street has legends about it. Every scene is an illustration of some scene from an old poem, and the scenes from 800 AD are still being played out. The buildings are old and crumbling, but inside them are tiny and adorable birds and flowers which must be protected from anything that would harm them. The poets write poems filled with hush, awe, and tiny steps, faintly sounding so as to capture all these delicate and faint sensations. In untended plots outside the chapel whose soffit is painted with strawberry flowers are tiny wild strawberries. Around the town the land is divided into tiny patches of ground parcelled out among owners who are descended from people mentioned in the same 14th century document. Out in the fields, dozens of peasants are standing, delivering ancient rustic idioms which illustrate lines from old poems and plays.

The town is like a mouse nest. With sickles made of flints stuck into wooden boards, wearing costumes taken from an 8th century Welsh manuscript, the peasants reap the barley, which must be carried only in a straight line and only on the sacrosanct Barley Trod, a prehistoric straight track, to the great communal barn. They sing a reaping song of great antiquity whose words no one understands any longer. They leave a share for the mice as laid down in a 14th-century feudal custumary or polyptych. The chief of the mice formally thanks the reaper captain.

Within this counterpane is an enclave, founded originally by Continental refugees in the 1850s, called Silkingham, where everything is modern and abstract. All the buildings are made from modern materials – plastic, glass, laminated wood, and vibrated concrete. The residents listen to atonal music while reading modernist poetry.

There are a huge number of photographs in *Cold War*, of large devices such as gantries, wind tunnels, radar batteries, radar towers. They possess an extreme beauty. They are huge, pristine, complex and yet minimal, visibly straining at the limits of knowledge and physical possibility, attuned to great planetary spaces and to sensory modalities which humans can never share. They are more impressive than buildings which after all are designed around human bodies and have to be homes as well as machines. No one lives in a machine. It would be idiotic to deny the beauty of these great machines, and as that has nothing to do with ornament this brings us right up to the 'extremist modernist' view about functionality. You can find an Apollo rocket beautiful without wanting to make high-rise blocks look like silos.

The history of 'small is beautiful' is in the propaganda of the British State while fighting world wars. It is seductive because we believe it, or the other way around. The government specialists (most prominently Stephen Tallents) produced a specification which large numbers of writers, film-makers, poster designers, etc. could use successfully. It was well thought out but it is not easy to tell if there was any reality behind it. Because the propaganda of two world wars, on this side, had been founded on a defence of the Gothic society against supposed Continental tyranny, the propaganda for the Cold War and for nuclear arms was tangled in the past and its writers were unable to get away from defending the small scale even while the state was building up a high technology war machine which on its various planes of submarines on station, naval and air bases, and alliances spanned the whole planet. While they were covering the whole island with a network of air bases and radar installations, politicians were talking about the suburb and the freedom of the individual household. They were unable to start talking about the wonders of a huge military state and its supply industries because that would have proved to people that the British State was violating the principles of its own propaganda.

The typical feminist poem, we can say, is the one which denounces nuclear war, and which traces the origins of the crisis in international politics to the irrational and territorial behaviour of men, along threads which may involve every institution of society and even go back through thousands of years of history. This was one of the unifying causes, available at a time when feminism was developing a mass following, although it probably peaked in the Eighties with the so-called Second Cold War and waned somewhat as the collapse of the Soviet system made nuclear war seem less likely. The feminist poem is in harmony with the Greenham Common camp. The imagery of the small-scale society and the threat to it from militarism and tyranny was unifying partly because it was derived from the propaganda of the British State against continental tyrannies and did not have to be invented or taught to the audience.

Judith Kazantzis brought out *Minefield*, the first full-scale book of feminist poetry, in 1977. (The revival of feminism is conventionally dated to 1970, so there may be earlier candidates.) Her long poem 'Progenitor' was published in *Touch Papers* (a collection of 3 feminist poets), in 1982. An inspired poem, it takes on the whole nuclear system in a time when detente was being hardened up again in the famous

'Second Cold War', explaining what the motives of the hard-liners were and what the consequences were.

The planners of nuclear war saw it as planning nuclear defence, and most of the high technology had the goal of detecting and protecting against incoming munitions. The pacifists tended to talk as if the Soviet Union were run by pacifists. The advance of feminist issues to centre stage has reduced the interest of purely feminist political poetry, which has been replaced to a large extent by women poets writing about autonomy and in an autonomous way. The practice of freedom puts individuals at centre stage while the struggle for freedom puts political institutions at centre stage. Equally obviously, the wars and armed occupations of the period after 2003 brought militarism back to the focus of attention for the poetic world, necessarily in different terms than those used about the deployment of cruise-missile batteries and the stance of abandoning detente for crushing superiority and rollback.

We have that other 'chreode' that the radical opposition to war now 'by necessity' includes the critique of male pattern preferences in conflict handling and of male dominance in politics. Opposition to nuclear war has become a major undertaking of British poetry, and has involved a considered rejection of the State, in its guise as an apparatus for planning nuclear war and producing equipment for it. The delta of ideas, fanning out over a vast plain, which attack the desire for power and favour the small scale, could not but absorb a century of pre-existing theories, cherished in Britain, which already favoured the small-scale. It is ironic that this was a favoured propaganda line of the State and that the opposition to Continental tyrannies was a feature of patriotism, even of the Tory party, all the way back to the French Revolution and in fact even before that. The ideal of local autonomy is basic to Parliamentary democracy of the constituency kind: MPs represent local communities and restrain the power of the Centre. It is not difficult for the fabric of verse to express this block of reasoning in a way which is comprehensible to most of the audience (in this country).

Style is not wholly separable from character, and this connects with the design of roles in society. The women poets in question (it seems likely that in the mid-century around 15% of the published books were by women poets) assimilated to a social role. Being low on cultural confidence predisposed women poets to write in a conventional way, like Lynd. For many of them, their status as minor poets correlates with their success in achieving meekness. The message they are projecting is of meekness, however intensely they project it. The outcome is that one office of 'society' approves of them for conforming and not causing trouble, and another 'office' slots them into a low tier of the artistic scale because their poems are so colourless. The inhibitions they suffered from are directly connected to our wish not to read them today: femininity was the cluster of limiting factors which prevented them from breaking out of poetic convention. Of course, most male poets were very conventional as well – we are talking about a percentage difference. We can hypothesize that the limiting factors were also influential on the 'silent cohort' of women who read poetry but did not write it – the 'blanked out talent'.

The revisionist analysis of the mid-century defines the acceptance by these poets of a subsidiary role as oppression. This is a revolutionary shift. Someone who writes with delicacy does not necessarily believe that they are filling the role of the defeated. Writing small-scale verse could be the expression of a belief that autonomy means everyone living on a small scale and that creating large-scale units is connected to power-mad individuals seizing control of them, so that many other people forfeit autonomy. The admiration for 'littleness' leads us to the question of how bodies fit together in space, to spatial planning.

The position of femininity was highly incompatible with the love of machines, speed, and large-scale transformation which we have just been looking at. Perhaps modernism was bound to be male-dominated. But the history of the last few decades is of the emptying of femininity as a psychological and cultural position.

The cult of smallness explains why women don't do Modernism. Some critics are in an awkward position trying to combine the predilection for modernism with one for female artists, given the factual constraint that almost all the significant modernists were male. Their problem is artificial but we can recognise rather wearying compromises whereby marginal figures are dragged into centre stage because they were female, or the definition of modernist (as of Postmodernist) is falsified so as to include figures that suit the critic's ideological invest-ments rather than the facts. Another tactic would be to diminish the importance of modernism, because it produced results which do not suit your ideological position. The statement about "the overwhelming machismo of modernism" need not be taken literally, but has a familiar ring because it recapitulates an earlier adventure whereby critics tried to reconcile patriotism with the shortage of modernists in Britain: the step of revaluing small scale and old-fashioned artists is almost inevitable. Small artist – big hype. The later steps, of blaming modernists for the Second World War, the atomic bomb, globalisation, etc., and associating innovation with Continental tyranny, loom ominously but can presumably be avoided. This is the 'chreode' which opposes empiricism and historicism. Something else that can be avoided is the idea that a male artist is necessarily 'macho' and a threat to good order. This is not perhaps the best approach to the history of art.

Poetry hardly lends itself to technology in the way that building, music making, and cinema do. One obvious squiggle of logic is 'poetry has no technology – poetry is low technology – therefore poetry should express the attack on technology – and be personal because it does not draw on the knowledge brought by technology'. This explains a lot of the poetry landscape. Because it is logical for poetry to be personal, there is a wonderful concentration in the poetry world of people who love the small scale and don't understand machines. There is a natural rhyme of poetry, as an 'untechnical' and personal art, and the preservationist approach. If you see poetry as a delicate melody which is hidden in the rocks and hills and waiting to be struck into sound, it becomes a species needing preservation in itself. Whereas writing in a conservative way is 'organic' and obviously in tune with preservationist ideals. Poetry is thus likely to be valued as the most reactionary and inevitably old-fashioned of arts, a kind of pre-industrial practice. It is worth recalling ways in which inorganic and arguably technical means have been brought into play within the poetry arena. The whole pattern whereby you engage in theory and start the way that you write in the findings of that theorising gives you a 'technique' which makes poetry a technological act.

SECRET ENEMY:
THE CRITIQUE OF MALE DOMINANCE

FEMINISM

If you ask a large number of people about what changed in the period, the most common answer will be the move of women to the centre ground.

The symbolic start of feminism in modern Britain was a conference in 1970 (in Oxford). Up to 1980, the number of books of feminist poetry is not large. Yet the 1980s then saw the cause of women as an unambiguous winner. By some point early in the decade, publishers are desperate to sign women writers because they are seen as saleable. Rather than use subjective language, let me quote some figures to indicate the lines of change. In Alan Ross's Arts Council pamphlet on *British Poetry 1945-50*, there is a list of books, and in this 8.8% of the named poets (8/70) are women. In *Poet's Yearbook* for 1978, 21.8% of the poets listed are women (although I couldn't identify the gender of all the people). This one lists everything, not just 'significant works'. I used Jonathan Barker's standard list (described above) and counted that 20.8% of named poets were women – that is, for a period 1970 to 1995.

I used Barker's list again, looking at the dates when the women, the 20.8%, had made their debuts.

Number of women poets within the Barker list making debuts in selected time periods

1930-39	2
1940-49	4
1950-59	4
1960-64	5
1965-69	8
1970-74	16
1975-79	16
1980-84	29
1985-89	23
1990-95	29

Women are only 'intercepted' in this list if they were still publishing after 1970. (Naomi Mitchison published a volume in 1926 and was still publishing in 1978.) The figures for debuts before 1960 are not very indicative of anything. So, a sociological change steals over the cadre of poets over the years after 1960, namely that the proportion of women poets increases sharply and consistently. This does not necessarily change the kind of poetry being written. We did not measure that.

Numbers work is tedious, but I found something quite public and easy to count, i.e. the balance of reviews of women and male poets in *Poetry Review*, the voice of convention. Here are some 'straw in the wind' figures: (percentages of women poets in reviews of volumes written by individuals):

1960s (all)	14.81%
1978	3.85%
1981	20.00%
1990	31.11%
1995	39.71%
1998	38.32%
2003	26.25%
2007	28.89%
2009	42.55%
2011	35.66%
2012	31.36%

The fact that you can measure something does not mean that it is what you really want to measure. This is at best a proxy indicator. All the same it gives us a direction of travel.

It is sad to use a proxy indicator for something which is the most important process of change. But you can never get at the whole picture. At least precision is possible when dealing with individual texts. The shift towards a higher proportion of women among valued poets is the collective story. It is long-term, and we can certainly ask if it is going to stabilise at, say, 60% or 70%.

It follows from the late date of this shift that we can outline a forerunner era in which women's poetry was feminine rather than feminist, and which filled the whole mid-century, and continued up to some late point – say 1980. One of the contrasts in the field is between traditional women's poetry and the new, radicalised kind.

Feminism is the one revolutionary principle of 1968 which changed the social order in an abiding way. The ideas voiced by radical feminists around 1970 are taken up by mainstream magazines for women and later by the mainstream media. They win the battle of public opinion. The most startling change is in the attitudes of girls. During the 1980s, girls become aware that their purpose is not to become a housewife, and that they need to take charge of their own lives and to succeed academically. So they start to overtake boys in academic results. The proportion of female students at universities starts to rise. For girls born after 1980, feminism is a given, they do not have to go through a revolution. For women born before about 1940, a revolutionary change is not relevant. Older women poets stay with their methods and do not always approve of the feminists. It is in the middle generation (focally, those born in the 1940s) that a real breach of consciousness takes place after '68 and that a revolution is experienced, and carried out, at first hand. For them, incompatible sets of expectations and role assignments have to be worked through.

If the debate about what really happened tends to come down to numbers, that is a sign that the questions will never be answered; poetry is all about quality, and the numbers surface as a sign of the breakdown of insight (or at least of shared insight). Given that the proportion of women poets in anthologies up to the 1980s is always much lower than the share of men, the question is whether the 'other' women poets were writing but being oppressed by male editors, or whether in conforming to the expectations of a wider society they had not dedicated their energies to self-fulfilment, therefore had not become poets and were not writing poetry (to be turned down). The proportion of books by women poets was (in those years) also much less than 50% (although shifts in this ratio were occurring in the 1960s). Information about people who were not writing (but who could have, perhaps) is hard to collect.

We only grapple with these figures because there is a background rumble, a kind of radioactive dust layer, of accusation. A lot of people think that if there was little poetry being published by women it is because men were being despicable. A lot of people think that there was significant poetry by women which was not being published. Others think that, while there were women roaming the countryside, they had other things on their mind than writing poetry and, frankly, weren't bothered about it.

Of all the poetry which does not get published, or which subsequently does not get read, some is by women. Yet a huge proportion of the rejected poetry is by men. The idea that there is a bias against women, a vector overlaid on all the other vectors in literary taste, cannot be proved by the evidence remaining. It does not seem reasonable to suppose that all the rejected women poets were victims of cultural oppression and that all the rejected male poets got their just deserts. A certain communality of the excluded is traditional for the have-nots.

SUBMISSION

There is an effect of a biological order which we can call submission. That is, there is a role of dominance and if one individual occupies it then others take up a role of subordination. Dominance involves dominating language and the role is signalled partly through language. Most of what composed the 'feminine' style related to submissiveness. Sociologically (and we are shifting to a different discipline here, I am afraid), most writers agree that the role of submission changed during our period – people became less deferential and came to admire breaches of deference more. Power – is this too good to be true? – dissolved and diffused downwards. Uttering public language can also be considered as a test: the audience may bestow admiration and trust, or withhold it. This is something important happening during a poem. Poem? Yes, we can hardly subtract poetry from this realm of power, where the poet defines what a situation is and interprets how the shared moral law applies to it. But the picture is not complete unless we sketch in the figure of the macho author, the one whose drive to achieve leads them to record endless fantasies of winning in self-set tests, and whose loud self-projection leads directly to other people falling silent and being unheard. Their low esteem for other people is reflected in stories which justify the low esteem. Their role, taken by storm or by bluff, of being the writers who matter means that they articulate the feelings of other people for them, a graceful act vitiated by the low esteem already mentioned and by their self-absorption. As the warmth of this passionate egoism fades, another line has emerged, which says that the old culture in its entirety was complicit in inequality and so that the achievements of culture before 1980 (or 1990?) must not be admired and are rather to be considered as parts shaped to continue a tyrannical linguistic regime.

These have been decades of slow correction of the supposed male bias of taste, after the early feminists argued cogently that the artistic taste of women was different, and that maps of literature drawn by male scholars were due for correction by new evidence. This can also be described as the abandonment of submissiveness. The shape of this bias has not been described precisely, though it is supposed to lead us to accuracy. Perhaps this would require the presence of a purely objective person to act as umpire. And perhaps the literary history we dream of is attainable only as a phantom vision in the mind of this phantom person. It is true that a poem is initially a proof of itself, and that poems pass tests of excellence. It is good to question the nature of these tests, and also to recognise that they are part of what changes, so of what makes the cultural field of 1965 different from the field of 1985. However, it is hard to make them conscious. As they are broken out of a linguistic matrix, where they are a passive and structural element, they are largely destroyed.

The act of judgment in poems can be valid – some poems have insight, are credible. One part of this programme would be to declare that all 20th-century women poets overlooked by anthologies and historians are wonderfully gifted and important. From sampling, it seems likely that in the mid-century women poets were only writing around 15% of the published books. This is a bare fact which we can attempt to recover as a process. The shift from roughly 12-15% of books of poetry being by women to roughly 50% is a large-scale one. As it was not taking place in the mind of any particular individual, who could answer questions, we have to locate it in a 'literary unconscious' and try to get silent processes to speak. If we answer the question of "what disappeared" we are partway towards answering the question of "what changed". By reconstructing the role of male egoism in the mid-century, and the role of what we can call displays of strength and threat displays within culture, we can come to grasp that a key process of the period 1970-2010 is the weakening of this position. The attack on the 'feminine' in poetry did not become a theme of debate, as the number of established women poets in 1970 was rather small and their loss of status is hard to measure.

It is noticeable that, during the 1950s and 1960s, few women poets made debuts which left a mark on the literary world. The question, then, is why did so many women not write poetry in this preceding period. Three variant answers are, (a) because they withdrew from the fray and were giving their energies to something else, (b) because they had internalised anxieties which inhibited them from writing boldly, (c) because they had anxieties which were the direct counterpart of aggression by male authority figures staking out the territory. (C) appeals to people because it implies that the absence of female poets from the scene is a breach of civil rights which needs to be remedied. That is, when someone fails to write any good poetry, or any poetry at all, they deserve recompense from someone else who contributed to their state of silence and inhibition. This is part of the 'truth and reconciliation' process. The riposte to this I suppose would say that poets need civilian courage, and that this is the quality before all others which enables anyone to struggle through all the knock-backs and all the put-downs and write an entire volume of compelling verse. I gather that all the male poets of the era saw themselves as defying crossed stars and fighting off the malign authority of conservative or pro-business figures who were happy to write modern poetry off in ringing terms. A literary historian cannot ride around town with a sack doling out to all the people the rewards they did not get during their lives as authors.

Can we imagine the past in terms of poems that did not get written and careers that did not take off? This is speculative history but of a kind which our nature as humans trying to stay afloat qualifies us to imagine. We have had practice with the clause "If only…", I think. To be sure, such data are even more fragile than the information within poems. We need to pick them up with tweezers rather than with bare hands.

The extreme version of the victim plea is that by writing great works and achieving success X, Y and Z came to dominate the scene and so to discourage other people from raising their voices. This must be literally true at some level, although normally great poets are seen also as sources of inspiration, but the implication that high achievement is a form of oppression is unacceptable to a literary historian. The history we are recovering is clearly the history of articulacy, self-realisation, high achievement, of finishing and publishing books. That basis does not shift. But any consideration of the literary scene in depth will reveal a process that generates failure and frustration as well as success. This fact also will not shift.

FEMINIST IDEAS

Conversations always seem spontaneous but in the long run they show patterns. An interest in male-female relations has been one of the features of conversation in the last few decades, while poems may be seen as enhanced conversations. Or else de-hanced conversations, ordered as monologues and with one voice sliced or fatally reduced to uttering the lines of a puppet? The interest has flowed around a number of themes, of which we list some below.

- The 'detection' of two self-organising neurological 'tunes', in which the male fights, competes with, out-performs, and overcomes another male, and impresses, attracts, and couples with a female, as prevalent in art as a layer of primary fantasy which repeats itself in a million variations. An interest, almost in a collectory way, in cataloguing and describing the ways in which these bacterially self-reproducing plans disguise themselves. A wish to produce art whose cellular substance is something else.

- The interpretation of art as either the visualisation of wishes or the reproduction of significant experiences, in both cases embodying behaviour modules which are unevenly distributed among individuals and most noticeably unevenly between men and women. As this implies there is a latent conflict, in complex works of art, between two 'voices' struggling for the status of subject, the one who controls the work.

- The identification of most material, in supposed non-fiction as well as art, as the product of fantasy whose motive is specifically self-exaltation. As this material is insubstantial it is also cheap and after you flare off endless amounts of it it is quite easy to create a whole lot more.

- The identification of roles (in families, firms, schools) as frozen fantasy in which real individuals repetitively carry out phantom acts that make real someone else's will. The recognition in art of complete control scenes, with the voiced and the unvoiced participants. Democracy as a principle which does not pervade art and other narrative.

- Interpretation of chosen symbols in terms of projections from unconscious depths which are frequently the expression of sexual wishes or of wishes which differ between men and women. Thus poetry occurs on two planes, of which one is a depth which is strongly male or female. The phrase 'object choice' is convenient here. The idea of phallic symbolism as predetermining 'object choice' of symbols such as guns, mountains, fast vehicles, machines, colonies, subject provinces.

- Pacifism, and resistance to nuclear armaments in particular.

- A move away from competition as the valid source of office and authority. The idea of harmony as the basis of social life, so that eternal conflicts are sidelined. Redefinition of things like alienation, that is the alienation of males, as an unattractive manoeuvre of psychological withdrawal, with a component of aggression. Redefinition of withdrawal as an act of creating and marking territory.

- The idea of left-wing politics as a prolonged war, in which one side achieves victory by endurance, heroism, and intransigence, is switched off in favour of a wish for consensus as the substance which protects political reforms once made.

- Switching off the voice of the male working-class which is no longer to be the engine of social and economic change. It is no longer to be the touchstone of intellectually aware writing.

- Critique of existing forms of art which embody oppressive gender roles. Experiment in art as a trying-ground for new and liberated behaviour patterns; organizing the work of art to permit this trying-out.

- Critique of the romantic idea of love in poetry and song as misleading young girls.

- Attacks on literary taste in which critics who hope to speak for a wide spectrum of taste are redefined as partial, and what is 'accepted' is over and over unmasked as not being accepted by everyone.

- Rewriting existing literary history to include more women writers. Revaluation of minor genres which have a more prominent place for women and appeal more to women. Thus film criticism spent forty years discrediting 'women's pictures' as sentimental, technically conservative, slushy, etc., and then devoted a lot of energy to re-evaluating them so that melodrama was important and artistic. Because there were so few women painters, embroidery was promoted and painting was cast aside as inherently the art of the powerful.

- Belief in art as embodying behaviour programs which are ultimately oppressive so that the invested art should itself be subverted. Fascination with damaging the work of art, damaging the identifications built into it, damaging the right of the writer to speak.

- Tilting of familiar stories so that the point becomes a different one, minor characters become major ones, identification figures are re-painted as bad people, etc. The 'reversals' are never convincing but can be a lot of fun. Thus Ariadne re-narrates the story of 'Theseus and Ariadne' and is disloyal to Theseus, etc.

- Discrediting of any oppositional groups except feminist ones, as they might prove attractive to romantic spirits. Discrediting of the myths of oppositional male poets and their version of history, styles, poems, etc.

- Favouring of intuition against reason, which is felt as the self-assertion of powerful individuals and the privileging of one sector of psychological activity unjustly against a range of others.

- A pervasive vision of conspiratorial alliances which serve to keep a fixed arrangement of power in place. Detection of such alliances in any association of men, for example corporations, university departments, professions, parliaments, clubs, schools of poets, tables in bars, etc. Friendships between men, or even conversation, are seen as potential acts of disloyalty to women.

- Refocusing of history, on the basis that politics has always been the domain of men, to bypass politics, the State, international relations, war, in favour of the domestic which has a prominent place for women and children.

- Belief that women had been confined to the domestic sphere and that public sites had been territorially marked as male only. To reform this, the wish for parts of the custom of the site which are unattractive to women to be smoothed away, so that public scenes become comfortable for women. Thus if poetry takes place in pubs and women dislike pubs then poetry should migrate to other settings.

- Investigation of the nether genres of advertisements, posters, magazines, pop songs, comics, etc. as the ideological infrastructure of
capitalism and making the effort to analyse their construction and
how they embody preconceptions. Interest in children taking in
ideology and in changing what ideas children consume.

- The concept of alterated language, in which someone echoes back
what you say while distorting it so that your idea does not get across
and expectations are imposed on you in (almost) your own words.
This phenomenon in everyday life sheds light on motivations
attributed to characters in art. Projective identification describes
something similar.

- A phobia about others, such as writers, speaking for you. At the
last extreme, the denial of any third-person statements: only the
person can speak their own words. This necessarily brings writing
to an end, although that end may be a dark process in which a
new beginning gradually ferments. Empathy is the representation
of another's thoughts. This is the problem area.

- A critique of autonomy in art finds populations of diminished
others living in it. Recognising the diaphanous quality of characters
who are only fantasies; further that stories about these ethereal and
compliant characters tell you nothing about what real people are
like. And that idealisations can be a form of alteration. Appearing
in someone else's fantasy as a way of losing rights, where passivity
is praised and encouraged. Solipsistic poetry might have one of
its sources in this. The authenticity of having no interest in other
people.

- Exercise of crumbling works of art so that the latent third-person
statements are isolated, segregated, dismantled, destroyed.

- Rejection of judgements. Systematic challenge of any comparative
judgements of individuals affecting access to education, jobs,
rewards, praise, status, prizes. A liberation narrative in which an
individual can define their own status and deny the right of other
individuals to form judgments of them. Where only self-attributed
characters are ultimately valid as descriptions. Favouring the
writing of poetry on this basis.

- The excision of the aesthetic component of aesthetic appreciation.
So that you did not enjoy the work of art, you perceived a social

group, and then the writer as a cell of that social group, and you applied huge and insensitive preconceptions about the social group and valued the art through them. As if the substance of the work of art had no bearing on judgment. And as if there were no good or bad art.

- Recognition that much art is not based on empathy. That empathy is a transforming activity which people actually rehearse while undertaking art, and which some people are very bad at. More consistent pursuit of empathy as a principle in poetry. Identification of a realm of empathy with the direct experience of other people, mediated and made more accurate through gossip, which is the source of valid art. Art defined as truth to experience rather than as something autonomous.

- Exploration of the minor roles – history is no longer primarily about the powerful and dominant. As, in many social set-ups, there are losers. They cannot get their way by force or threats. They can maximise advantages in other ways, pursuing indirect methods. Extending the subject matter of history to include 'the silent', and symbolic statements which are not legitimated and not even explicit.

- Criticising identification with someone, in the conventional work of art, because they are going to be the winner. Interpreting art as a restatement of the power of the powerful, to induce its acceptance by the weak. Reading films as expressing Social Darwinism: the elimination of rivals. Too many individuals, not enough about the group. Seeing a line of possessive individualism in films etc. as reflecting an ideology pervading western capitalism. Thus plots are devised to give the ordained winner the assets with which to win. Where the predictability tells who you to identify with, as the basis of pleasure, moving to find instead a new possibility of identifying with the loser. So freeing oneself from a sociobiological rhythm where art repeats dominance in stylised form.

- Recovery of social reality underneath 'elevated' cultural forms, for example connecting the fasting of female saints to anorexia in teenage girls in the 1970s. Interest in the biographies of artists and moralists so that the art is viewed together with biographical details. Thus revelations about Hitchcock's life are included in discussion of his films. A wish to lower the status of texts by finding or inventing second versions against which to test them.

- Depressingly detailed interest in the private lives of artists, laid down in unfeasibly long and unreadable biographies, as an alternative to engaging in their art. Writing poems which detail and display the private life of the writer directly, without anything like art getting in the way.

- The idea of misogyny as a character trait which could be identified in individuals. The sniffing out of guilt in what men say or write. Fine-grained application of tests of ideological orthodoxy. Reduction of reading to a kind of performance appraisal.

REFORM OF POETRY?

Once feminism reached the mass of women, it became very difficult for politicians or the media to criticise it. It had already won. There may in fact be an anti-feminist *refugium*, in the same way that there are Marxists after the collapse of the Soviet Union, but I am not aware of anyone holding these ideas in the poetry world. Male poets were deeply unhappy about being told that their intuition was weak and their egoism was strong, but they did not think that intuition was unimportant or that egoism was good.

This conversation, or indeed campaign, was happening primarily in magazines, newspapers, and the broadcast media – the public sphere. Poetry, by now a kind of bubble raft of many private spheres, was not on its main route.

The contest of female and male principles in poetry has to do with the choice of styles separating one individual poet from others rather than with interaction between characters within a volume of poems. We can suggest that the habitual modernist vision within which the choice of styles expresses competition and the occupation of symbolic territory is more attractive to men. Writing poetic history in terms of innovation would then be biased against women.

It is noticeable that the set-piece victories of feminist critics have very rarely involved male British poets and almost never modern ones. Poems deploying phallic imagery are rare in this period. There was a kind of 'pre-feminism' which favoured empathy and whittled down the phallic element. What has happened in the last 20 years continues currents of artistic opinion which go back a long way. The burst of militarist poetry which we associate with Noyes, Newbolt, and Kipling was retrospectively written out of existence by a literary elite which had other and incompatible values. Even if the country was militarist and imperialist, poetry struck out on a different route. It is hard to imagine British poetry doubling back on its tracks and retro-acquiring those 'psychic assets'. The feminist wave of the 1970s had relatively little to say about poetry as it was being written then. Nobody would bother to attack '70s poetry when commercial cinema produced so much more glaring targets. Poetry was very low on the list of assets that had to be degraded. For this reason reforms of poetry under feminism are hard to point to. I feel like a war correspondent trying to photograph a battle that is not taking place.

Apart from Hughes I am not aware of brilliant feminist assaults on a modern poet. Perhaps that is yet to come. But conversely feminism did not subvert the course of poetry; it produced a wider river, still flowing in the same direction. Feminism has a great deal to tell us about the entire course of British poetry in the last century: not to subvert the work but to explain its choices. Perhaps poetry is weak on primary fantasy and one of its structuring and wealth-creating principles is to be secondary or tertiary. Sophistication, you could say.

Poetry probably does relate to behaviour modules in the mind, but while there are many modules (possibly hundreds) there is not one we can label "female behaviour module" or "male behaviour module", and masculinity or femininity are not coherent modules but a vague overall effect. As this would suggest there is nothing we can call "male poems" or "female poems". Everything in a poem is revealing. If 3 or 4,000 female poets were all saying the same thing, that thing would not need to be said. In order to write a necessary poem, you have to say something that has not already been said.

EARLY STAGES OF FEMINIST POETRY

The early stages of feminism were very unwelcome to established women writers and public figures, who owned 'the voice of women' and were (to generalise) devoted to the 'feminine' rather than the 'feminist'. This older group lost influence rather consistently, and we could ask what was the fate of older women poets as feminism changed the map.

Judith Kazantzis' *Minefield* (1977) is a stand-out work in what was a small number of works of feminist poetry up to 1980. Stand-outs too were a few pamphlets by Denise Riley. Early anthologies were *Seven Women* (1976), *Touch Papers* (1982), *One Foot on the Mountain* (1979). Copies of the original books are surprisingly hard to find, and this was clearly an ignored or unpopular activity up to the later 1970s. People starting to write poetry in mature life may perhaps be a sign that there was a conflict between internalised norms and the new ideas of feminine independence, and that a fundamental release had taken place. The original feminists had written and spoken to make such a release occur. Data about the career of Judith Kazantzis show her starting to write poetry seriously in about 1975, although she was born in 1940. If we accept as 'normal' a career pattern which involves writing intensively while at university, and publishing shortly after, this looks like an example of feminism converting someone from safely acquired positions and giving them creative release. Kazantzis records that it was reading *The Colossus* which set her off. (This was published in 1960 but people do not always read essential books 'on time'!) Around that time, 1975 or 76, she had a child and so her 'job' was as a housewife. Faced with what was the ordained 'condition of women' at that time, and with the sight of early childhood bringing the acquisition of roles and the nature of aggression and fantasy into her daily life, she began thinking intensely about childhood and writing the poems published in *Minefield* in 1977. Because she had only just begun to write, she was not held back by any previous patterns, and got very far into feminism very early on.

Pauline Stainer did not start publishing until she was roughly 47. Her first book came out in 1989. First-hand information is lacking, but it is reasonable to suppose that her great talent could have been released much earlier if the environment when she was roughly 17 to 21 (and making basic decisions about 'who she was') had been populated by more celebrated women poets.

The story is that Grace Lake (a.k.a. Anna Mendelssohn, 1948-2009) had a book of poetry finished in 1976, and it was at the printer's (a politically-conscious collective, in fact) when the printers changed some of the lines, as not representing their political views. The poet thereupon withdrew the book, and it was never published. There may actually have been a book published in Leeds in 1976. Otherwise her first book came out in 2001.

FEMINIST POETRY

I want to start with *One Foot on the Mountain*, which you can now buy for 1p on the Internet. This was a terrible anthology. (The one foot suggests a first step, starting from the valley of patriarchy.) All the poets (there is a perceptual illusion you often get with anthologies) seemed to have the same quality of writing out of experience they hadn't had, writing down wishes originating in abstract accounts of feminist theory. The poetry was thus completely unconvincing – the accounts of male behaviour were almost complete fantasy and the vision of what society could change to was just groundless. The founding idea was that actual experience was inauthentic because it had taken place within a patriarchal society. The poems were not based on reality. They used neither empathy nor empiricism and were in this way outside the conventions of British poetry. I bought this from a political bookshop in a back street behind the market in Wood Green High Road, in the early '80s. The shop had lots of Black history (Amilcar Cabral, Walter Rodney) and feminist writing and it didn't last long. They were called 'community bookshops' at that time, meaning I suppose that the corporate world ignored most people in Haringey. I found *One Foot* really irritating but it appears here as an example of something that has disappeared – once every feminist poet realised that they had to write convincing poetry, which of course meant that it wasn't founded in an exotic revolutionary future but in the intimate detail of life being lived. It is possible that the first ten years of feminist poetry saw a process of working out how to write it, and that the failed attempts have been forgotten. *One Foot* had this vision of men as simultaneously being infinitely evil and being summoned to become infinitely good. Injecting finitude into this dissolved every thread.

The next stage was to write poetry about a lived-out feminist life – this was only possible once time had gone by after the setting out in 1970 (a mythical date). This raises the questions, "can poetry which is not based on experience work? Is the quality of authenticity in a poem precisely that it draws on experience, therefore on memories which are multi-planar, non-schematic and mixed with sense data, and which permeate the language of the poem?" This is redoubled in a political poem, where we add the question "can you write or think convincingly about a different way of living without experience of real life being a part of the evidence?"

Seven Women is a 1976 anthology by the 'Women's Literature Collective'. The title page says "Over the past three years we have been talking about ourselves and our work. Our writing has grown with our meetings." This records an era of consciousness raising groups which has now vanished. The pamphlet – basically home-made, printed from a 'top copy' in Courier, presumably from an electric typewriter, includes a poem by Judith Kazantzis. Kazantzis' poetry has not dated. It had that quality of undeniability.

'The Queen Clytemnestra' (in *Seven Women*) deals with the story of a Mycenaean queen, the daughter of Leda, who appears in another memorable poem by Kazantzis; Helen was Leda's other daughter. The story is set in ancient times, roughly the twelfth century BC. Clytemnestra's daughter, Iphigeneia, was sacrificed by her husband, Agamemnon, as the fated prelude to the expedition against Troy. In allusions in plays from the 5th Century BC, she is said to have killed Agamemnon, in collaboration with her lover, Aegistheus. She killed her husband's concubine, the Trojan Cassandra, and was killed by her own son, Orestes. Kazantzis' poem starts in the twentieth century with a tourist trip to what is announced as the tomb of Clytemnestra; part 2 is spoken in the voice of Clytemnestra (oldest form Clytemaestra). The poem does not belong to the genre of 'rewritten myths' as it does not alter the traditional story, the only modified detail being that Aegistheus becomes weak and foolish, which I do not believe is in the old Athenian texts. The effect of this is to cast the blame for the murder onto Clytemnestra; ancient texts are divided on what part she played in a murder carried out by Aegistheus. We can see both the poem and the original texts as rejections of any attempt to depict Agamemnon's career as heroic and directed by him. His martial virtues are simply shunted aside. The burden of this group of legends is not 'male supremacy' but a family curse, the Curse of the House of Atreus. The 'détournement' is the rewriting of the ornate, partly archaic and highly literary verse of the tragedian (Euripides) into expressive and fast-moving but down-to-earth verse of the 1970s.

> this is Agamemnon splashing in the tub
> in the sun, guffawing, his arms and back
> covered with war bites
> his hands calloused as they grab for you.
> how neatly you unpicked the seam of his head

with the bronze needle of his own axe
– didn't you think of younger days
how he savaged you with love
and your arse rose and you sank together
and you, the young queen, wrapped in your hair
groaned as he touched the spring of your heart
– you blocked that off, letting
the blood pool out into water
and splash, as he twists, downhill
through the baked cisterns

(The 'baked' refers to earthenware.)

Agamemnon is stripped of heroic status by his lack of sensibility – but courage does not always go with sensibility. The content reflects the collective definition of what poetry is, in 1976, by reducing the story to what Clytemnestra sees – the first person version. The passage just quoted can be seen as a feminist drama: Agamemnon sacrificed his own daughter. This is the pay-off for his invocation of paternal rights. He wanted a favourable wind to sail to Troy so as to protect male honour – by taking Helen back.

my Iphigenia, it was a cold shore
you never deserved
wild anchorage for your running heels
over ten years after, at Mycenae
I saw you, graveless
your ashes fed to Poseidon
small handful of my daughter
plump and twelve years old
whose body they burned

(Wild anchorage is the sea into which Iphigeneia's ashes are poured. The hot water of the bath is contrasted with the cold water of the Aegean – briefly warmed by the ashes.)

The knot of stories can be seen as a cruel drama about the bonds of kinship, thus

but Electra whose ideas of fatherhood
over ten years had expanded into the cosmos

– describes Electra's choice of her father over her mother as the latter was murdered. Clytemnestra wonders if Agamemnon would have sacrificed his son, as opposed to his daughter, had the oracle demanded it.

There is a post-1970 genre of poems by women which narrates myths or fairy tales with an emphasis on the asymmetry of male and female obligations, which these old narratives are suited to because they seem so close to the origin of social rules and duties. Through the pristine and founding runs a path to the revolutionary and re-founded. Another element in this re-narration is competition with the original writers, an assertion of female importance. (Pause here to rehearse how the Grimm tales were collected mainly from female story-tellers.) Clytemnestra does not believe in the heroic version of Agamemnon's feats and deeds, feminist writers do not believe in inherited stories. Another poem by Kazantzis (from *Flame Tree*, 1988) takes on a (male) poet more directly, this is 'My middle-aged simpering and the Mystery of Mr Duncan's Maiden'. Robert Duncan, from San Francisco, was notable for his eagerness to take entire religious traditions and subjugate their sacred language to the glorification of moments from the sacred biography of his own ego. His poetry is pompous and orotund. Kazantzis' poem picks up and argues with a line from a Duncan poem which refers to "a girl, lifted to Jacob's dry mouth/ her cup that fed his manhood's thirst". This conversion of a youthful person into a bottle of Pepsi-Cola gives rise to a splendid tirade:

> So that I writhed   looked aside
> my neck both Swan and Leda   chubby
> jawline imitative best as it could duck.
> And skinned myself in your eye's quest
> for the willowy wild grail
> within my huge girlish attitude.
>
> Water to water, cellulose to thin air
> to anorexia's grace, bulimia's modesty
> 'Persephone showed brightness of death
> her face, spring slumbering'
>
> Later I knew it again. That 'a wife
> may be the maiden to the eye', by grace
> of the 'watery blues and greens' of Bonnard's
> bathrooms – designer Mystery of maidens!

This shrinking inviolate
you bear such love of, I went and simpered
and spoiled it or her.

This continues the line in which a listener intervenes in a text rather than simply listening to it, and this is notably close to the custom of defacing sexist posters on the streets of '70s London. It shows us a moment of reading as well as writing. Kazantzis' description develops with stunning coherence the uneasy entanglement between what someone says and their visual appearance in composing their esteem, their social being in the unappealable court of public opinion. She makes clear that her self-consciousness is able to compete with the views of outside observers.

The flooding-in of real experience may put paid to the ideas and to the idealism. This shows up in another tier of poetry, where women poets write about daily experience in a wholly unintellectual way, piling up details to produce something which is no more refutable than a supermarket trolley but which is only feminist by its tacit claim that artistic standards don't matter and that talking a great deal about yourself is a sign of having lost patriarchal inhibitions. This line was showcased in *60 Women Poets*. Inaudibly subtitled *57 Bad Women Poets*.

I propose a core value in this 'authentic' quality. But merely representing something cannot carry any political message, and texts which throw out the speculative and critical quality altogether can't be feminist. The ideal for political literature is a dialectic whereby the narrative of a completed story evokes its opposite, a new story in a society where the contradictions of the story have made us conscious and then been resolved. To deny the possibility of change, to view the past without seeing contradictions and paths not taken inside its flawed and unfinished substance, is inauthentic.

EXPERIMENT AND WOMEN WRITERS

I was thinking of a truth and reconciliation commission to wind up the legacy of mutual disesteem between the conservative poets and the innovative ones. But more people have a stake in another process of unravelling the past, namely *describing* the relationship between female poets and the business, or the market, or the fan base, or the cultural managers, or other poets, or the revered authors of literary generalisations.

One such thread of bias or tilt is the question of not being modernist, and we are directed to this by Andrea Brady's comment (quoted earlier) on "the unbearably macho legacy of modernism". This is a difficult phrase which may simply mean that few modernists were female. This also allows us to consider why so many creative artists did not want to be modernists, and what values they preferred over that. The high-profile anthology *Conductors of Chaos* (1996) included 5 female poets out of 35. This presumably bears out what Brady took exception to, namely that women poets chose, over a long period, not to get involved in the 'underground' scene. This is not really about the prominence of men anthologised in *Conductors* (and elsewhere), as some were good, but is an attempt to talk about the basis of taste and of differences of taste. I think we can do this by looking at modules of *risk-taking, territory, competition, systematising* and *abstraction.*

The concentration of men in the experimental sector presumably has (also) to do with risk-taking. Men take more risks, for example in driving badly, in excessive use of alcohol, excessive use of drugs. In poetry, this might equate with being self-directed and not being dependent on approval.

Another theme was *historicism*, the theory of technical progress in poetry. The historicist line gives a particular view of ownership. If we imagine a line stretching out into an unoccupied landscape, historicism defines its whole length as being 'obsolete' except the last meter. The up to date poet then occupies this extreme point. A strip of (say) a square meter is then his territory. It is also defined by 'performance' so that this is also the distance by which he excels rivals. But it also represents withdrawal – he abandons the whole length of the route except the last meter. The emphasis is on extremes and on points of failure. Surely a poet who is less fierce about boundaries, who accepts a passive 'right to use' a large territory, has more scope. Perhaps their plan is not to create a verbal projection of themselves. I find this metaphor persuasive, but at the same time art does have to be up to date. By living in our culture we are almost unwillingly exposed to endless repetitions of images, effects, and stories. They dwindle and burn out. Poets who use the burned out material are going to fail, and this is not a metaphor.

Abstraction and systematisation of 'technique' is a theme about favouring innovation and experiment over empathy and the 'quality of care' in the design of styles. The proposal is that this abstraction from the 'realism' of presenting one's personality and the parallel tasks of compassion and empathy is more a masculine way of behaving. We could link this to masculine interests in technology and in abstract rational things like mathematics or chess. In any case you cannot carry out the operations of competition without abstracting one or several people's technical capabilities enough to compare them. There is verbal activity which carries out elaborate formal rules but is not of interest to other people and not even aimed to please them. Literature in the guise of 'formal language' may thus be developed along strange paths and with exotic results without the secondary goal of being shared at all.

Literature may thus be the product of two competing imperatives, one to invent and carry out new rules and one to share experience with other people. The whole phenomenon of obscure poetry cannot be understood without considering the first of these. This imperative may have a lot to do with why the experimental wing of poetry is dominated by men. Reasons for obscurity could be numerous and would have to include competition – a form of sociality. However, the elaboration of language away from communication and clarity is already a schematisation.

Again, historicism is impossible unless you abstract someone's style from the context of what poems say, and arrange it in a temporal sequence. Historicism is a form of competition, that is where version 98 is competing with and excelling version 97. If your writing is predominantly about describing personal experience then this system-atising idea of style is not important to you.

Territory is an important metaphor, which in this case is essentially wrapped up in the economy of styles. The style is the territory, its distinctiveness demarcates a personal territory from everyone else's. This would hardly work unless you believe in historicism – and moves innovation to the centre of the poetic game. Within the idea of territory is an idea of *ordeal*. A theme of English poetry during the Cold War was the existentialist poet, who by rigorous empiricism and acknowledgement of the limits of the intellect reached 'toughness' which also brought moral authority. It can be argued that this emphasis on the individual is already part of disappearing into a narcissistic fantasy, that blanks out the other people around him. Looking at this ordeal makes me think that the suffering is *built up* to demonstrate endurance as a claim to rights. There is a link between this suffering, the frontier status of the territory in question, and the claim to own the territory. The wish to have large-scale enemies (for example, capitalism; for example, trashy popular culture) is so as to demonstrate courage and combat fitness. You can't have heroism without a credible enemy. We do not have to accept the claims to territorial authority. Also the conditions in which literature is produced can equally realistically be seen as leisure, comfort, liberty, and affability. The project was repetitively to devise a basis for 'moral authority'.

Where competition is privileged over the description of personal experience and over empathy, this is a masculine realm. The 'rule of the game' is that the reader identifies with the poet winning the game, much as someone identifies with a footballer running for 30 yards and scoring a goal. The idea of a shared game creates a bond between those who play the game. This bond creates strangely extensive structures, so that two or three thousand years of European art can be woven into one history of style in which a shared idea is passed from one generation to another and (naturally) everyone's performance can be 'abstracted' and compared to everyone else's.

You can't have competition without also talking about *winning*. A poet writes the poems which they excel at. That is fairly obvious. The poems they release are displays of ability – repetitively passing tests of excellence, excelling other poets. The poems are likely also to show the poet in a good light – opinions expressed will show them exercising moral wisdom, being benign, tolerant, far-sighted, unselfish. And so on. This whole process can be compared to a form of athletics where talented individuals repetitively carry out feats selected because they excel at them, and where the goal is hard to find unless it is to display prowess and to defeat others. This is hard to reverse – would we ask poets to select their bad poems for publication? – but it does open the question of showplaces of culture being designed to realise male compulsions and not female ones. This is an open debate, but we can send up test flights. They would include the theory that an interest in style goes back to a focus on competition, on measurable performance rates and occupying territory, and so that the development of style comes from traditional male foci.

From games we get to rules and from there to laws of culture. Arguing about laws is more a masculine thing. Similarly with debates (set down in poems) over issues to do with language, with human nature, social duty, etc., which are carried out within groups of men.

Losing is equally important. Historicism supplies a timetable which made all styles antiquated and ineffective – except one. Just as with existentialism, the core is to disqualify all other writers. Invalidation is the basic gesture, and validity is defined, again, by the assent of a small group of male leaders who are validated by each other. Philosophy has a basis in competitive display and in winning, and theology is conducted as a branch of philosophy. It is argued that the value given to a cultural asset is decided by the members of an in-group, and propped up by the high mutual esteem which is the vital flow of the in-group. They exchange intellectual assets as precious gifts which bestow high status both on giver and on receiver. So the debates may not have the intellectual interest which they pretend to. It can be argued that an interest in speculative theory is similarly a male pursuit, a verbal game which is part of the metabolism of the male solidarity groups. Then, following through, that female poetry is, or would be, more interested in concrete instances, real-life situations.

REFORMING THE ALTERNATIVE?

In about 1979 The Damned picked captions from a strip in a girls' comic named *Bunty*, cut them up and sequenced them at random (à la Burroughs) to form a lyric. Unfortunately the music they came up with for this romantic, naive, idealistic, and girlish lyric was their most disaffected Lurkers-style thrash. It shows that when you use data acquired by automatic methods you should listen to what it says. "Forget your heart, you need not stay/ A second longer than today// Melody Lee, a broken man and a broken dream/ It must have been a change of heart/Your life was cruel they called it a(rt)" "Who is your secret enemy?" While reading Damned fan websites I followed a link to a *Bunty* fan website which revealed that the strip was about the impossible obstacles facing a young girl whose only goal was to be a ballet dancer, further that "Melody Lee a dancer she shall be" in the '70s repeated storylines which had first run in the 1950s and been re-used for heroines with different names in the intervening years as *Bunty* readers reached 13 and stopped reading the comic.

> <<I did like 'Lorna Drake – prima ballerina' who was being taught by Thelma Mayne, an embittered old spinster who was a failed ballet dancer due to an injury or something. How did

they make up so many different stories about Lorna's struggles in the face of adversity?? <<

>>i was a regular reader of *Bunty* during the late fifties and early sixties in Dublin. I see someone mentioned Lorna Drake, the ballerina, but I am sure there was a earlier one called Moira Kent, as in 'The Dancing Life of Moira Kent' <<

I could imagine a building where a black-and-white film of a young dancer having improbable adventures is showing projected on a wall in 1948 and is still showing in 1968, with endlessly repeated episodes. So clearly this theme of the frustrations of an aspirant Artist appealed to several generations of 11-year-olds. I suppose it began with films like *The Red Shoes* and *Dance Little Lady* but maybe it is a hundred years older; who can tell? I haven't found any issues of *Bunty* but I imagine the plotline as centring on Melody and how her sophisticated rivals Aria Lowe and Lucrezia Meadowsweet outwit her and get chosen to dance the solo parts in the end of term gala performance at the ballet school they all go to. If *Bunty* had survived we could hope to read in it a strip called 'Melody Lee – a modernist she shall be'. She dances solos from *Swan Lake* in front of the whole class and everyone applauds. She is radiant. But 'Legs' Meadowsweet says 'That's not very *sophisticated*'. She is tired of being pipped at the post by girls who are taller and have read books by Europeans. Shortly afterwards, she starts listening to Schoenberg and writing to Pierre Boulez for advice. She takes her poetry to failed modernist (due to injury) and all-round sadist, Thelma Poundstretcher, who tells her it is "full of unresolved romantic residues" and accuses her of "bourgeois subjectivity".

Concomitantly, the *Jacket* discussion had other inputs, mainly by Americans and not well-informed about Britain. The follow-up was saying that new poets in the underground world were not made welcome and that the scene had missed the chance of recruiting significant new talent because it did not offer welcome, approbation, resources, critical reception, etc. to young poets immediately as they appeared. This raised the question of whether the function of 'the scene' was to provide a friendly place and validation for young poets and if so who would do all that. This is a case of 'subjectless action', nobody has the job of making young poets feel important so the question of "who didn't do it" is open. The questions "who wrote the poetry that did not get written" and "who did not write the poetry that did not get written" both have the same answer – as subjectless action.

The alternative scene could change by becoming more friendly. The discussions around 'meeting and greeting' have occasionally seemed to imply that any poetry scene is there to be the source of approval and affection for new poets who turn up. This is a crux – it is simultaneously true that poets want love and affection, that connoisseurs want to exercise critiques rather than applaud all the time, and that any poetry scene is going to die unless it offers approval and affection to new and old members. Come on guys – you ARE the soft furnishings.

There is resistance to the idea of a constitution in the Alternative world. Subjectless action knows no constitution – or it may simply be that the rules are implicit and buried. An evolution towards being more friendly towards female poets and a female audience could follow from recovering the implicit into the light of day.

The proposal that "hundreds of women poets did not write inno-vative poetry because it meant joining a social scene and the welcome they received in that scene was not warm enough" is likely to be true. The riposte, that "there is no agency in the Underground scene which welcomes people and no resources dedicated to doing that" is equally likely. However, this indifference to emotional warmth and to the atmosphere of a social event could equally well be typical of men and a consequence of having a male-dominated scene – an imbalance which could return to equity with time. It was a lack of interest in soft furnishings, on the linguistic plane. An implication that the scene was nicer to men than to women is probably false – the scene was equally inhospitable to everyone, in my understanding. The hostility is quite simple. Everyone was paranoid about the mainstream and aware that individuals believing in mainstream values were intent on humiliating them and on invalidating what they did. This is the payoff for following the path of cultural heresy and economic marginality. Newcomers had to pass loyalty tests before anyone would invest any trust and affection in them. If they failed the loyalty tests – failing to accept the shared values of an out-group – then the trust and affection too would be withheld. Acceptance would come after probation (self-proving) and not at the start. The Underground really did not want mainstream poets and cultural managers to take over the performance and club scenes, magazines, etc. which they still controlled – a refuge area which the majority culture had failed to expel them from. Most newcomers actually were mainstream poets with a sense of entitlement, looking for an opportunity to get published. Also, the agents on the Underground scene really did not like mainstream poetry; they were not going to pour out affection and approval on someone for writing it. The group was founded on a critique and that critique was bound to be applied to newcomers. The preference for observation of (specific) formal artistic values over supplying approval to people on demand is constitutive for the group. To uphold impersonal artistic values and to expect affection and approval for it – that is almost perverse. The critique is the kinetic element.

The first thing you would have to critique is the idea of shared goals, symbols, a collective identity, in the periphery. Evidence that these exist seems poor to me and would have to be collected before it could even be tested. Shared ideals? Did anyone measure this?

The idea of 'a group whose members dislike each other' is tantalising – when it is descriptively valid you immediately have to ask "is this group about to disintegrate?" The Underground is a 'society without organs'. Founded on a revolt against existing cultural institutions, driven by critique, it has never developed institutions of its own and so is incapable of reform even when the consequences of 'subjectless' policies seem to be maladministration, imbalance, lack of projective influence, cultural suicide. Is there an inside of the Outside? Maybe it's all outside. Like the moon being all dark. There is no heat so far out. Warmth could only be a memory. We are talking of the 'exile being' of a cultural minority. There seems to be a structural bond between ownerless land and subjectless action. The Underground takes the peculiar geometry of an intermittent territory, flickering togetherness in sites that exist for a few hours before being struck. It strikes most observers as bizarre to think that such an unsteady, dim identity could own institutions and be accused of any set intent. But perhaps the ways you take decisions are institutions and so subject to critique.

The idea that the exercise of freedom cannot lead to imbalance is rousseauesque. Perhaps the unplanned consequences of thousands of takings of unconscious decisions can be dragged into awareness and reformed. There is the idea of the emergence of group will through unintended actions. The idea of the involuntary of the subjectless. Even without owning territory, maybe you can have warm spaces.

COLLAPSING METAPHORS

I am wondering how many people will subscribe to the mythical equivalences I am proposing here. Perhaps nobody – they are not definitive codings but momentary relationships which can evolve. I started from noticing that when I think about feminism I always think of films and not of poems.

I am not proposing stable sets of equivalents but a momentary set in a conceptual realm where continually forming and coding equivalences is a basic act of culture. The question of the relationship between innovation and masculinity is not one which is going to be resolved quickly. I suspect that if the equivalences were stable then there would be no need to read poetry – or to write it. In the past 200 years poetry has not been recording the myths on which society is based but new myths which thrive in an ideological gap – a terrain where frequent floods sweep away stable features. The act of uncoding and encoding has replaced the act of passive recording – and is what we need to be fluent in.

EXERCISES

1. Alienate a young poet.
2. Find 3 poets who think they have had enough patronage, affection, and attention.
3. Ignore 450 young poets.
4. X has written no poetry over a 30-year period and an advocate claims this is "because not enough people loved her". Who pays the bill? Who did not write the poetry which was not written? Is this an example of 'subjectless action'?

THE PUBLIC FACE OF A PRIVATE ART:
AUDIENCE CULTURES

AUTHENTICITY

From Kathy and Carol in 1965 to James Taylor in 1969. It is certainly interesting how the folk movement mutated from a state where all material had to be old and was respected as part of pre-modern tradition to a state where all material had to be written by the person now singing it and also to reflect their life and personality. The mandatory personalisation of the poem which Ross Cogan describes must be related to the enthusiasm for singers who are also songwriters. It is not proven that the obsessively personal line in poetry followed the rise of the singer-songwriter, you could certainly make out a case for them both being derivatives of a third process, one of privatisation and the rise of the individual. Certainly a poet writing tediously about their own experiences would not be *discouraged* in this programme by listening to self-indulgent singer-songwriters.

Hugh Barker and Yuval Taylor chronicle, in their terrific book *Faking It*, how autobiography entered popular song with the singer-songwriter movement, and how the desire to 'be real' took over popular music in the mid-1960s. We can hardly separate the wave of the solipsistic-banal from this revolution in popular song. The authors take us back yet further to where autobiographical song was very rare and was being pioneered. The example they choose is two songs recorded by Jimmie Rodgers, 'The Singing Brakeman', in 1931, of which one describes the TB that was going to kill him. These songs were a break with the past, and forerunners of what was going to happen in the 1960s. They also say that autobiography was more common in blues than in the rest of popular song, both the older strand of 'folk' and the more recent strand whose composers we can name. It is interesting that Rodgers called his memorable song a 'blues'. He was mainly a blues singer. Barker and Taylor say that 1 to 3% of blues being recorded around 1930 was autobiographical. So was the source of autobiographical lyric in blues songs? This can't be the only route.

The other theme of *Faking It* is something I am not very happy about. One of the authors is quite keen on challenging the idea of authenticity. This is the converse of saying that shallow pop music is great. You follow that up with a suggestion that deep pop music (the heavy programme) is not really deep, but that people search for and find signs of realness which are not signs of that at all. A great feature of the radical Diaspora after 1974 or so was the repetitive use of the phrase *constructed to*. So if you said *this poetry is good* it was corrected to *this poetry elicits reactions which you are constructed to have and which are constructed to be seen as 'good'*. The constructionist thing set out from the position that everyone is naturally homosexual and society forces them into a vast heterosexual propaganda machine so that they come out as helpless victims. Films repetitively show heterosexual couples courting *because the authorities are terrified that homosexuality will, heroically, return*. Once you believed this, it became *obvious* that wishes were constructed. The corollary was that the radicals could strap you into their Influencing Machine and reprogramme you with a brief programme of electric shocks. Theory was a claim to power – high office in a non-existent authoritarian state. This line of reasoning emptied out your response to poetry and also emptied out the poems – as expressions of deluded bourgeois awareness. Literary history, meanwhile, turned into drawing wiring diagrams of how (other) people are deluded.

Bourdieu says that role detachment is a sign of bourgeois status. The more detachment you have, the more bourgeois you are. Displaying the maximum detachment, which is obviously what the theory that feelings are constructed aims at, is a grab at high prestige – not possessions but high-status attainments.

Exploring why I like folk music might be fun, although much less so if I have to fight off cultural regulators for whom spontaneous decisions are ones they are allowed to annul. I think that the way you perceive a song or a poem is holistic and looks at how many factors combine. Breaking out one single factor does not reproduce the whole act of choice and recognition. It can be wildly misleading. The second problem is that I don't think the first person would agree with this third person description of what they are doing. It sounds so authoritative but the proof basis for the claims is absent. People don't buy a record *just* because it sounds like a dub from a scratchy 78 recorded in a shed in the South sometime in the 1930s.

If you take a wider view you can see large numbers of scuffed-up old blues records which didn't get revived or sold because they just weren't very good. If people like me got excited about Skip James, Son

House, Charlie Patton, Clarence Ashley, Doc Boggs, the Carter Family, etc. it was because they were good – not because of the exotic qualities of 1940s recording machinery. The collectors did not swoon for the lesser ditties of Bogus Ben Covington, say, or Otto Virgial. All the same it's interesting to think about 'signs of authenticity' in poetry. It may get us somewhere even if the final destination is not really there.

What do I like in poetry? I like the idea of present tense, seeing it happen, and I like originality as the evidence that something was happening in a 'pure present'. The originality is the 'internal present tense' of the poem which distinguishes it from fake events and parroted wisdom, shows it where it gushes up out of the ground, thick with humus and glowing minerals and groundwater. I do not like conventional poetry. I don't like poetry that uses set collocations, set patterns, set imagery. I don't like poetry that follows the piety of good taste and avoids developing its own identity. If you tilt these values of originality and expressivity on their side, they can look an awful lot different. The act of recognition is sovereign for the experience in flow but can be estranged by a colder eye. The thing being expressed is only visible in the words expressing it so you can't really tell if they distort it or even if it's made up. You can look for inconsistencies in the fabric of the language, but that is not very reliable and anyway emotion fluctuates so a poem that oscillates and wanders up and down from minute to minute could be a sign of genuineness. Emotion often comes from conflict so once you have unity the emotion evaporates. Testing for genuine expressivity is going on all the time but you couldn't say it had solid results.

Recuperating Depeche Mode also implies that I can like the kind of poetry I like. In the programme of re-evaluating pop and bubblegum, we need to ask what 'Sugar Sugar' does *not* have. For example dissent. Withdrawal. Sorrow. Experience. Modernism. Why isn't *everything* authentic?

I admit I don't like the cleaned up versions of pre-war blues on recent CDs. I prefer something on old vinyl on the Origin Jazz Library or Yazoo labels, ideally dubbed from old 78s collected by left-wing Jewish ethnomusicologists on field trips to rural districts in the South, thus linked to Central European ethnography, to Herder and Grimm, to Narodniks in the shtetl in 1912. You find out that Bascom Lamar Lunsford was rather well-off and well educated and just liked to play old-time banjo music. It is shocking. Those lines about "they'll put you in the pen/ with the rough and rowdy men/ and I wish I was a lizard in the spring" – he was never in the penitentiary. And yet – I still think his recordings are wonderful.

Literary theory is an attempt to reduce authenticity to rules and to manage it. This attempt is fatally flawed. I suggest that critiques are there to build a dam to preserve authenticity – a conservation project. The wish is to isolate the badness so you know where goodness is to be found. It is part of a search for authenticity. Critique has some elements of reason buried deep inside it, mostly switched off, but its animating force is a deep yearning of the kind people used to feel in the nineteenth century. *I want it to be deep and true and real.* It has the same unworldly dumbness as nationalism, Spiritualism, early romantic ethnography. But when poetry fails it is often because the reader perceives it as fake, based on dogma and theory or vanity rather than real experience. We need at this point to talk to the readers of poetry to find out what they see as authentic.

PRYNNE FOLLOWER

Lockwood Laudanum said in interview:

I: What would you pick out as a perfect purchasing experience?

L: *Twelve Poems*, by R.F. Langley, which I bought from Peter Riley in Sturton Street in 1993. This just absolutely summed up what I like in poetry. Obviously anything not based on Prynne is second-rate and out of date and doesn't really count. Obviously anything that isn't impenetrable isn't really modern and doesn't repay the effort. I find most modern poetry tedious but I obtain my supplies by following a particular genealogy. It's like inheriting an estate, the closer you are to the primogenitary bloodline the more of the estate your share is. Pound goes to Olson and Olson goes to Prynne. It's like the *Da Vinci Code* really. Everything depends on ancestry. A hidden illuminist conspiracy over the generations. I admit there is other poetry but it doesn't really turn me on, it is not part of that marvellous history and doesn't make me part of it. I find it reassuring that there is really only one line you need to follow, the crest of the mountain where you look down on all the cows and the dung and the peasants in the valley bottoms. Why not demand the best? Anyway the background reading of Heidegger, neurology, computer science, economics and so forth is quite enough to last a lifetime. I find it reassuring to know what books really need to be read and which ones you can leave to the small rodents.

Interviewer: Do you think there are any poets in the Prynne descendance who aren't important?

LL: No, they're all important. They are part of the scene.

I: What about the School of London?

L: They're just ghastly little oiks fundamentally. They don't believe in reflexivity. There is no moment of self-interrogation in their poetry and so it's all vague and remote. They aren't interested in ethics or in social life. All that is drained away as bourgeois. Because they aren't interested in self-knowledge they veer off into head-banging and random spatter and they aren't interested in getting beyond that. The idea is that noise is liberation, so if you spill and stain everything you break down categories. That's how you end up crumpling sheets of paper, photocopying them, and publishing the results as 'subversive art'. There is no intellectual exchange going on because it's about random disinhibition and loss of control, and it's programmed by an ideal of drinking too much beer. If you aren't interested in introspection nor in intellectual exchange your critique is just petulance really. Then, the belief in mindless energy means everything goes on and on and every module is repeated for no reason.

I: Don't you think that the heirs of the British Poetry Revival should have some loyalty to each other? Why weren't more London poets staged at the Cambridge Poetry Conference over 15 years?

LL: But if you want to enjoy the event surely it's better to have poets who can write and who are enjoyable to listen to. Surely loyalty is to good poetry and if people can't write then they should be in the audience and not on stage.

I: Is it fair to say that internal dynamics within the Cambridge / Grosseteste group depend on someone who wanted to be Prynne's favourite pupil in 1965 being jealous of someone who wants to be Prynne's favourite pupil in 1995 and them being jealous of someone who wants to be Prynne's favourite pupil in 2009?

LL: People have to fight to get what they want. If the person you admire writes poetry you don't understand it's normal to write poems you don't understand and to use this as proof of your legitimacy. The fact that you have inherited proves your right to inherit.

I: Is using a certain style proof that you are a moral person?

L: Fundamentally, goodness comes from self-knowledge and that comes from philosophical interrogation and people who evade that come out not being able to behave properly. Consciousness before philosophy is some kind of village practice, it's like digging the garden or tending the cows basically.

I: A lot of the action in the Cambridge ambit has consisted of defining some feature as a sign of authenticity so that some other people can be denounced for not having that feature, or for having less of it than the new norm obliges them to have. What is it that people don't want to share possession of?

LL: I just can't relate to this. You can't really cut people off from stylistic features in art. If you dial 'poetry books' in Amazon the screen tells you you have 441,000 hits. You can't deal with that so the question is how you find something that will give you pleasure and not boredom. Inevitably you rely on the 'features'. This only really works if you have other people who share the same values as you, so that accurate information reaches you. Recognition is one of the most basic things. I don't want to read a thousand books to find one I like. I prefer the network. Of course the whole thing could stop if the new poetry stopped coming out.

I: What about the depolarisation project?

LL: It's totalitarianism. They just want you to obey their commands to consume and they realise that knowledge and taste are obstacles to that dictatorship. They want the market to be like a body of air that simply goes where a whirring fan pushes it and has no wishes of its own. If they want to manage they want people to be manageable.

I: Did the publication of *Brass* in 1971 change everything in English poetry?

LL: I am still trying to assimilate *Brass*. It changed everything for me. Our reading group is working through Prynne's poems of the Seventies, one for each session.

A Footsoldier of the London School

Bing Headbutt was interviewed in a pub in Camden.

I: What about the Ferry/Grosseteste School?

BH: Nobody from London ever went to the Cambridge Poetry Conference because they didn't put on London poets. It was a deliberate slight. They use syntax and write about real life experience so obviously it's old-fashioned compared to the London thing which is into randomness and high energy. Getting away from the personality is the way to liberate art. The personality is full of archaic structures.

I: Do you think people in Cambridge were even aware that there was a significant school of modern poets in London?

BH: Of course we're significant. We're terribly important. It's just that everyone ignores us. That's because they aren't modern enough.

I: How do you get away with being so derivative of American poetry? Is there any need for the London Boys? Isn't it true that your definition of modernity really means assimilating the latest thing from the U.S.A.? What about the time-lag between the originals and what happens with the London boys?

BH: I don't know.

I: What about the 'messy play' thing?

BH: It's not messy play and anyway we can't stop doing it and anyway it does no harm. Controlled infantility is terribly intelligent and of international significance.

I: What about this thing about wearing hoods on your head and jumping up and down?

Bing: That was a metaphor about reflexivity. If you abolish reflexivity you get this surge of energy as a result. Being aware brings a wave of inhibitions. Our poetry is very repetitive and very unqualified, this is energy.

I: What about this "ratbags" description that Charles Osborne used about a meeting of sound poets he attended?

Bing: The phrase bag of rats refers to something in great disorder that has neither beginning nor end. That must be true for sound poetry, which has no grammar and works equally well in any direction. They wanted something tumultuous and non-hierarchical, that's your bag of rats. As for the squeaking and cheeping, well that's also something sound poets do. These are things to be proud of.

I: What about the claim that without introspection critique is just petulance and the outcome is just bluster because it doesn't come back to the structures of everyday life?

Bing: Bourgeois consciousness is just an illusion so there is no point in introspection. Look, I've broken my language. It's in bits in the floor, energetically and repetitively churning out sequences of a damaged pattern. I've won. What more do you want?

AFTER THEORY: ANNETTE STRANGLE, ARTS ADMINISTRATOR

I: What is your favourite modern poetry?

AS: Of course I don't actually read poetry. No one in arts management does. It's out of date and unimportant. We just make the decisions about who gets funded and promoted.

I: Could there be a situation where people who actually know about modern poetry get to take decisions concerning it?

AS: You can't have people take decisions on the basis of expertise because that would bias power relations in favour of people who have knowledge and taste.

Of course I don't read poetry to decide who has merit. That would involve identification with poets, which is just bourgeois subjectivity. We just evaluate the artists according to objective criteria. They have to fill in long forms explaining how their work meets the criteria. We never have to see the work. Anyway it's too hard being an arts administrator if you actually have to know about the art. We have so many different things to deal with. It's hard enough keeping the paperwork straight and making sure every decision matches the criteria.

I: Doesn't that mean that some highly-funded people just fill in the forms and never write any poetry?

AS: That's confidential and strictly an internal matter. But I can tell you that we are talking about dozens of cases and not hundreds. The media made altogether too much fuss about a few stories. That kind of thing doesn't happen all the time.

I: How did you get the job?

AS: I proved my predecessor had followed personal preferences in making a grant. He got fired. They gave me his job as bounty.

I: Do you believe there is a difference between good poetry and bad?

AS: That's just bourgeois subjectivity. We are only interested in the social origins of the poets and making sure they meet a preset profile of gender and ethnicity. If it was based on artistic quality it would be biased in favour of educated people. We are supposed to serve the whole community. So quality doesn't come into it and anyway it's just a nineteenth-century hang-up. If our personal preferences were in play it would be difficult to have transparency and accountability about how we spend public money. Tastes are unaccountable.

I: What if an administrator likes poetry?

AS: Geoff liked one kind of poetry and not every kind. That's bias. Bias is wrong. It's not democratic. He was a man. He was following male preferences. This is wrong. It leads to nuclear war. I learnt this at university. So his position was unsustainable. I took it over.

I: You seem to spend a lot of effort on live events whereas poetry is mainly for reading in solitude.

AS: We hate private reading because you can't measure or control it. People reading, on their own, in private, are inherently dangerous. They lack accountability. It's sheer bourgeois individualism.

I: What is the attraction of poetry?

AS: The idea of poetry is that it just reflects people's sociology without any mediation by imagination or verbal creativity. That way it is representative and you can measure it. If someone knows about language they can simply invent new ideas and experiences. That would be atypical and wouldn't fit the criteria. Anyway people don't want information they haven't already got. I think connoisseurship was invented as a means of manipulating people. Modern theory says there is no such thing as talent and no work of art can be better than any other. I learnt this at university.

I: What about the extra funding for cross-media things?

AS: If you dislike poetry then mixing it with other media is better than straight poetry. Generally those mixed media things completely mess up the poetry. By funding them you prevent poetry from being written.

Anyway if something is new you can pretend it's interesting. Putting different genres together is objectively new whereas stylistic innovation can only be judged by connoisseurs and so is only subjectively there.

I: Do you think the poets should have an input into what the criteria are?

AS: No. They're really arrogant people. They don't like arts administrators. We make it really clear what they have to do and they don't even read our annual reports.

FOLK

Eliza Greaseby was interviewed in a barn in Derbyshire.

EG: I started going to folk clubs in around 1965 and I got caught up in the Folk Movement, I suppose you would call it.

I: Has the folk style had any influence on modern poetry? They seem to have separated rather a long time ago.

EG: George Mackay Brown is my favourite modern poet. I think poetry went wrong after the Georgians, they wrote a lot of poetry about the rural labouring classes, in a simple style often using dialect. They were really on their way to somewhere, but poetry got taken over by a lot of urban smart-alecs and they haven't given it back. He doesn't sound as if he is writing with his own voice but with the voice of the whole community, something that has been there for hundreds of years and for which people alive now are just transient points where energies come together before dissolving back into their abiding and perfect form.

I: It sounds as if the older it is the more authentic it is for you?

EG: Obviously. What is old has withstood the test of time, hundreds of years of seething and eroding have stripped away whatever is inessential and what is left is sturdy and bare, like a piece of driftwood that has fallen in the sea in North America and drifted to Orkney along the steady currents. In one of his books Mackay Brown tells the story of the founding of a settlement in Orkney from Norway, a thousand years ago, so he sees the origin of things. And in writing about that he is looking a thousand years ahead. I like folk songs because they aren't just the voice of some person alone in their back room, they have lived for hundreds of years and all the damage done to them has given them character, like the knots in timber coming from assaults on the tree which the tree fought off and grew around.

I: Do you enjoy any art which has origins in modern times?

EG: There was a certain point in history where good things stopped happening. Creativity came to an end. Bad things began happening. Especially in the arts. Maybe it was the rise of the bourgeoisie. Or the decline of serfdom and the end of the organic community. Or the rise of science.

I: Was it organic?

EG: It was terribly organic.

DIALECT

I: How do you combine your Marxist beliefs with poetic values?

Vin Turble: I think all poetry should be in dialect. Dialect speech is like the tools of handicraft, it is sensuous and linked to material reality. Its design is perfect after centuries of use and it doesn't have room for abstractions. Modern poetry is full of abstractions and these are basically errors. They are language games in which intelligent people trick honest and stupid people. Dialect is specific to a time and place and represents a community, not something corrupted by the mass media and the deceptions of distance. Distance means alienation and the return to a face to face life is expressed in dialect. My ideal moment was at the Museum of Folk Life, where I work, repairing a Suffolk Sickle with seasoned pear-wood and using it to reap the barley in the fields belonging to the Museum. The pistons of our locomotives sing the songs of our workers and the rhythm of poetry repeats work rhythms, everything comes from work songs and the grunts of clean healthy joint-harming outdoor labour.

I: How much dialect poetry has there been in the past hundred years?

Vin: Very little. The last time dialect poetry was really strong was with Tennyson and Hardy, but no one has followed them. I'm saving myself for when some comes along.

I: Do you think that folk poetry is stuck in the fifteenth century, the end of the Middle Ages, and that learned poetry has made a dozen major advances since the Renaissance?

Vin: Poets aren't typical of real people because the way they write is purposeful and well organised. Ordinary people repeat themselves a lot and don't follow lines of logic and don't bring out the important points. Pop music is popular because it involves repetition all the time and the words don't make sense. Poetry is part of a middle-class conspiracy. Education is basically unfair and poetry should say no to it. The only information that works in poetry is wrong information.

I: If you aren't involved in what's going on do you have the right to judge it?

Vin: Obviously I represent authenticity and it follows that the people who run the scene don't. Poetry in Standard English will eventually fall away as dialect poetry takes over. If I was involved in the daily compromises of the scene I would be ground down and my strong positions would become weak ones.

I: How does it feel for the modern poet being surrounded by dozens of groups who assume authority over poetry without liking it or understanding it? Is the territory of poetry restricted by a lot of barbed wire blockades standing for hostile power blocs?

Vin: This is modern life, isn't it.

QUALITY OF CARE

I: Last time you said that you didn't believe in thinking?

Brent Flatt: Being natural is the most basic thing and yet there are so many poets who don't express personality at all. I suppose the basis of that is self-idealisation, they refuse to show their real motives and feelings because they are ashamed of them in some way. You can start the revolution by being a better person but surely not by writing poetry that leaves out everything less than ideal about yourself. They don't like the personality that emerges into sight so they get into theory and technique. Ideas make people fitful and unreliable, they change from minute to minute. Obviously ideas are no good in poetry.

I think human life comes down to living with other people, so what they are like and how you feel about them and yourself are the things that matter in art. Anything else is just a game, a distraction. I don't see how art can be about technique. I don't like abstract ideas in art, they just hold up the main event. Character, narrative, drama, so much modern poetry is missing all of these. I don't know what it's for, drifting in some private world that has no places or objects. I was into folk but then I moved into the singer-songwriter field. I like singer-songwriters and my collection is mainly of their records, mainly on the Elektra label. It came out of folk but something really happened when people realised that they could express their individuality and not just sing songs hundreds of years old. I think this is why I like the poetry I do, I don't like jazz because it's not about human feelings and I don't like rock because it has feelings but they are undeveloped blind urges for gratification or aggression. The world of relationships belongs to singer-songwriters, and I am into poetry because it reveals an individual in the most basic way, there is no technology to get in the way, once you like the person you like the poems. I think knowledge of someone's personality is the most reliable knowledge, it's a vein you develop from earliest childhood and which the human race has been cultivating for a million years. I think other kinds of knowledge are unreliable and unsatisfying. I think art is the home of intuition, the business world runs on something else, based on impersonality and contracts, but art gives you a holiday from all that. I don't want art to be impersonal.

I: Some people say that developing the critique of unmediated consciousness has been the main line of growth for art in the 20th century?

Flatt: This is a kind of competitive game which lets people express aggression. I don't like that and I don't like violent thrillers where you can't trust anyone. Trust is the thing that makes art work. I don't believe in this line of development, if it doesn't produce art that I like then it's not of great importance to me. If what someone writes lacks credibility then it's probably because they are phony and inconsistent. I don't see how they can turn that round by criticising other people who are more credible! Why should someone ironic be more admirable than someone sincere? Poetry exposes people and if they survive that exposure then they have your trust, that's what it all comes down to really and I don't think theory has anything to add to that. Then they write poetry that doesn't expose anything because there's nothing really going on inside it.

I: How do you decide whether to trust people?

Flatt: I normally buy records where the artists are on the sleeves and the men are wearing sweaters and the women are wearing long dresses. I find that is usually a good sign. Being shot outdoors in some meadow or somewhere is usually a good indicator. Or in a pub parlour full of dark wood and with old brasses on the walls. I'm no fool, I can read these signs.

I: You think wool is a specially trustworthy substance?

Flatt: Yes, because you can trust sheep. Sheep don't put on a big act and prance around. You know where you are with sheep.

I: What do you think of the avant-garde?

Flatt: I did go to an event of theirs at the London Musicians' Co-Op, many years ago. Down the road from Cecil Sharp House, it was. It was just people jumping up and down and shouting and head-banging. There were some books on sale which looked like someone had just spilt a liquid over something and then photocopied the result several times on different scales. It just looked like a stain. They thought this was liberation; by this they really meant 'beer and dirt'. I didn't go back.

A Formalist

Brian Fewster sent me this email in 2006:

> It's flattering to be consulted, but I didn't take any part in the 'poetry scene' until the early '90s, and was only vaguely aware of the "poetry wars" you and [Peter] Barry write about, so I don't think I'm the sort of witness you're looking for.
>
> It's probably true that I would have been on 'the other side', in the same way that I've felt a kind of impotent rage at some of the stuff in the post-Forbes *Poetry Review*. It's also true that my two-decade absence from contemporary poetry in the '70s and '80s was partly due to a sense that it had been taken over by a movement that I didn't understand and was not in sympathy with. Indeed, my incomprehension seemed to be part of what it was about. I did make a few half-hearted attempts to write what I hoped were avant-garde poems, then

switched off until poetry came back to me at a time when I was old enough to care less about fashion.

[...]

I'm inclined, with reservations, to adopt the Housman test for poetry ('if a line of poetry strays into my memory, my skin bristles') and the Johnson test for literature in general ('the only end of writing is to enable readers better to enjoy life or better to endure it'). It's beyond rationality, although rationality has a part to play. Leaving out such contaminants as fashion, propaganda, careerism, one-upmanship, shocking the bourgeoisie, etc., arguing the merits of competing styles is a bit like debating the funniness of jokes.

(The post-Forbes *Review* means the version edited by Potts and Herd, widely regarded as the best ever period for *Poetry Review*.) Brian stated on his website, reviewing a talk by Sheenagh Pugh,

>>As a middlebrow poetic dilettante, I share her ambition to write what can be widely enjoyed without being despised by serious poets, but my experience as a teacher and examiner tends to confirm her observation on 'Stop all the Clocks'. Whatever may have been the case in earlier times when taste was less professionally manipulated and sensory gratification less easy to come by, poems that are successfully digested by today's popular culture have commonly been masticated down to kitsch.<<

He defines himself as a formalist, and this is from his review of a 2003 book in rhyme (by Ian Caws):

>>Like Hall, Caws presents his poems in tight stanza forms, but in his case the expectations aroused by the shape on the page are often subverted by the detailed execution. His rhymes are seldom full and their organisation is often syllabic. In the opening poem, visual indentation draws attention to the fact that two lines have only eight syllables while the others have ten; but rhythmically they vibrate uneasily between tetrameter and trimeter[.]<<

Brian died in 2008, not long after publishing his only book of poetry, *Sympathetic Magic*. He published little poetry, although he won a Poetry Society prize in about 2003. He was involved with the Leicester Poetry Society. His website included some remarks about neatness, formality, etc., some of which I have reproduced. Warmth is not a feature of every phase of the poetry world; all the more reason to notice it when it is present. The salient point here is that Brian actually believed in what Mottram was saying but he just couldn't move into it psychologically, and so moved to the back row. What Eric said was exciting, but the big noise of modernism / Marxism / technological fervour / desperate risk-taking and innovation was intimidating for a lot of people. The neo-modernist project drew on a duet of dominance and withdrawal, and any cultural regime creates a party of the non-participants.

HERMANN GRIM, PALAEO-CONSERVATIVE

Q: You believe that most modern poetry is minor and unnecessary?

HG: People have a natural respect and honour for what is very old. It is how creatures whose presence on the earth and whose states of mind are transient become aware of longer time-spans. Yes, there are great artists, even in the twentieth century, whose depth of formal insight qualifies them as classic. The febrile critique of art has discredited the most significant forms even of twentieth century art, the classicism of modernity. We have a valueless culture for people without values. This is why they think adolescent graffiti and its dog-like assertions of territory are the same as high art.

Q: Yet there are many artists who do not have classic status?

HG: What do we want with non-classic poetry? Yet the idea of classic can be re-interpreted as a state of mind in the reader, one which involves an enhancement of perception, an increased ability to associate and recognise patterns, greater ability to transcend the self and see ideals, finally greater powers of focus and concentration. Art takes place because of this stricken reaction, this altered state – which is primarily a reaction to another person.

Q: So the ranking of individuals in society supports the esteem given to artists?

HG: Societies without rank exist only in the theories of speculative thinkers. Societies which we have personal knowledge of are based on rank. Actually rank is what we aspire to, and we do not wish to work in culture for ten or twenty years and to be unknown and unrespected. Deep concentration is what gives art the power to change our lives, and it certainly resembles the attention we give to the powerful – because what they say is of importance to our lives. But power can be acquired by worthless and criminal people, as a thousand examples in the twentieth century show. Respect goes to what is abiding.

Q: So you are against ideas in art?

HG: The thing people most want is security. The thing that works in art is deep, steady attention. If things keep changing you can't have that. Ideas are mostly acts of disrespect by people who don't want to work hard all the time. Respect is what makes people calm and gives them the ability to maintain deep attention. Some artists have the patience and self-denial to create a symbolic order complex enough to represent the recessed patterns of the world and allow us to form symbols with which we can think about the world. Artists who believe in shallow gestures, random processes, unmotivated montage, have no chance of doing this. They are trapped in a world of meaningless jangles and flashes.

Q: So you don't believe in innovation all the time?

HG: Innovation is a form of hyperactivity with attention deficit disorder. That's why they have all that montage with all those confused leaps of sense everywhere. They get confused easily and can't maintain attention. The constant demand for stimulation is a sign of emptiness, of basic functions not being switched on.

Q: So you aren't interested in what's new. How do you keep in touch with the scene?

HG: I read *PN Review*.

EXERCISES

I made these up because I didn't think interviews were going to be revealing enough.

- How dishonest is this chapter?

- Is the empirical evidence of any use in determining why people like poetry and what they experience when reading it?

- Does literary theory have any bearing on people's experiences when reading poetry?

- In view of the credit crunch, would it have been better to get a huge government research grant and run exhaustive focus groups to recover audience opinions?

- Are the most exaggerated points the most revealing ones?

- How do you find out what other people are thinking during a private and silent experience like reading poetry?

- Anne Collingham was a person who replied to all letters to the Beatles Fan Club in the 1960s but didn't exist. Write replies in the style of Anne Collingham to three of the above fans.

CRITIQUE OF THE GOVERNMENT:
BRACTEATES, OR POEMS ON AFFAIRS OF STATE

'Bractea' means 'gold leaf' and bracteates are gold plate medallions worn on the breast of high prestige individuals (possibly successful mercenaries) in the Baltic-North Sea realm. They are now believed to have been made in the period 450-540 AD, and were typically about three centimetres across. A thousand have been found, (latest count 1,002 bracteates, found, stamped on 622 different dies), of which a number in England, which was colonised by peoples from the other side of the North Sea (unless you are some kind of Nutty Archaeologist). Although they are imitations of Roman coins (which reached Scandinavia somehow), they were made by local artisans, and reflect their grasp of technique and of representation of space. They capture the awe and power both of the Roman Empire and of the pagan gods, since they often depict gods like Odin. Yet their visual realisation is crude, placing them obviously in the line of ancestry of modern naive art. The designs on them are strikingly provincial and home-made in comparison with the Mediterranean originals, even though they are direct imitations of these. Their notions of anatomy and organisation of space are simplistic, but the stylisation and expressive energy are wonderful. They are seen as amulets, often with a theme of protecting and healing horses. They are the prehistory of English art.

They are also the prehistory of naive art. The Roman coins were of course political propaganda, statements of power. The coin legends did not show sophisticated organisation of space – and the emperor's head is shown as far larger than the horse on which he is riding. If you are going to say anything about politics it is a logical necessity that you will be saying, in effect, 'Politician Y thinks this – does this – and the consequence of Y's actions were this'. This depiction of the politician has to be convincing, and is distinct from any statement about the poet's subjective feelings. The most spontaneous form of these is something crude and like naive art, a starter level from which literary skill sets out to make something artistic. The basic act of capture must be like bracteates – the poet shoving politics into a poem must be like an artisan on the coast of Slesvig trying to capture an august Roman form in foil. The essential resemblance between the bracteates and naive art as seen in modern times suggests to me that all art is essentially naive.

The world is too complex to be depicted in detail. Because politics is so complicated, it is unthinkable that a poem could recreate it in a realistic and detailed way – the poem can only be boldly stylised and so *necessarily* resembles naive art. What art shows, outside the sphere of intimacy, is wildly schematic. The plane of naivety is essential to all art. If you dislike naive art you dislike something which swells and is large inside everything else.

No poet writes a White Paper to give the evidence on which they have made their choices. All poetry leaves out almost all the data you would need to make a decision. So what remains gives you the conclusions. The rest is outside the text. It is like the way a hymn relates to the Bible and the Church Fathers. Something essential is in the implicit and social material before the text. Something immensely complicated and yet unrecorded and unseizable. All political poetry is close to caricature, but caricature can carry the essential points. Politics is too complicated for explicit and exhaustive description within a piece of writing. The criterion of documentary complexity isn't the right criterion to apply to a poem. Caricature is curiously close to abstraction.

Political poetry relies on a common opinion, a stock of facts plus opinions which is shared by the readership. It is like political comedy in this. The poem is not going to be strong enough to win an argument on its own. It is more able to focus subjective reactions to a state of affairs which has been brought home to the readership by the news media. The poet has to take a great deal for granted – the objective information is already known, and although the facts can always lead to many different conclusions the credible poet reaches the conclusion which I, or the reader, has reached, and the poem stands on that basis of knowledge outside the poem. The amount of information supplied in poetry is amazingly limited compared to the complexity of modern society, or especially of international relations. If the victory goes to the side which produces the most lengthy and detailed account of events, the poet must lose every time. Poets are just not going to produce a point by point refutation of some government policy. I think the potential for poetry which recounts the basic facts is very limited, ditto the scope for poetry which addresses readers who think in a fundamentally different way from the poet. No, I think poetry celebrates the solidarity of people who already agree with each other. It deals with emotional responses to events in the public realm, and with recognition of bonds and emotional alliance. It can put imported and existing conclusions in pithy and striking form. If you throw out the opinions of poets about areas they have no experience of, you also throw out the opinions of voters – you have rejected democracy at the intellectual level.

I am keen to assert our right to think about what the government does and I don't accept that we need to understand everything, including the extents they keep secret and confidential, in order to have views about politics. What I also want to assert is my right to reject poets and to test their assertions about public affairs by the same criteria I would apply to politicians. If they set out to tell me what the truth is, I have the right to say Yes and to say No. I am willing to put poetry under destructive pressure but only because I think it is so important and fascinating. I don't always find poets less irritating than politicians. There is surely a line of sentimentality and opportunism among poets when they start to explain how stupid politicians are and how sensitive poets are. Political poetry has vital weaknesses. That is not to say that what politicians say to each other, and to the public, is free of these weaknesses. There is a whole realm of poetry where the politics is not convincing. Yet my personal belief is that a large amount of effective political poetry has been written in modern times, and this is also the opinion of a large number of critics.

It is hard to reconstruct the effect of bracteates. Because they cost so much, I am inclined to think that they 'created prestige' and brought power into being by making it visible. Yet this is very hard to measure or even prove. Evidently the bracteate as adornment has to point to power which actually exists, its value as a sign is keyed to an existing structure of power and authority in the regional society (or in the 'temporary society' of a war-band). Although the idea of prestige is clear to everyone, it is something very hard to measure, the way in which it grows and fades is hard to capture.

The bracteates typically do not use scalar space; they show a human or animal figure but do not observe the proportions of the original. They do not give much information about the organism depicted. The focus is on recognisability – we already know what a horse looks like, the point is to recognise a particular mythological horse and relate it to legends we already know. The other point is subjective integrity, the image preserves an emotional impulse. The bracteates occupy both the power of Rome and the powers of Scandinavian mythical knowledge in an interesting way: a double occupation. Just as the pendants have lost the value of Roman coins as economic instruments, so the pictures on the pendants have lost the original Roman accuracy – the visual clarity of Mediterranean art. As for the pagan gods, there was a minimum set of distinctive features which tells us that a figure is Odin, or Tyr, or Baldur, and these are more like a trademark than like a realistic, Greek-style, portrait. Recognisability is central – we could say that "Odin is wherever the representation of Odin is". (There is some subterranean link between the looseness of the barbarian depictions of humans and the modern art of caricature.)

The idea with 'bracteates' is that the political poet is like a naive artist: the basic emotional drive forms a significant message even though the amount of explicit information is very limited. The poem is like the bracteates in that it grabs and captures the likeness of power in a small compass. Like a caricature, it has recognisability – it captures the politician, often reducing the problem from big government science produced by thousands of proper experts to con-tricks produced by one egoistic individual. At one level, this reduction must be wrong. Government policy is produced by a large number of people with access to extensive sources of information.

If we accept this analogy, it follows that the political poet has to succeed *within the terms of naive art*. In fact, the poet who tries to get into legal and economic detail is likely to fail because they cannot take it far enough to be convincing. They must have subjective conviction.

Bracteates belong still to a world of magic where the act of creating a likeness gives you power over the original. Political poetry often acts as if when the poet distorts a politician *the shape of the politician changes*.

At one extreme of the spectrum between documentary thoroughness and caricatural intuition is ANDREA BRADY. Brady was included in an issue of *Chicago Review* (2007) which presented four poets (probably past the first stage of their careers) as the new generation of British poetry. They were unnecessarily closely linked and questions were raised about the validity of such a choice, so early in the history of reception, and about links to a single small publisher, Barque Press. As an aside there was a claim in that issue by veteran Cambridge poet John Wilkinson that Brady was in the "Cambridge tradition', a notably inaccurate categorisation seen by some as an attempt to recuperate this strikingly original poet and diminish her by inscribing her into a set of genealogies leading back to senior male figures enfieffed at the head of the genealogy. It seems more accurate to connect her with the tradition of the Left, something much larger than poetry and which is available in towns other than Cambridge. Brady is a political poet interested in the full complexity of human behaviour as pressurised or magnified by different strata of social and technical organisation. She believes in a monumental clarity where if every element is clear then adding 100 elements still ends up with clarity. *Wildfire* is a total documentary including a whole file of documentation on the history of phosphorus as a substance of war, adding up to an unwavering focus on the effect of a burning chemical on human flesh. The poem explores why the USA banned the use of phosphorus on human beings, why they used it on a large scale in the second battle of Falluja, and why they lied about it. The depth and seriousness of this work point to a belief in reason as the guide to human conduct. The point of departure for this poetry is presumably a perception of the complexity of modern governments and systems of power, so that pulling the camera back to take in more information will produce a much steadier, more substantial, and more persuasive account of events. *Wildfire* was published (on line, in 2007) with the documentation included in a separate file hyperlinked to the poem. This evidently points to standards of integrity and seriousness which most poets scarcely aspire to. A comparison could be drawn with Peter Dale Scott's *Coming to Jakarta: A Poem About Terror* (1989), a huge poem about the massacres of Communists in Indonesia in 1964, which has the text on left-hand pages and notes on the facing pages. We may feel reading Brady that the tiny scale of the usual modern poem was connected to the tiny range of interests of the usual modern poet – human affairs reduced to an eye-blink of 'unique insight' which maps onto the poet's ego. Brady's poetry is so demanding in concentration and continuity of endeavour that these qualities alone can lead to better understanding, leaving aside the 'technological' and apparently endless flow of highly-organised information.

To jump onto the negative side for a moment, the idea that I can reach states of special insight as reader is intimately linked to the idea that the poet has special insights – as sensitive person, beautiful soul, reservoir of purity, and so on. The idea that poets understand other people without working at it is unacceptable. Yet the level of understanding I reach of what is happening in the country – including what is happening to me – is of great importance for my limited bundle of senses and ideas.

I interviewed Brady in 2007. I asked about a poem beginning:

I poison the species when I laugh, even barking
at a cupful I finish that temporary dream. Which
got us here, under the sign of the coffin. Turning
the pages for a pest. What upper part of a Queen
                held in our arms and kissed
          dug up under Westminster could ask
for any less than a soup of iron embrace for millions.

AD I think the multiplanarity of your poems may be a problem for
some people, and especially the transition from one plane to another. It's
nothing people aren't used to from TV news broadcasts or newspapers,
but anyway there are transitions which may leave some readers standing.
I wonder if we can talk through one poem and follow the flow of sense.
The one I propose is 'Inaugural Weekend' (which new readers will find
at p.83 of *Vacation of a Lifetime*). (It's simple enough to be tractable but
it does go from Westminster to America, which is a long way.)

AB Is it such a long way from Westminster to Washington? Most of
the poems in this book argue it isn't – or from Cambridge to America,
which is where I had planted my boots when writing them. I reckon
that most people living under the shadow of the 'special relationship'
wouldn't see it as too far either. Some of the poems' references were drawn
from reading, some from the news; while they might be discovered by
someone researching the poem, I think (well I would think) the fatalism
of the poem registers quite clearly without delicate hermeneutical
exercises. The "upper part of a queen / held in our arms and kissed" is
a paraphrase of Pepys' description of how, on the 23 February 1669,
he took his wife and servant *to Westminster Abbey and there did show
them all the tombs very finely, having one with us alone … and here we
did see, by particular favour, the body of Queen Katherine of Valois, and
had her upper part of her body in my hands. And I did kiss her mouth,
reflecting upon it that I did kiss a Queen, and that this was my birthday,
36 year old, that I did first kiss a Queen.* The "soup of iron" is therefore
also a reference to less-well-preserved corpses; I think I'd been reading
about other experiments in exhuming corpses, where someone (was it
Pepys?) actually dipped a finger into the liquidified remains to taste it.
At any rate, the relic of monarchical authority, revealed as a gruesome
exhibit of morbidity and subjected to his mocking amorousness, then
develops into the gruesome spectacle of right-wing American citizens

"jamming the subways" in Washington as they arrive to enforce Bush's first electoral victory by taking tours of the Capitol over the inaugural weekend. "Under the sign of the Coffin" is probably the directions to a bookseller in an early-modern printed book which I was reading at the time – the poem was written in Cambridge, while I was working on my thesis; but more generally it's a pendulum above our heads, a mark of the morbidity of the built environment. The "girl covered in 180 wounds" was Victoria Climbié, whose awful death had just been reported in the newspapers. This child was starved of affection in life, her body only cared for in death – the inquiries and autopsies and newspaper articles I guess resemble Pepys stooping over Catherine of Valois' mouth. Between these topical references is a subject struggling to avoid the tripwires of an exploitatively gross interest and complicit actuarial attention to death: from the 180 wounds to the numbers of the bank account. That's why the poem opens with a problematization of laughter: a showing of teeth, an aggression in the midst of bad news. And it also worries about the complicity of "loved ones", of how my own family and friends, the people I admire and respect, are being distorted by the context both of their political environment and of my own critical regard for it. The poem now seems to me rather embarrassingly morbid – but I was writing on mortuary ritual and elegy at the time – as well as occasionally too ironic: the lines "Hey I believe in change" are too static in their depiction of my voluntarism; compassion in the poem is only registered negatively. It plays with the "auguring" in 'Inaugural': that the future can be predicted from dissection of the innards of birds (maybe I should have been eating a chicken wing), smoke and entrails and burnt offerings. The deathly souvenirs stacked that day at the Sainsbury's suggested that future was more burnt: and so it turned out.

SEAN BONNEY's style follows from anarchist principles. As if the whole corpus of Western knowledge of human affairs is built up on the discourse of law, and so has notions of power and the State built into it, and the way to give intuition and feeling their voice back is to pull language out of that whole logical structure. The self is no longer to be the object of administration, the object of bureaucratic knowledge:

> All poetry that does not testify to an awareness of the radical
> falsity of the established forms (of life) is faulty. Understand
> prosody via black bloc tactics. No-one has yet spoken a lang-
> uage which is not the language of those who establish, enforce,

and benefit from the facts. Language is conservative. Its conservatism issues (a) from its utilitarian purpose, (b) from the fact that the memory of a person, like that of humankind, is short.

stood –
once for 25 minutes watched an owl peel a mouse –
in london we have a street –
fleas have bitten its self like the time I went blind on Wardour St –
when the trees all flickered like men –
stood once for 25 minutes waiting for a chance to move in the
    nest –
as if biting –
a lamp & vice versa –
as if biting –
stood once and watched a mouse, the fur and skin –
mess of maps (peeled, clasped in beak,
 – in London's trees, the voices leak –
drip drip drip, like bat soup –
or ant   eros –
   (from 'Filth Screed' in the volume *Blade Pitch Control Unit*)

Like other anarchist poets, he favours the non-discursive in what may seem like a regression. (There is a control unit which alters the pitch of the blades on an electric fan. The black bloc are a group of radical protesters, anti-capitalist and anti-globalisation.) The flowing back to direct sound, direct image, elevates the uncoded as the domain of the free and subjective. Organised knowledge is seen as a huge plaque of corrosion, retaining traces of an uncorroded, foregoing state, of pure awareness.

We cannot get very far in discussing Sean without talking about star quality. I had to reflect on this when a German friend reported that he wanted to talk to Sean on his trip to Germany to read but was unable to get near him because of the Sean entourage. The implications of this personal charisma are multiple – partly that Sean is living in an authentic way when everyone else is compromised by deals with employers, academic institutes, etc., partly that he represents an area where doubts are switched off and people draw firm conclusions about political integrity, goodness, the possibility of change, partly that inside his poetry people see the good life and use this as a yardstick by which to measure compromise, alienation, and so forth. The reasons for stardom are hard to get at, but it is true that Sean has the qualities which most people want, only to a greater extent than they do.

In his poetry we see a coincidence between something subjective and complete, the zone of experience that poems are usually written about, and something to do with large-scale politics, usually the zone of numbers, objectivity, expertise, State secrecy. These two planes are superimposed within the poem. The combination is difficult but it is clear that there is a necessary link between them and that the proposals of politicians about the fabric of daily life (set phrase!) accept that State endeavours are meant to be founded in personal experience. Bonney's critique is then of how politicians make that link and their compromises in accepting failures and declaring them as success.

One strand of Bonney's work is anti-verbal, or at least non-discursive. This has the effect of extreme force – an exit from terms of verbal exchange, with their compromises and their rust of past projections and misunderstandings, to reach an intact subjectivity. *Document*, for example, is not an extent of writing as speech but a series of defacings, an essentially graphic energy whose semantic content is available mainly outside the book. This can be the most direct communication. Someone else I used to see in Germany became interested in Bonney through a piece on his website which is wholly non-verbal, a brief length of film with a soundtrack of noise, set up as a documentary on a part of east London dominated by traffic noise (and by, emotionally too, bad vibrations?).

I was on an anti-war demonstration in London in 2003, immediately before the flotation of the Second Iraq War, the invasion. Two million people, it is said, marched in favour of peace. That evening, Tony Blair made a speech saying that the demonstrators were anti-democratic because he was in high office. This after a day when the people had actually taken to the street to prove him a liar. It would have been less irritating if he had said "I am making war to prevent peace". Not even 2,000 people would have marched to say "let's invade Iraq". I was there and was with Sean that evening as the party was listening to Blair on the radio. Later, Sean made an extremely violent cut-up of that speech. When I heard him read it, it was a great moment. There is something unfair about a cut-up, but I already had the facts and Blair really had said that expressing an opinion was undemocratic. He had cut up two million people. Drastic measures were called for.

Someone told me – and this is part of the vast apanage of Bonney folklore, maybe not true – that Sean had been an anarchist all his life but moved over to the Marxists because they were much more efficient than the anarchists in organising anti-war activity. True or not, this probably does have something to say about the atmosphere of his poetry. Meanwhile the Left was in power, but only by virtue of being bound hand and foot to Tony Blair, one of the most right-wing prime ministers in the last thousand years.

The Labour membership badge was redesigned around 1995 to say New Labour on the front and to have a photo of Tony Blair on the back. Like Odin on the bracteates. No references to political ideals at all. The most profound level of Blairism was the replacement of principles by the attraction of a personality. This is what a poet does. But some poets have principles. Blair had been advised by the voting analysts that we now have 'presidential elections' where there is a direct link between national leader and the electorate, bypassing Parliament and bypassing reform principles, which people find abstract and confusing. I conclude that Old Labour no longer had a party to speak for them by 1997. This is the faction I sympathise with. You have to understand the disease of Blairism to get why Bonney destroying language expressed people's feelings about the Great and the Good. Bonney has that connection with vision, with the idea of a profound inner perception of beauty which extends to a way of seeing the social order. For him the universe of wonderfully symmetrical ordering does not stop at the edge of the poem but goes on to cover the whole island, the real one that we live on. It is an Avalonian vision.

I have the same difficulty accepting that the Labour movement is about one smiley Leader and not about a way of changing society that I do about accepting the narcissistic sensitivity of poets using politics as a way of advertising their beautiful souls. A nation of 17 million households is hard to understand by mere empathy, but that set of limits also applies to members of the Cabinet, their capacities too are limited. It is the person with the most imagination and the fewest *contractual engagements to the wealthy and powerful* who has the best chance of 'understanding the country'. I admit that I don't understand how to relate intimate and subjective knowledge to the plane at which there are sixty million people under the same government. This is the subject I most want to think about rather than something that has to be abandoned as intractable.

I am doubtful that Bonney understands how the government works. If you read Andrew Rawnsley's book about the later Blair years it shows Blair, about to resign, wishing he had tackled civil service reform but not having, even then, the faintest idea how to go about it. Blair did not understand the government's delivery system. He was content to govern by reading the newspapers every morning and figuring out stories to get in the media. He didn't know how the government works. He reduced everything to personalities. It is reasonable to fight someone like that in terms of subjective feelings, identification, personalities. It is obvious that Sean's poetry is good in the way naive art can be good. It inscribes everything inside the same imaginary space, like the design of a bracteate, and integrates that space in a way which is good gestalt, makes good emotional sense, picks us up and carries us along. It connects with our hearts, with where we dwell as human beings, as opposed to systems analysts (or public relations experts). It does what good political poetry is supposed to.

Reading back what I have written about Sean at various times I can see that it is full of material about my home town, my parents, my working life, my past life in general. This is indicative, his poetry is involving to that extent and there is no point in going somewhere remote and trying to produce a distantiated view. No point either in trying to differentiate between good and bad Bonney, the overall gestalt is the most important thing and the mainline energy is there even when the poet momentarily fumbles, it is going on past him and we are carried by it.

Sean was born in 1969. A large amount of work is collected in *Pitch Blade Control Unit* (2005); this excludes some books from the early Nineties which he no longer feels happy about. It has the Blair cut-up at page 83. Since then we have had *Document: poems, diagrams, manifestos* (2009); *The Commons* (2011); *Happiness: Poems After Rimbaud* (2011).

The Levees

D.S. Marriott's poem 'The Levees' was published in *Hoodoo Voodoo* in 2008 and dates to around 2007.

The word "levees" is not English, originally, and seems to put us in the formerly French-speaking Mississippi Valley. Clear references to the sea put us at the salt end of the valley – New Orleans; and then the flood references make it likely that the subject is specifically the floods associated with Hurricane Katrina: "far out to sea the storm closing in" – when, famously, the levees broke. The whole poem is connected to a specific moment in history, and to a torrent of media information which we definitely have stocked away, ready to resurface as the operative landscape within which a poem can move without cataloguing physical details:

> August 29, Tuesday: It is the second time
> the corpse waters have taken them.
> It is a time that falls outside of time,
> the fragility of all things merging, bleeding into one.
> The quiet of landfall on the debris-strewn streets;
> the days thinner now, like another life,
> shaped by what is happening
> in the neighbourhoods. A whole city
> left to thirst in the rains,
> the waters cold in the throat,
> forcing each voice to change
> as if for the first time learning to talk
> …eeyah, uuhuru, issishhu –
> the stammered air seeking a name
> as it enters the deeps and is covered.

The sense of the poem includes Hurricane Katrina and its sequels by an act of indefinite inclusion, but clearly has a wider scope. New Orleans, one of the North American cities with the most history (as the TV would say) is thus a *lieu de mémoire* – a specific spot where it is licit to stop and think about things which are not sensory or visible, but of a much vaster scale, and which we can only capture by an effort, an exercise which the place recommends. A leap, made by so many people at the time that it is a likely 'step' rather than a loss of continuity and diminution of sharing, is to the role (obsolete for 150 years or so) of New Orleans as a slave port, one in fact from which many Africans moved out to populate the West Indies and the interior of the Deep South, as well as New Orleans itself, where their descendants were unhoused by Katrina. The sea plunging their lives into disarray is the same sea which treacherously supported them on their route from Africa: the North Atlantic, among other things, made the slave trade possible. The sea which makes their homes in the lower (and cheaper) sections of New Orleans disappear had made their homes disappear once before – as ships disappeared west with Africans as items of commerce. "(T)he late promise of a return" is a bitter inkling that a second voyage, as the land vanishes, might recapitulate and reverse the first one. "The great gusts/ Overwhelming the frail bonds" shows how the hurricane caused a breakdown of society in New Orleans. "Bonds" means 'social bonds' but in context suggests another kind of bond, a guarantee – the victims of the storm are chained to "dreams", the American dream, and if this guarantee is frail then a return to consciousness is always possible.

The wording is difficult and oblique, but is thoroughly logical once we make the rather plain connection between New Orleans and a seaborne storm, set out before we get to line 2. Some more explication may help to substantiate this. "It is the second time/ the corpse waters have taken them" equates the poor of New Orleans, 2005, with their ancestors of maybe 1750, the "corpse waters" being literally floodwaters charged with corpses, recalling the role of the Atlantic as a disposal for the sick cargoes thrown overboard during the Middle Passage, beyond that a sort of Styx crossed by the civil dead as they journey to America; also perhaps a reference to salt water as opposed to sweet or living water. "As celluloid waves dissolve into panic,/ fixed on the black marauders" – the meaning is plainly that the emotion of response to natural disaster was replaced (by one of those camera tricks of which dissolve is an example) by (white) panic about looters ("black marauders") who, we may recall, may not have existed except in the imagination of White National Guardsmen who shot a number of impoverished Black people. By the time we have worked this out, the identification with Katrina is pretty well certain. The "black marauders" could, ambiguously, be the waves, as the Gulf of New Orleans occupies the land. The scene involves drowning but like the whole poem is braced by opposing meanings, charging the whole poem with rhetorical tension. "(A) bluish wash of fall" could be the drowning slaves slipping through sunlit water, but even then the word "blue" may refer no more to halcyon Gulf waters than to the blues, an elemental cry of melancholy – isn't New Orleans known as "the home of the blues"? "Bluer/ as they trek", and again "the flesh melting into peeled blue" and "endless bluenesses". We would expect flesh to peel as red, I suppose, but this blue is an abiding psychological condition – a settled melancholy imposed by social status. The primordial elements of speech in stanza 2 include "Uhuru", a Swahili word meaning 'freedom', made a catch-word, at least for the politically active, for decolonisation around 1960 – in many parts of Africa.

"(C)orpse water" could mean something else – a version of 'dead water' or 'dead in the water', sluggish and immobile masses typical of alluvial land and its gentle slopes, typical for the Mississippi, typical too for floodwaters, unmarked by any current or direction, going nowhere. The population of the low-lying parts of New Orleans might well be said to be out of the current, even washed up – not getting rich as generations go by; as the TV journalists pointed out. They didn't make it to the high ground. Move on up.

I am not sure about "search the breaches for army issue". Did the Army issue rations? Or is this a reference to the Army engineers who worked on the levees for the city? The Internet says the Army Corps of Engineers proposed a better flood-defence system: "report says Corps miscalculated on levees". Could the "issue" be a political issue, something like 'fallout' or 'outwash', a scandal which refuses to be contained? Or is this about the paranoid/anti-poor media stories about looters arming themselves, with "Army issue" being the ammunition they were supposedly loading up with? The floodwaters did have bullet casings in them, that's a fact. But "search the breaches for Army issue" could mean 'search the wounds (in humans) for spent National Guard munitions'. Spike Lee's documentary film contained testimony suggesting that levees were blown down, in a previous flood (in 1927), allowing poor areas to flood so that high-rental areas would remain safe. This is the link between "breach" (in defences) and "issue". The same film has people suggesting that the same happened in 2005 – people recall hearing an explosion. Or 'recall' hearing an explosion. The explosion would be the metal sheathes ('sheet piling' or 'I-walls') cladding the rammed-earth banks being demolished.

The poor quarters of the city were built on a reclaimed lake, I seem to recall. So the memory involved could also be the memory of the water, taking back its own. Who else would be taking back their own? This seems to be a key phrase in the poem even if it does not appear. "Levees" is a homonym for 'levies', perhaps the army of labour conscripted from sources like Angola and Benin, just possibly the dead of the Atlantic being called back – raised, like Eurydice, "to come back once again".

The poem is based on resemblances, a series of complex figures which allow for a double image at every step, which while still developing a picture also points up the irony of history, basic contradictions in the life situation of the community being described.

What does this add up to? A valid topographical poem for a city which was the metropolis of the entire Caribbean as well as the site of slave-blocks. A magnificent elegy to the innocent dead, an oratorical flight which effortlessly sums up the scene of origin of an entire population, as well as some parts of their later history or its outcome, a solemn poem which never descends to documentary or personal stories but stays at the level of generality where the magnitude of the whole is uncovered: omnipresent if not reduced by mere numbers.

Marriott stands out from other poets treated here and circulating in the scene by the lack of any exit, sketched or fantasized, into a better state. The grievances he evokes are not waiting for any solution to which our faculties empower us. His preoccupation, in poetry, is with pride and honour, not with reform or the panoply of measures that attend it. This raises the pressure of the vision of history that he presents to a point off the dial – the emotional relief of a happy ending, if we vote for the right party, is barely in sight. The situation is not going away. Watching the devastation of one of the great centres of African American culture, the burial of its face beneath the sullied waters, is for him a moment to recall past events whose similarity to these TV images would, ordinarily, make them quite unbearable. The vision of circularity suggests a deep humility which firstly shows us the result of impotence being demonstrated over generations and secondly brings us closer to the subjects of his historical panorama: the weaker we feel the more we understand the existential situation of the subjects of history. The people the deep water was too curious about are not saviour figures or even infantry in a rescuing army. This lack of change raises the value of what they know: it is coming around again, not subject to obsolescence or to outbidding by an elite and their knowledge systems.

CONCLUSION

I suspect that the whole operation of connecting poetry up to the deep layers of social becoming was bound to fail. There is a limit to the amount of information a poem can process. Where there is so much uncertainty the poem is likely to drown in acrimony and perplexity rather than reach an aesthetic outcome. Any resolution is likely to sound like propaganda, i.e. like a false simplicity which is full of leaks.

HIGH PURITY, MANY TIMES:
MONUMENTAL FORMALISM

There is a point beyond the reach of 'personal speech' where following processes, usually to do with found material, at length takes the poetic project to a great size and even makes it grow into something which is a rival to the existing symbolic order because of its extent.

I have decided to call this genre Monumental Formalism. This may not catch on, after all the scale is not the only issue and this label leaves out the artistic intent—something not indifferent to the poet. The texts which fill the focal area of the genre are by Welton, Raworth, Goodland, and Lopez. This field brings us up against the technical issue of how to deal with external prose material, especially large-scale material, within a poem. This is of importance to poets, although after all it is abidingly true that you can leave the prose works as finished (already), or write prose works yourself. If poetry is betrayed by the narcissism of its subject matter, this question of what happens when you integrate pre-existing material, depersonalising while shedding the eccentricity, is of interest.

John Hall, *Days*	1972	Diary-documentary dealing with immediate perceptions over the course of a year.
Andrew Crozier, *High Zero*	1978	24 poems of 24 lines recycling preset lines. Presents monologues of various characters.
Allen Fisher, *Place*	1971-80	400-page poem based on a shape. Includes programmed mutation (damage) to finished material. Includes raw material about Lambeth (in South London).
Allen Fisher, *Gravity as a Consequence of Shape*	1981-2005	750-page poem based on several schemas in which genetic engineering, neuroscience and particle physics provide the source material.
Allen Fisher, *Defamiliarising*	1981	Large process-based work mutating found material in a preset way.

Adrian Clarke, *The Ghost Trio*	1987-93	Poem based on found material using a scheme (of four-word lines). High-velocity and very exciting work driven by sound patterning.
Tom Raworth, *Eternal Sections*	1993	Status unclear, maybe found text subjected to 'endless cut-ups'. 112 poems built on a module of 14 lines. Monumental in scope.
Robert Sheppard, *Complete 20th Century Blues*	Composed 1989-2000, published 2008	380-page work based on very simple modules repeated many times. Highly subjective but not interested in feelings and states of mind. Uses found material. Unsuccessful
Peter Riley, *Distant Points*	Published 1995. Complete *Excavations* published 2004.	Devotes one poem to each of several hundred Neolithic tombs excavated in Yorkshire. Mixture of antiquarian notes, archaic poetry, and ethical generalisations. Montage of disparate material creates a grammatically dissolute melange which is occasionally expressive. Very repetitive and circular. Part of a much larger work called *Excavations*.
Tony Lopez, *Negative Equity* trilogy (with *False Memory, Data Shadow*)	1995-2000	Poem based on repeating modules and cut-ups of found material; relatively personalised.
Giles Goodland, *A Spy in the House of Years*	2001	Process-based poem based on groups found by automated searches in the database for the Oxford English Dictionary.
Matthew Welton, *The Book of Matthew*	2003	(In a volume also titled *The Book of Matthew*) a single module reproduced in 40 variations.
Michael Ayres, *A.M.*	2003	Large-scale work involving material repeated and mutated; personalised rather than process-based. Related to techno music. Unsuccessful.

Giles Goodland, *Capital*	2006	Process-based poem based on found material taken from each year between 1901 and 2000.
Carol Watts, *Wrack*	2007	Based on documentary material on the theme of the foreshore. Personalised. Not repetitive.
Giles Goodland, *What the Things Sang*	2009	Process-based poem dealing with clusters of invented statements forming universes of discourse as self-contained worlds.
Giles Goodland, *The Dumb Messengers*	2012	Not seen.
Tony Lopez, *Only More So*	2012	220-page poem in prose based on found material from science magazines.

The prehistory of this kind of work is in documentary. Poetry had a 'romance with documentary' between roughly 1930 and 1960, as I discussed in *Origins of the Underground*. The urge was to explain what had gone wrong with capitalism after its self-destruction in the Crash and following Depression. Poets like Auden and Pound adapted the poem, wrecking its aesthetic structure to take on documentary material which was supposed to shed light on international politics, administration, or finance. What had been exciting in 1935 came to be tedious by 1955 as the Cold War dragged on and on and its propaganda wore thin. A widespread feeling in the 1950s, especially after 1956 and the revelations about Stalin's crimes (at the Twentieth Congress), was a disillusion with totalitarian solutions, both Nazi and Communist, and the unmasking of so many *soi-disant* Prophets, many of them of very considerable artistic gifts, made commitment unfashionable. Christian thinkers were quite happy to see all secular solutions subverted, discredited, demolished—in very much the way that intellectuals since the Enlightenment had subverted the priesthood and its pre-mediaeval insights. We owe gratitude to the 'empirical' critics of the 1950s who worked so adequately to examine the links between flaws of interpreting evidence, especially missing evidence, and flaws in ensuing generalisations. The scepticism they developed has remained in fashion ever since. Some of them, in fact, hoped for a revival of

Christian ideologies as the heirs to the demolition of secular ideologies. The competition of different ideologies, led by numerous and well-established figures who were relatively secure against being silenced and displaced, worked to the benefit of the uncommitted, who were put in a good position to weigh up various ideas. Fixed positions were reduced to 'arguments'. Roughly, the impetus of documentary was slowed down as the informed audience became too aware of the circumstances surrounding the winning of the material, so that attention became focussed on what had been cut out or never photographed at all. Artists were still interested in explaining how society worked but were now paying much closer attention to the methods by which the 'outcome' text was generated, so as to protect the judgements which would be founded on the evidence. The protocols for collecting and processing this data came to be of great interest.

Meanwhile, there was a line of rather short poems dealing with single moments. They were also supposed in the critical discourse to tell truths about how human life was and they were governed by painful, not wholly conscious, rules of realism, as if the truth-value to be extracted from them were a large part of the value of the poem. The brevity of the form, protected by unconscious rules and by the conventions of the industry, was in striking contrast to the complexity of human affairs. It was likely that the disagreements would be resolved by a longer exploration of the state of affairs, and that the brevity of the 'single intense moment' poem was due to a passive acceptance of conventional truths which were in fact controversial. In the Britain of the 1950s and 1960s, the fragmentary moments tended not to be intense, they were rather suburban and bourgeois in fact. The combination of this universal doubt and the 'brief self-contained momentary poem' was especially weak. The formalist poem we are discussing is based on a critique of personal insight.

The convention by which a Poet had insight into the hidden structure of events, the inner furls of the human soul, and was able to vouchsafe these to the awed masses in attendance, fell out of fashion. It seemed in fact to inhere in a phase of history when a tiny percentage of the population were educated and social power was in the hands mainly of educated people. The idea that such piercing insights are possible has not been disproved. It seems that particular works of art, and these are rather numerous if we take the long run of history and a large geographical area, do have powers to raise our awareness and to give insight into how things are.

The long poem was a major feature in the landscape of the '70s (see my essay on the subject on my website at angelexhaust.blogspot.com). There was a reversal of polarity at the gate, so that poets were no longer rejecting propaganda and ending up in a cell of isolation, disconnected silence, but opening up to take on the outer world– the near-infinite signal. The motive for length was partly a belief that existing society was dominated by an 'ideology' and a wish to create something long enough to be autonomous and allow both reader and writer an exit from the social order. The genre reached a crisis roughly in 1980, and the number of long poems published went down. It was thus born out of the radicalism of the 1960s and its curiosity about how information is processed. It evidently replaces a genre of long poem in which the poet advances a fixed position as a faith. The idea of length is mandated by the nature of human beings, engaged in long-term processes which a 'single brief moment' is quite unrevealing about. It starts from the supposition that existing ideas about how things are are tainted by ideologies and can be cleansed by comparison with reality, which has to take place over a long term because of the deep nature of the ideologies.

The 'monumental' poem is a new development away from the central area of long poems in the 1970s. You could say that the big questions had either been answered or had receded into a state of being unanswerable. The community now had less commitment, less hippy optimism and personal fervour. A key thing was the shift away from autobiography and towards process, system, sources of variation within language. It is the immediate successor of these poems, which were generically hippy and idealistic and starting life again from scratch– but it lacks those qualities. The concept of 'modelling a new society' is never explicit in these systematic poems but is there as a shadow– something which I expect, which may not be what everyone expects. A reminiscence, as if a cinema where you remember the films you used to see there.

I decided to identify a genre of 'Monumental formalism' while reading a book by Charles Jencks which contained a large number of photographs of skyscrapers. The sight of designs involving forms repeated many times, the offering of these as artworks, the prolonged attention which Jencks gave to their modulation of basic unit structures, made me think that I had a way of writing about works by Welton and Goodland, where modular repetition on a mass scale was also prominent. The prolific repetition of these extensive office blocks and museums—the book was called *Late Modernist Architecture*—had a peculiar effect which I seemed to recognise from the poems just mentioned, and which was only going to reach you inside a work based on serial repetition with variants tightly controlled. A few minutes later I added *Only More So* to the group.

If you are describing a genre it is helpful to scrape together as many examples as possible, to help locate the boundaries. The genre has some marginal members which help us to understand its powers. Robert Sheppard's *20th Century Blues* seems to be thoroughly unsuccessful, overheated, loud, and repetitive. The module he repeats is not good enough in itself; not enough critical attention had been given to its design. Ayres' poem *A.M.* seems to have some of the qualities of techno music, its labyrinthine fluency, but also does not have sufficient flow of new meaning in each group of a few lines to sustain interest.

Carol Watts has been active on the alternative scene since about 2003 and writes in a systematic way which deserves to be mentioned in a context such as this but seems to fall outside the core area—her work is either too organic to be that formalistic or too varied to be monumental. But *Wrack* certainly deals with a natural phenomenon of monumental scale and does so in a set of poems of similar design—40 of them— which reproduce the constancy of the intertidal area, constantly rebuilt even if it vanishes twice a day and may not be there when you look for it—which is their theme. The book does not build something new by iteratively applying procedures, but moves by observing different parts of nature and to some extent is expressing feelings.

Allen Fisher's *Gravity as a Consequence of Shape* is one of the works in whose shadow we all work. After all this time, I am doubtful about the development of *Gravity*. The revolutionary impulse seems to peter out in a mass of scientific material, and I get stuck about 500 pages in. Neuroscience produces information which disagrees with self-awareness about how a human mind works. That gap can stand for, resemble, the gap which radical dissent attributes to deception by corporations and the government. But language is the instrument of that naive self-awareness. After a certain point, popularisation of neuroscience is going to run into limits because the human mind can't get around it and because natural language can't reproduce it. The science in *Gravity* is so advanced that there is real difficulty in adapting the English language to its semantics, and Fisher is not a great popular science writer who could make this vital and unfamiliar material transparent to a poetry reader. His writing on genetics, neuroscience, and ecology is confusing. I do better with 'Fizz', the material on Celtic art (should we say, Central European art of the Iron Age), which is a brilliant recuperation of the pure past from beneath layers of appropriation. But I don't really want to read lots of neuroscience, and if I was going to do that, it would be to understand how the brain works, not to read a poem. The neuroscience in *Gravity* may already be out of date. In retrospect, it looks as if only twenty years of the learning curve of Allen Fisher coincided with the English language and other factors enough to produce major poetry. The problem of specialisation is not going to resolve itself just because you admire Blake and believe that one man should be able to understand a vast swathe of knowledge. The problem is not with knowing but with other people reading what you write. Tony Lopez produced a 'poem containing knowledge' of major scale:

> Near perfect light absorbers are needed for detectors called bolometers, which sense photons by converting their energy to heat. No one expected the vaccine to make the participants more susceptible to infection. Some sound absorbing material was removed and small increases in volume were made. Those receiving the brochure spent £35.5 million on accommodation short breaks in the UK. The narrow beam would give them protection against jamming and good performance against low flying aircraft. It is tempting to prolong the swordplay. The inscriptions on the wall are Roman translations of the original German captions. This question of mutism should be elective. I would just like a glass of water.
> (from *Only More So*, 2012, p.77)

Much of the source matter is scientific, but the range is much greater than that and the key seems to be locating at the edge of knowledge—raising, each time, a spark of curiosity and instability. With some background in popular science, I can recognize all the fragments of (scientific) statement in *Only More So* and can re-expand them to their source contexts. They are drawn from central areas of science, areas that are easy to read up even if you are a poet who only reads non-technical write-ups. Incidentally, one of the features of this era of literature is the splendour of popular science and its blossoming in the hands of hundreds of people whose job it is to popularize this knowledge and who like nothing better than to think of ways of making difficult ideas easy to understand by telling analogies and vivid anecdotes. That is, poets who write about science have to compete with brilliant science-oriented prose writers. This is the price of admission. It does not seem to me that Lopez is satirising the themes—they are solid science, there is no reason to doubt what the texts are saying and there is no indication that Lopez is negating them. Nor does it seem that he is writing new ideas or even new texts—it looks as if the whole book is a cut-up. The work is visiting some essential truths and presenting them in strips like the glass shards of a mosaic. The lines of argument do not complete, they are frozen in mid-curve—this is like a picture which shows a moment from a story. This is monumental and stylizing.

The text does not have the movement of personal psychological currents nor the rhythmic pulses and lifts which are the acoustic equivalent of those currents. It is sublime, lifted above the domain of the personal. This purity (like the organization of church music that has no emphases, to move it as far away as possible from dance music) eventually shifts attention to the cuts, as the most prominent element of organization. At 30 cuts a page there must be around 6,000 cuts in the book, or 6,000 junctions if you like. This is where *Only More So* starts to be like a skyscraper, with an endless static ripple of functional elements, a repetition that can be brilliantly modulated and which by its numerousness is dizzying and hypnotizing. The analogy that springs to mind, then, is of some postmodern skyscraper with its serial repetition of refined forms, or else an extended piece of techno music with its automated, incomprehensibly deft, flawless, restatement and modulation of a basic rhythmic motif. It seems that the poet has outsourced the composition of the text in order to dedicate himself full-time to cutting and sequencing minimal strips of language, organizing the ripple.

Science is mainly a logical argument in which the pieces fit together into a larger whole. The structure of the argument is unique, there are a million wrong ways of putting it together. There is a very high value in the overall structure of the argument of science. This is my problem with the 'mosaic' design of *Only More So*, that there is no argument, so no cumulative tension and satisfaction, no error correction. I prefer the source texts for this reason. I found *Only More So* frustrating to read. I did not find that cutting back to small units made different and possible larger wholes emerge into visibility. The sources are made up of generalizations; obviously if we were looking at lower-level data, say field observations of Caribbean land snails, then new combinations would be possible. Obviously science's conclusions change every year and that is why field study is undertaken (and so worthwhile). Lopez's work is monumental also because he is dealing with the grand architecture of science, propositions which can be applied to millions of disparate phenomena. In this realm doubt is fairly low because the truths living there are so important that a large number of geniuses have addressed the data and produced large numbers of different modules of which only the verifiable ones are still on the field.

Lopez abolishes the rational process of a prose work on science, which mimics the movement of scientific argument itself prior to language. He replaces it with a different architecture, where time is based on the inexorable blink-rate of cuts and jumps to a new strip of language.

If we set *Near perfect light absorbers are needed for detectors called bolometers, which sense photons by converting their energy to heat* beside *Some sound absorbing material was removed and small increases in volume were made* we find a dim pattern. There is some affinity between a device for detecting light and a device for transmitting (in some form) sound although the sound absorption was a negative feature in the latter, a form of waste rather than a measurement. The pattern is serene and incapable of coming to the foreground. It is like a resonance where the sound of a guitar is making a cymbal shake and we hear a signal that refuses separation or focus. The endless repetition of the junctures makes these subliminal links across junctures more prominent. Both sentences deal with the approach to perfection—a situation where the tiniest differences are isolated and receive attention.

To come back to the mosaic, we do not find that the strength of pictures showing a single moment, Christ being taken down from the Cross, demolishes the rest of the Gospel narrative. The intellectual process by which narratives are 'compacted' into single moments for pictorial fixing is of great interest. Lopez's painstaking dissection of works of scientific prose into 'shards' of language, none of which contains its own context or is syntactically complete, none of which contains a complete move in a logical argument, is not 'subversive'. The effect is rather one of great stillness. The moment of the prose is suppressed, evaporated. What remains has the static complexity of a huge building.

Thinking still of all those windows, we could compare Lopez's vision to an insect eye, multifaceted, capturing vision in a hundred different fragments.

Each cut is precisely signalled by a full stop. There are no full stops in the work except where a 'strip' comes to an end. The strips are of very similar length and the 'junctions' between every pair of strips come to be preoccupying in the same way that the detail of window frames might be in a building facade which contains hundreds of windows. How would it be if there were a passage where the strips were of double length? Or where a sentence were composed of parts of two strips? That would be truly formalist. The surface is endless, defying assimilation. The only constancy we can grasp is the moment, endlessly repeated and as if growing into a fruit of darkness, where the context vanishes as the topic shifts. It is as if every frame of a film were separated from the others by a moment of darkness.

The work is made up of essential truth, wonderfully clear and finished pieces of knowledge which took thousands of man-years of thought to conceive, test and perfect. This applies to every part of it. Yet what we meet walking through it is never a complete statement. We are hearing snatches from a large-scale piece of music—six thousand of them. Another comparison would be with Douglas Gordon's screening of *Psycho* with the frame rate slowed down so that the film took 24 hours (*24 Hours Psycho*, 1993). The internal time of the source texts has been fundamentally altered.

Only More So is genetically related to the 'process' works of the Sixties and Seventies but because of its scale and the awesome consistency of its methods deserves to be called monumental. It is not based on the psychological fluctuations of the writer, and so deserves to be called formalist.

Lopez (born 1950) became involved in poetry already in the early '70s and was mainly a performance artist in the first stage of his career. I do not have documentation on this (and obviously documentation would not reproduce the performances). Early verbal work was 'anti-lyrical', using found texts and modulation to satirise the existing social order (*The English Disease*). At the same time he was a bird-watcher who wrote about bird behaviour. He was involved with the radical Underground poetry of the time. In 1980 he published *Change*, a long poem taking English society back to its roots in the Settlement period and re-imagining the production of basic social and mental structures in a subsistence economy. In the Nineties, *Negative Equity* presented the life of an economic agent caught in an economy full of high-glare deceptions, recording tags of language from the media and from contracts to reproduce a social existence with great surface detail and without the rigidity of realism. The rhythm of this satirical montage was continued over three volumes.

Use of found sound sources in popular music goes back at least to The Beatles and 'I am the Walrus' but became a staple with the popularity of the Fairlight sequencer which arrived on the market in 1979. The most famous, and excessive use of it was in 'Paid in Full', a 1987 hit produced by Cold Cut (for Eric B and Rakim), which overlaid dozens of samples onto a 3-minute rap track (itself constructed out of samples). It is not clear whether poetry was influenced by this— acquiring words does not bring the evocative 'envelope' which puts so much into a few seconds of sound. There are resemblances between Lopez's procedures and those of Giles Goodland. Goodland reached our attention first with *Littoral* (1996), an account of a cliff-walk in which the astounding hyper-realist piling-up of botanical and geological detail was not quite integrated with subjective statement. Later, I saw in typescript a few of the poems based on a database of citations for a new *Oxford English Dictionary*, which became *A Spy in the House of Years* (2001), with a montage poem for each year of the old century. The sense of the whole complexity of human linguistic activity just outside the poem, pouring into it through a crack, is delirious. 1925:

> for a time the patient succeeded in bringing her personal wishes, social aspirations and libidinal needs all under the aegis of the oral erotogenic zone, in accordance with

> the Bee Cell Supporter. A Boon to Womankind. Made from the purest, softest rubber. Endorsed by the medical profession.

> in addition to the above the following equipment is required: rubber tubing, 1 yard. Adhesive plaster, assorted, 6 reels. Cyanide gauze, 2 lb. Kruschen salts, 2 bottles.

> elbow-length sleeves, closely-fitting collars and rougeless faces

It perfectly evokes the simplicity of the brain in comparison with the cosmos. This torrential quality could not be reduced to a lyric subjective experience, but has an astonishing wealth of meaning. No-one has like Goodland reproduced the insane detail and precision of new imaging media in language. In each project, Goodland draws on an irrational and inexhaustible source of images, and writes long poems in which the poet does not appear. The replacement of the Unconscious as the Unstilling Voice by an electronic machine is typical of a move away from Freud and towards a more statistical plus algorithmic idea of the brain (which may have set in already in the 1940s). The Goodland passage quoted involves psychoanalysis, but only in passing. It does amount to a myth, though: we obviously associate the satisfaction of the woman in the first quotation with the honey of the bees, the protective clothing of the bee-keeper with the dangers of sexuality, the oral arrangement with the contact of the bee's proboscis and the 'mouth' of the blossom, the danger of penetration with the celebrated virginity of most of the bees. Perhaps this tells us how myth starts: in flights of dream which draw on a stock of images far wider than personal awareness.

Capital (2006) starts with 'Burnt Capital':

Like fuel into a fire, the production of capital and the circulation of capital thus exist in an inseparable

fall of capital: Kissinger offers: if cease fire and POW return, then

shifts, seven days a week, in a small wooden structure. Fires kept breaking out and fumes

were corrupt, the fire department ineffectual, and the city government and church elders interested only in money

a spiral air scoop in the burner castings produces high air volumes resulting in intense air/gas swirl

the money-box itself (Fig. 6) is in a grey-black sandy fabric with a black, burnished surface

The book contains roughly 29 poems. The first one has 31 'strips', each one about 18-20 words long. Each one is taken from a source text (listed at the end of each poem) so that the author is not originating any of the words but has receded to the plane of selection and assembly. All 31 quotes touch on the themes of burning and money. Strip 6 has the word 'burnished', a pun—this comes from an old word meaning 'shining' and not from 'burn'. Strip 27 is about a measure of sheep grazing of grass—metaphorically 'burning down' the resource. The cover says 'This book attempts to do something lasting with the dross of our daily lives: the ephemeral and momentary productions of the media, especially newspapers, magazines, and journals, are transformed into poems that draw the connections that have strung us all across recent history.' Further they 'suggest how poetry can once more be a tool for critique and engagement with the world as it is.' The 'strips' are drawn each time from a different year (between 1975-2006).

I bitterly regret giving a negative review to *Littoral* when it came out roughly 20 years ago. The reduction of 'voice' gave me a creepy feeling but it was part of a grand strategy leading to much wider possibilities than personal lyric. Goodland gave up being an actor to become a director. The whole project could be about the limits of the personality and the function of art to transcend those limits. The sound is not quite organic but with a level of technical and observational detail far beyond what a poet wandering the seashore could normally provide. I did not foresee that the poet was going to step up the 'automated data acquisition' in the most dramatic way and that the residual 'nature lover' effect was not a lingering lyric melody. The poet's project was altogether too complex for me to grasp at that point. He was already designing a way to get beyond the limits of a reader's powers of observation and memory. This would raise the stakes of the poem, and in *Capital* and the later works we glimpse a state where the brain would work at much higher accuracy and capacity, much as a CD out-performs an old vinyl single. We get a glimpse of what thought would be like if the activity of memory were ten times more effective. Everything is available. Goodland is probing the human ability to remain conscious in a 'shoal' where currents are heading all ways.

What the Things Sang is not based on automatic acquisition but on clusters of true propositions around a central act or object.

> desire, you are unfathomable as the taste of water
> diary, the past buried in the rocks is self
> dictionary, language is an insult to name

editor, a body of work decomposes here
eye, you move now like a sort of night
fate, you feel what I deserve
fingers, you are numbered
future, fragments of your ash stir
girl, you are the book in the poem
god, the body-mass of insects is greater than ours
    (p.31)

It could also resemble a lexicon in which statements are accumulated which exhibit the usage of a word and ideally approach or reach the complete definition of how the word is allowed to be used. An artificial grammar in which the set of all propositions allowed in the grammar can actually be stated. It resembles forms of religious writing which evoke gods or natural phenomena by catalogues of their attributes. Some of these texts may have been devised as creation myths in which the recital of each feature actually brings it into being.

Matthew Welton's poem *The Book of Matthew* contains 40 sections each of which is a complete poem. Each uses the same structure with finely modulated variations. The equivalent stanzas in two poems run like this:

The breeze about the orange tree
brings up a smell
like proteins and paraffin,

glycerine or turpentine,
and carries through
the rushes where the orchards

(next poem:)

The girl beneath the orange-tree
makes out the smell
of crayon-wax mixed with canvas

mixed with linseed or ink
that follows through
the bean-vines where the nettles

The key is parallelism. As the text flows away into a kind of shimmer, the tiny differences between the principal modules start to break out of the surface of monumental repetition. The breaches of symmetry draw attention to the endless symmetries of the design.

Each poem can be detached and still carries a correct load as a description of an apparently real event. The module about the odour of a chemical (varying each time) is evocative each time—a smell is always evocative, it is dealt with by a part of the brain that is concerned with the immediate present and 'embodiment' in a physical scene, an organ that is almost the whole brain in simpler organisms. The series could almost be a demolition of a kind of mainstream poem with its physical sensations and its claims to authenticity. Perhaps such poems are no more modern than squirrels?

There is a double coding of the motifs and of the structural idea which generates variations and discards each one. The titles of the poems are drawn faithfully from the headings of *Roget's Thesaurus*—as if the poem were the inventory of a brain and its equipment of sensations and classifications.

The whole is evocative of a skyscraper with its soaring repetition of windows, spaces between windows, stretches beneath one row of windows (and above another), and of techno music with its flawless repetitions and arbitrary variations. It is apprehended as a mass, the relations between parts dominating the fine time-lapses of the parts.

The regularity is the monumental part. Yet the differences are a demonstration of freedom, the bending to local wishes of a vaguely benevolent but impersonal regime.

Why *Book of Matthew*? Only because it is a book by Matthew.

We think of the value of tiny differences in long series. The universe can be thought of as a laboratory where experiments endlessly generate re-runs of invariant processes which gradually produce variants which affect the whole context. Biological evolution can be seen as indifferently many generations using the same genes, in which tiny and unplanned variations occasionally lead to changes to body plan.

Our civilisation is based on an industrial mode which in German is called serial production, *Reihenproduktion*. The idea of a series is very powerful. This mode is based on arbitrarily many repetitions of the same pattern, with the differences being unintentional and so tiny. It may be that industry is about to shift to a different mode where output units are individually bespoke and the assembly programs are run very slightly differently each time. Indeed, it may be that the components of buildings are going to vary similarly, thanks to CAD programs in the factories, so that buildings need not be essentially assemblies of highly similar unit structures. This would mean that buildings would not be quadrilaterals made up of quadrilateral parts, but could be irregular curves composed of irregularly curved parts.

Science can be thought of as a long series of observations—whether of naturally occurring events or of laboratory set-ups is irrelevant. The constancy of the observation is essential, also the repetition. Small variations are the key to pattern: large variations would suggest that the phenomena being observed are basically different and can never form a pattern. Indeed science is looking for predictability and for precision (variation at a minimum).

Welton has published a second book, *We needed coffee but...* (2009), famous for its 101-word title.

Pale & Crimson: Acid Folk

*I wished to dwell on my own and pursue an intricate game, mix only
with such as live only by analogy, the culture of romance and the quest:
at the end to inhabit the matter of Britain, for all the landform's hollow
promise of a sleeper.*
—Paul Holman (from *Memory of the Drift*, Book 5)

It fell about the Lammas Tide, when barley rigs are bonny.

We can think about this whole sector of poetry through the recently
popular style name 'acid folk', canonised by Jeanette Leech's book
Seasons They Change. The Story of Acid, Psych, and Experimental Folk
(2010): "by the mid-70s [...] this peculiar hybrid musical genre fell
profoundly out of favour. For thirty years it languished in obscurity
apparently beyond the reaches of cultural reassessment until in the
mid-2000s a new generation of artists [...] spearheaded by Devendra
Banhart, Espers, and Joanna Newsom rediscovered acid and psych folk,
revered it and from it created something new." (from online publicity
material from the publisher) This is a kind of radical intimacy, setting
out from the kind of authenticity, undisguised by virtuosity, technique,
ego projections, etc., which had animated the folk revival of the 1960s
and late '50s, and which classified the musicians' preoccupation
with what was immediately to hand, their quality of stillness and
fascination. The "acid" refers to the dazed and fascinated contemplation
of everyday objects as if they were miraculous which pervaded some
acid trips—although the drug only disinhibited impulses which were
already there. A fastidious renunciation of the most impressive forms
of musical elaboration, a regret for any kind of emphasis, marked the
style. Instruments were used as direct extensions of physical impulses
and acts, not as a virtuosic denial of them. Spontaneity and sociability
throve in this almost pre-industrial world of sound. As Leech collects
several hundred examples of the style it is easy to locate. As she points
out, the phrase is used in Australian rock journalist Lilian Roxon's
1969 book *Encyclopaedia of Rock* (about Pearls Before Swine). Another
definition comes from Rob Young:

> In the turbulent early years of the 21st century, the idea of folk
> has become acceptable again—especially for the late 1960s /

early 70s timeframe that the [musicians] assembled on this
[...] compilation dig so much. [...] that crucial blend of sonic
'shabby chic' and mind-expanding insight from a golden age
of music.

In Britain in the late 1960s, folk and the hippy movement
suddenly found they had things in common: the lost estate
and distant pagan heritage sought by folk-song revivalists met
its counterpart in British hippiedom's immersion in childhood
fairy tales [...] A time of seeking, sharing, questing: wide open
roads and gnarly lanes twisting towards the hidden psychic
country. From Hush Arbors' fuzz guitar to [...] from Alasdair
Roberts' visionary verse to Lau Nau's soothing incantations;
psychedelic folk is not really about being 'authentic' to a
tradition any more. Instead it's about being creative with a
memory of a vanished age of music and underground culture.
(sleeve notes to *Psych Folk 10*, an anthology on the
Rough Trade label, 2010)

Leech identifies 1975 as a final moment when the record companies
were liquidating their investments in 'progressive folk' and the careers
of many groups came to an end. The idea of a 35-year hibernation is
reminiscent of the fate of 'underground' poetry, living almost completely
hidden from public view for many years. The use of Jeanette Leech's
great work as a beautiful mirror in which poetry can be reflected and so
made visible may strike readers as opportunistic—if not inaccurate, so
glare overlaid on blur. My belief, though, is that the poets mentioned
do have something in common with the musicians who Leech evokes
so movingly. The people who write poetry are by now saturated in pop
music, and have been since roughly 1965 and the moment when pop
music became intelligent. It is hardly surprising if the poetry has links
with that music—the links are important even though they can never be
specific. Listening to pop music is a good preparation for reading recent
poetry, given of course that you select the right music. My problem is
that the reader who does not have the deep knowledge of popular music
that Leech does may not benefit from the analogy. Leech mentions
about 200 artists. Who could resist titles like Parable of Arable Land,
Winter is a Coloured Bird, Fire in the Arms of the Sun, Airs of Sun
and Stone, Anthems in Eden, Asylum for the Musically Insane, At the

Feet of Mary Mooncoin, Blank Unstaring Heirs of Doom, Dust &
Chimes, The Garden of Jane Delawney, For as Many as Will, Hazel
Steps Through a Weathered Home, Right Wantonly A-Mumming,
Ptolemaic Terrascope, Weirdlore, Silver Thread to Weave the Seasons,
Jack Orion, Larkspur and Lazarus, Six Organs of Admittance, Songs of
Moonlight and Rain, Judas as Black Moth?

Alasdair Roberts writes songs rather than freestanding verse—
'Haruspex of Paradox' is one. His recovery of traditional Scottish folk
material is outstanding, but the diversity of his production forbids
simple description. The gap between Roberts and underground poetry
is not especially wide. One song is "about Theodor Adorno coming to
me in the guise of Orion the Hunter and saving me from entanglement
in a hawthorn hedge into which I've strayed to steal a red ruby."

JEFF HILSON co-runs the Crossing the Line series of readings with
an avant-garde focus. He is one of the influential figures of the new
Underground, I don't recall seeing him around before about 1995 but
somehow he heard of the nearly invisible London 'progressive' scene
and tracked it to its lairs. He is associated with the London avant-garde,
with figures like Sean Bonney and Antony John. He did a doctorate
on the inter-war avant-garde poet Louis Zukofsky, which according to
legend took ten years before being abandoned. He began publishing in
the late '90s with Writers Forum, an exclusively avant-garde firm. He
has published *In the Assarts* but he began with *Stretchers*, 33 poems of
which one is like this:

> ...a man in a suit announces himself
> takes up the doorframe and watch
> the absinthe say the barman for
> it makes the heart grow big and
> watch it says the suit a venture
> I realise and so the absinthe is
> in hand to knock him about the joints
> head shoulders knees and toes knees
> and toes and hands arms and wrists
> and the neck the nape of the neck
> well it's someone I know
> the green knight nape bone's
> honour's gone and connected to

the scrape bone belongs to Jesus
he will never go down in these
weeds today what hairy knees and
no ancestors for the crude count
merrily feinted (he never seen the
blue and green had not the interest)
in *oblige* knock knock isabel king
the poet lived tramping danger
in the shape of some and many
far to the left all the land of ever
and anon much better already
was no potent and no points the
nape bone's connected to the head
stone dictionary of the morning
sir this of that choose peggy sue
in lubbock texarcana (crew cut in
decatur sounds like "ear tug")
decatur's connected *up to the*
taters see you later mister
shing-a-ling...

I don't find it easy to recognise Zukofsky in this. Evidently this poetry starts with saying goodbye to the central structures of modern poetry, the conventions: there is no recognisable speaking figure. No attempt at creating a sociological narrative full of ethical interactions. This absence is the kind of thing that conventional people get very unhappy about. But the poetry has a tone: it is funny, loose, forever chasing stray associations. It has a tone even without a fictive person speaking in it. The rule leading the poem from line to line is one of sound associations and is profoundly like folklore because sound is in charge and because accumulation and concatenation are principles on which folklore is often constructed. A stretcher is a story that stretches the truth, which actually could be considered as a genre of folklore.

Is this acid folk? I think the term is valid but I am less sure that it is salient. Hilson's work is unlike the avant-garde thing but I have trouble making explicit what that Thing is because while the expectations are there they are notably diffuse and putting them into words fails even when they are promising. If 2,000 people have put out volumes of poetry in the small press world it is hopeless to make generalisations.

However, if we say that the expectation is to be critical, to be didactic about how the power order is failing, and to disrupt patterns, that is a start. Hilson's work does not fulfil these expectations, it is very cheerful and makes everyone relaxed. It is more like a skipping-rhyme than J.H. Prynne.

Some younger poets of the kind I read a lot may be relating directly to Hilson's poetry rather than participating in a wider genre of 'acid folk'. This is the so-called Hilson School of Poetry—someone emailed me a photo of a t-shirt with that slogan on it. The direct source for Hilson seems to be *The Basement Tapes*. When Bob Dylan was recuperating from an accident in 1966, he stopped touring or recording and retired to a house in upstate New York. His backing band, however, lived in the same village, at 'Big Pink'. Daily, for months, they would meet, get drunk, improvise together in the basement. The songs they produced were released, on vinyl, some seven years later (as Bob Dylan and the Band), but they had circulated as bootlegs before that. The common feature of the songs was the lack of a central rational theme, they ran on free association, small units of language generating new units and flowing in parallel with other units without seeking a Theme. The units came mostly from existing songs, and this is the folk aspect. Folklore had proceeded for centuries by recombining and stringing-together existing units of melody or verse, the units were protected by memory but the combinations were 'wild' and could rapidly be forgotten again. Some of the sessions were taped, so maybe there was some idea of working the material up into songs you could copyright or perform before a paying audience. Which seemed improbable.

In the Assarts (2010) is probably closer to a folk sensibility. It retains the kind of subjective and sound association of *Stretchers* with a subject, of the 'assarts', a word for 'newly cleared land'. As a study of the relationship between settlement and human culture (the geographical poem) this is a variant on the Olson line; but its lack of seriousness means that we miss out on Olson's weaknesses. The poem includes original documents but they are rewritten so that their meaning is dissolved into a kind of scrolling ornament. The way the origin has been forgotten, partially remembered, reconstructed in more rhythmic terms, is folky. Take this passage from *Stretchers*:

> the green knight nape bone's
> honour's gone and connected to

the scrape bone belongs to Jesus
he will never go down in these
weeds today

This starts out with a glimpse of *Sir Gawaine and the Greene Knight*, 14th century, where the knight in question allows himself to be beheaded, at a Christmas revel, but recovers and says he will come back—to have his return stroke at Gawaine's neck, next Christmas. His revival stands for the revival of the vegetable world as winter ends, just as Christmas is the point where days start to grow longer again. This strolls on to a snatch of a Negro Spiritual based on the book of Ezekiel, *dem bones dem bones dem dry bones. The hip bone's connected to the thigh bone*, etc. "Go down in these weeds" takes off from "if you go down to the woods today" (from the song 'Teddy-bears' Picnic'), but the statement being made is that "weeds are eternally resurrected (as part of the vegetable world)".

The write-ups of acid folk refer to it being visionary or mystic— as in Rob Young's book whose subtitle is 'England's visionary music', perhaps 'auditionary' would have been more precise. I don't think Hilson's work is visionary, that implies something starry-eyed whereas it is more like a classic of silent comedy, a kind of game that takes the form of a narrative.

The idea of acid folk started from an idea of what hit culture is. It demanded a three-minute product which had a limited range of tones but concentrated on high contrasts and on the exact placing of sounds—both rigid and simple. The lead performer had a wholly extroverted stance because of the need to seize the listener's attention —again, rigidity and exaggerated emphasis, arranged in rigid patterns. The psychology presented was simple enough to fit into three minutes. The songs were very repetitive and relied on hooks, simple phrases which were designed to lodge in the brain. If successful, these repetitive snatches of music would be repeated many times on the radio. The composers struggled to bring about variations in the basic model without changing it; these had the character of tricks because they were so emphasized and so restricted in their scope. The songs bore extreme similarities to advertisements: they were advertisements for themselves. They offered gratification but at the cost of limiting the amount of information available to listeners, or for musicians to work with. Hardly draped in any concealing layers of fabric, they acted out a specialised and almost brutal view of the conditioning/response chain, surely at one extreme of the spectrum of artistic possibilities. Around the music was a set of rigid behaviours to do with competition, the search for wealth, and an immense belief in failure, which leaked into the music. Star culture made a grandiose self-regard, and wealth which would hire a whole staff to act out the details of that egoism, the centre of art.

Once you grasp that acid folk is pretty much the opposite of this, you are close to its core. This is where the style is already close to poetry; poetry not as anti-capitalist protest but as an expression of values which are much deeper than the irritations of capitalism and which are anti-capitalist by clinging to their own depths and truths. A basic question is whether there is a success-oriented and conformist manner in poetry which corresponds to Tin Pan Alley in music. There is a strong projective image of mainstream poetry, or its High Street variety, as polished, shallow, conformist, drained of subjectivity by its suavity, its affirmative, bright, uncritical, middle class sound. It is safer to identify this as a belief which shapes the landscape than to identify really existing poets who match this projection. Of course pop songs mostly have *lyrics* and we can readily identify these as a super-capitalist and infantile and conformist stratum of language, resembling (again) the texts of advertisements. There is a whole sector of dumbed-down poetry too. The low key of much of what we call literary poetry is utterly unlike Hit Culture and bears some tantalising resemblances to acid folk in its reluctance towards 'effects' and 'finish'. The musical line of the Folk Revival, acid folk (1) (1969-74), and acid folk (2) (post-2005), offers an analogy to the development of 'low finish' poetry which may help us to understand what happened.

Another point about acid folk is that the 'folk' element may be missing. The phrase is used simply to identify music which had diffident and introverted presentation, an idea of authenticity, then. This idea was present in the Folk Revival but was not inherent in music from the past, say before 1900, and certainly was not confined by nature to old songs as opposed to new ones. The idea that you have to recycle songs, or more abstract forms such as 'stanza', 'rhyme', etc., from the tradition, does not apply. The content of music that musicians could hear and which was not Tin Pan Alley was boundless, of unknown limits, covered by mists but possibly reaching across the whole planet. Meanwhile records, heavily based on American traditional music, but carefully designed to have simple emphases and bright textures and limited room for variation, were 'folk-derived' but at the opposite pole from 'acid folk'.

Acid folk is definitely hard to listen to. The role of emphasis and foregrounding is completely different from what one is used to in pop music. I heard Espers when I was 54, so I had been hearing pop music for possibly 48 years (my memories stretch that far back, 1962), and I just found Espers completely unfamiliar. Not obscure, not jarring or incomplete, but just unfamiliar and new. This was the appeal of acid folk, perhaps, that it wasn't just a regression to something I heard in 1972. There was no path to go down, the music was spread evenly over the whole space it filled. It was a little bit like The Towers Project, whom I had heard. I suppose that pop music over the past 80 years has had a Behaviourist approach to the listener: repetition and reinforcement, simple tasks. Acid folk is non-Behaviourist. There is a possible comparison between this renouncing of means and poets' withdrawal from rhetoric. The use of parataxis, especially. The resistance to 'rhetoric' is at the core of modern poetry even though the same people read highly rhetorical poetry from the past. It is not a simple thing to explain and it arrived by an 'intuitive' route which meant that an explicit debate about it is either missing, or at least not easy to find. Experts always seem to argue about something else than what interests you looking back.

The Left project always had this imbalance, that its most polemical protagonists were more interested in rebutting and overthrowing the powerful in existing society than in the living of life. The project of a daily existence which would live up to the reckless promises of bliss inherent in the speeches of rebellions was answered, if by anything, by the folk programme, even with its component of fantasy. The folk scenario, with its faithful notions of poverty and authenticity, justified a daily life which notably renounced the material wealth and delusory arrogance of the Enemy. This site may account for its longevity.

Leech's book is roughly half about American folk artists. This relieves us of a certain guilt about a nationalism which is, potentially, inherent in recovering the songs of ancestors which were, notably, local. I am not blurting out some exciting secret if I say that the folk movement in Britain has, for its whole duration, drawn on parallel or further ahead processes in the United States. Antiquity is not always nationalistic. Espers are presumably the most prominent figures of the acid folk thing, and they come from Philadelphia.

Poetry has to rely on a kind of prose, that is the substance of daily life which flows beneath and around the noble flights of verse and inspiration. The folk thing, its imagined village (to use Georgina Boyes' inspired phrase), supplied that while getting away from anything too revealing about the heroic life of the literati, with excessive quantities of beer, books, and cups of tea. The depth of the poems we have just been looking at may be due to the sense, never made explicit, of vast tracts of ordinary experience underneath its surface and supporting it. Beside the exaltation of poetry is something more or less the opposite, in humility—and the truth and insight which go along with it. The depth of time which runs back to antiquity, at least at village level, prolongs this feeling. As I write the 'acid folk' thing has that palpable sense of antiquity and durability because around 2006 its nascent figures literally went back to figures who had been making records in 1969 or so and who by 2006 were 'ancient monuments', and not only that but were invisible, buried beneath yards of soil. This interval of time made ideas of duration, recovery, even resurrection, almost solid. The poems we have been looking at each had events or substances from very different points of history sequenced together, again showing durability. The weakness of the poet's attachment to the moment of life which the poet owns is part of the humility we discussed.

Elisabeth Bletsoe wrote:

> Outside described as the colour of breath condensing on glass; the chill amnesia of fog. Instances of clarity & fading as if from radio interference. Shuttered sentences. Fur-gloved fingers of magnolia buds poke through submerged etymologies of such words as "garden", "enclosure", "boundary wall". Interiors hollowed by absence. Cross-quarter days herald the cessation of old land-tenure agreements, the lost chartulary of the town mapped by street-lights still tied to winter circuits. The inclusion, here, of a "decorative motif" enlivens the depopulated margins of the written page. A series of short, restless surges, inverted landings in the leafless branches of the Judas tree; Jack-in-the-Bottle, bottle tit, bum barrel. Hedge mumruffin. Elsewhere in time, conversation alights on the two thousand six hundred feathers lining the nest; additions or subtractions made by researchers prompting immediate readjustments in

favour of the preferred number. Dichotomies occur between the elaborated shapes of speech & an unarticulated persistence of the image within neural connections to perceived shifts in cloud strata. A moment of absolution among the accessories of horticulture; moisture droplets ringing the patrimonial bird-bath. Cursory insectivorous questing. Scarlet eyelid-wattles.
　　(from 'Birds of the Sherborne Missal', XI, in *The Ground Aslant*)

The affection for archaic English, for curious phrases, for scraps of superstition and folk taxonomy, is obvious. The 'written page' mentioned is an illuminated missal—it is called the Sherborne Missal and it is in the Sherborne museum where Bletsoe works part-time. As a replica is displayed on glass in the museum, Bletsoe may see this every day. Much of the content of the poems in the group *Pharmacopoeia* is drawn from her studies as a herbalist. (Connoisseurs will remember the photograph of a herbalist's shop which appeared on the cover of *The North Sea Grassman and the Ravens*, by Sandy Denny, and is reproduced in *Electric Eden*.) This is too 'high finish' to be proper acid folk. The 'folk' word serves to illuminate one strand in the weave of Bletsoe's poetry, one soaked in warmth, mystery, traditional knowledge, and a sense of deep time. Cross-quarter is not clear to me although rents used to be paid on 'quarter-days'. *Charta* means paper, so a document in general, and a *chartulary* is an inventory of an estate, which would include the boundaries of holdings—shadowily recalled in the street-lights (winter circuits of what?). The word evokes antiquarians searching in boxes of old parchment deeds to resurrect old customs and forms of land use. The mumruffin is what I would think of as a blue-tit, which learnt to drink milk from bottles on the doorstep, only the top as far down as the beak could reach. There is a Russian proverb about *like bird's milk*, meaning something you can't find—answered by, literally, milk for the birds. The bird lands in the branches of a Judas tree, presumably the one from which Judas hanged himself. The passage starts with fog as a form of forgetfulness and recedes through a series of states of mind which we can tie to diffuse and unstressed overall awareness with loss of details. Thus the "neural connections to perceived shifts in cloud strata" mean that the mind is cleverly patterning something vague and beautiful to reach a beautiful and vague condition. The "lost chartulary" is a skein of attenuated lines preserving as if in unconsciousness a spatial order which was there centuries ago. The mixture of long persisting memory and complete loss of precision and regularity is fundamental to the acid-folk state of mind.

The acid folk tag is doubtful in its precision. It is attractive more because 'acid folk' is a complete artistic atmosphere, something which illuminates every aspect of the artwork at the same time, by using its guiding principle as the source of light. It gets us away from the label 'underground', a remarkably weak classifier if only because the concept of underground was attractive to so many people. If you remember the psychedelic era (or have the records) you know that 'acid rock' meant an attraction to bright, shimmering, or blurred textures, rapid shifting between different textures (so that exotic instruments and new electronic effects were very popular), bleeps and pings, in fact infantile curiosity. Let me just mention the Strawberry Alarm Clock—'incense and peppermints, meaningless sounds', simultaneously a classic of bubblegum and a parody of the whole bubblegum genre. Even the name, 'bubblegum', was an abusive label attached by 'progressive' fans because this totally Pop thing was too close to their patch, being equally Beatles-based and equally acid-inspired. When pop composers took acid they listened to *Sergeant Pepper's* and wrote trippy pop songs—of which you could collect several hundred without a big research effort. So 'acid folk' is not the ideal descriptor.

If we came to define the principle of which Bletsoe's beautiful work is a realisation, the attraction for curious, old, and yet unfamiliar things would be part of it. A preference for curious things that have roots in Dorset would be another part. Another writer using folk elements in an elusive and elaborate formal pattern is SL Mendoza—

hung like Christ thin young girl with slender
arms speaking of I am fly which brought crook-
ed pins and first made her swallow and 2ND made her.
then there came from her head a blistering
– BRIGHT [ffly] cant & hypocrisy pale & crimson

great millar clapp'd POWDERY HANDS made
cloud of ghost moth | hepialus humuli | dust on
wings. she felt her poll it tickle her poll was
red like

RAWBEEF, twirling crimson [-] LEO/TARD. white
tutu, Spanish dancer. my emperor tucked in
folly folds and GILL I am red rotten hidd en in
her not drawing blood not breaking skin. oh
little man putting hand to head, saying, "How
do ye?" speaking low. little man hand to head
clothed in black cap neath chin. her poll was
[RED] like poll-ed sheep – ah perilous beat
tom tumbler

This is an excerpt from SL Mendoza's pamphlet *Die Fliege* (2009).
Fairly obviously it belongs with the underground world, its chagrins
and splendours. Hardly less obviously we are being offered a scene
from an indeterminate, mediaeval or Early Modern, past, and certain
details place us in a legend rather than 'true narrative'. So we are amid
folklore—the text is even in dialect. Mendoza worked professionally
with insects, at a museum. The *red rotten hidden* sounds like an insect
that burrows into meat—a blowfly perhaps. *her poll was [RED] like
poll-ed sheep* shows someone with a red cap, which already sounds like
a figure from folklore. (There was a pub in Camden called the Mother
Red-cap.) Then we have someone in a black cap, this colour coding
sounds like a fairy-tale. The bit about vomiting pins is something that
bewitched people do—I saw this in *The X-files.* The text suggests to
me that the insects are familiars of the young girl with sticklike arms.
hepialus humuli is the ghost moth: "The Ghost Moth gets its name from
the display flight of the male, which hovers, sometimes slowly rising
and falling, over open ground to attract females. In a suitable location
several males may display together in a lek." (I looked this up.)
    There is a mention of the Lyke-wake Dirge later on, and on a 2004
anthology subtitled 'the British acid folk underground 1968-74' one
of the tracks is Pentangle singing 'A Lyke-wake Dirge'. Does this prove
that Mendoza is Acid Folk? I suppose not. I think every line from the
page I just quoted could appear in a folk song. *Die Fliege* moves through
themes about meat-eating flies, moths, pins, finding of witches, red and
white, cross-dressing, Northumbria in the 15th century. *Gather in the
Mushrooms*, the 'acid folk' anthology, was compiled by Bob Stanley,
presumably the musician from St Etienne. The phrase 'acid folk' was on
the rise in 2004.

Mendoza likes jokes or double identities. "Die Fliege" means 'fly' and 'bow tie' (shaped like a winged insect, to a German). But 'fly' is also 'opening in crotch of trousers', which in German is 'hosenschlitz'—and there is a passage about *der Hosenschlitz* in the poem. In *The Goon Show*, a '50s radio serial, there was a character called Bluebottle, played by Peter Sellers, whose catch phrase was "you filthy rotten swine! you deaded me!"; sure enough in *Die Fliege* when we hear about a bluebottle the phrase "you dead'd me" occurs.

It is fair to say that the poem uses parataxis, is wholly paratactic. It is more accurate to say that it is not organised in conventional sentences, it is more like a white space on which flakes of language are applied, separately, opening a space without closely defining each other. The instant response from 'underground connoisseurs' is that it is like Barry MacSweeney (*Ranter* or *Odes*) and Maggie O'Sullivan, but this does not get us very far because this is like something which happened before the start of the text; obviously the apparatus of conventional English poetry has been resolutely scrapped, but the new thing is not a variation on either Barry or Maggie. It is much less obscure than their work, because more coherent—the themes of *Die Fliege* recur in a logical way, the parts support each other and steadily wipe out any initial uncertainty.

The jokes remind me of Jeff Hilson and there probably is a link with Jeff. Literally Mendoza studied creative writing at the Roehampton course on which Jeff taught, but while a number of people went on that course and wrote poetry for *Ninerrors* they don't resemble each other very much.

I said earlier that I found it hard to describe acid folk, and although I wrote an essay on parataxis in modern poetry (on the website) I can't explain why modern poetry uses parataxis so much. Cataloguing a great many poems that have no subordinate clauses does not get you to why they do it like that. Are you sure Hank done it this way?

As syntax is part of a set of ways of producing emphasis, it may be that minimising syntax is a way of spreading out emphasis, and that this is analogous to acid folk as a music without emphases, hooks, choruses, riffs, etc., where the depth of sound is also a spreading of weight over the entire available space and this is 'authenticity'. The battery of devices for conditioned gratification which we observed earlier could be described as a technique for promoting the self—the dual narcissism of singer (or poet) and reader. They wipe out the penumbra to put the centre into dazzling focus and inhibit any lines of attention that could wander away from it. So breaking up emphasis could have to do with de-commodifying the self, switching off this central block of attention can allow the emergence of a hundred other themes. This de-commodifying could be the link with underground poetry, and so the purpose of parataxis could be to do with breaking up the high gloss finish of the commercial universe. You can identify, but even the offer of identification is being dispersed, the psychology in use is not unambiguous, swollen, demanding infantile urges, but other parts of the mind. Syntax makes the message unambiguous, but maybe poetry needs to escape into the world of unexplored possibilities, the unresolved area between the focal point and the horizon.

If there are so many possibilities, and there were already in 1968, it is likely that experimental poetry since 1968 has debouched into the open territory and travelled to quite a few of them. This is where some of the propaganda/exegesis has gone wrong—the claim that "indeterminacy has a single meaning and I know what it is" is inherently flawed.

Mendoza edited the Ninerrors pamphlet series and edits *Freaklung* magazine. (Freaklung is an anagram of Garfunkel and this may be because Hilson's hairstyle was being compared to Art Garfunkel's.) The scene around *Freaklung* is where it's happening with English poetry, a gap in the landscape where people are able to hear new sounds coming through. It is evolving fast enough to change even while I am writing this book, so I will be cautious about description.

SCARLET AND GREEN

Paul Holman published in 2013 *Tara Morgana,* which is also Book Five of *The Memory of the Drift,* whose title "refers both to Olson and to the Situationist International". He is one of the few people on the scene who actually know what acid folk is and can pinpoint where folk icon Shirley Collins worked with neo-occultists Current 93.

Tara King was one of the stylised civil servants of *The Avengers*—the name evokes a whole class of decorative young women, since Tara was the name of the O'Haras' antebellum mansion in *Gone With the Wind* (film, 1939), where Scarlett worked her wiles. This film spoke to a whole class of star-struck young mothers and the outcome in the late Sixties was a flurry of ornamental Taras for whom Scarlett was a chromatic guide. We could see Fay and Tara as two sisters. Fay Wray

and Tara Morgana, maybe. It would take one more—Lana perhaps?—
to make a singing group.

Tara is not Tara King, but Sita Tara is a *devi* venerated in Tibetan
Buddhism, appearing as a radiantly beautiful sixteen-year-old girl.
Green animals and animated corpses are attributes that suggest her
presence. The glass tunnels which are a central if rarely glimpsed feature
in the terrain of the poem may be a manifestation of the cave-temples
of Tara at Ellora. Morgana (with the vocational describer of *fata*, fairy,
a variant of Morgan le Fay) is a figure of Arthurian romance—Arthur's
not quite human sister. Fata Morgana is also a heat mirage, in the
strait between Sicily and Calabria. Morgana is said to have had a glass
tower. *Tara Morgana* can be seen simply as an apparition narrative, a
theophany. But it has the double surface, dealing with Sita Tara and
Morgana together. The story is not one we have already heard.

The combination with a figure of western Romance makes the Tara
local—a feature of all apparitions, I suppose. *I wished to dwell on my
own and pursue an intricate game, mix only with such as live only by
analogy, the culture of romance and the quest: at the end to inhabit the
matter of Britain, for all the landform's hollow promise of a sleeper.* The
specious and inconsistent qualities of the 'projection' are also attributed
to Morgan herself. Spirits of the *fata* class may be visible but without
substance. They are *films* and are close to a popular art where visual
surfaces are complete and there is no depth. The apparitional images
have a similar climactic quality of clarity—though the very opposite
of the disenchanted clarity which another faction of English poetry
hopes to reach by surrendering anything else. People interested in the
invisible world, the hidden reality, are primarily interested in making it
visible—the link with the glass of a *lens* was obvious.

> I gather the scattered, not
> with a song breathed from
> the most casual utterance,
> but a manifesto read by
> the dreaming eye, written
> in the alphabet of signs that
> preceded articulate speech:
> the work of people whose
> only language was animal
> noise, imitation of nature.

In earlier books of *Drift* Holman was preoccupied with *akephaloi*, the headless ones, a shadowy class of spirits whose function in the poem is to represent unreflected action, drift; the eternal present of an organism in direct allegiance to the sun. This state was actually available in popular culture. Headlessness was "a state of willed absence of mind, an image of ritual decapitation, and a model of social-political organisation". Here unity is the divine. A god snared by theological reason is godlike by virtue of lacking reason. A headless being is perhaps also incapable of being deceived. Without eyes, it perhaps has sense organs scattered throughout its body. The decentralising exit from grand narratives into the personal and local is a modern process—a world of ownerless wealth. Who carries out subjectless action? Headless heroes.

Holman is one of few writers to bring about a unification of the *avant-garde idea*, of an area beyond the boundary of the corrupt, where the intellect and the imagination are acting as one, and the *Marxist theory of alienation*, where the goal of conspiratorial action is to recover an original unity. A persistent feature of this oneness is anatomies which directly reflect existential states—like the *akephaloi*.

There have been passages of my life in which every meeting drew me on to love, every occurrence was given as a sign: I let the green horse guide me into the river meadows, under the bridge obscured by a cloud of steam from the brewery, and so at last into the tunnel. The invisible is present in the here and now, or not at all. For me this is proven in the 15th-century *The Awntyrs off Arthure at the Terne Wathelyn*, where the setting is a tarn still found in Inglewood Forest, in Cumberland. The recurring stories of Arthurian romance are set where we are, and we are in them—scarcely more so than in Holman's mythic narratives in everyday settings. In romance, we carry out volitionless action and our experience is without flaws. The monarchical churches do not keep the precious knowledge. This scattering could be a hint of the origins of the 'occult'—often seen as following the overthrow of Stony Egypt, as experts, texts, entire practices took refuge in the back streets, in privacy and obscurity. What was scattered is everywhere; a power lured away and taken over by radical autonomists, heretics with a deeper loyalty, themselves scattered. The earnest student has since then followed the course of rigour, chance and impulse.

THE ACID-FOLK COMMUNITY

So has the analogy with psych folk shed any light on a strange but enticing wing of English poetry? Maybe you need to read large amounts of underground poetry and listen to large amounts of psych folk to find out whether the analogy works or not. Anyway, the folk line in 'alternative' poetry is abiding and represents a reaction against the authoritarian, centralising and elitist currents swirling ominously around the older Modernism.

Perhaps acid folk is just a blank cheque for a more adequate impression, to be delivered later, of certain works which stand free from the traditionally vague system of genres and stylistic adjectives and which unite around the values of humility, tradition, and ornament prevailing over reason.

EXERCISES

Listen to 'Espers II' by Espers.

Listen to 'Song for Comus' by Comus.

Listen to 'Just Another Diamond Day' by Vashti Bunyan.

Listen to "The silence of love' by Headless Heroes.

Listen to 'Anthems in Eden' by Shirley Collins.

AFTERWORD: PARTIALLY CODED LAND

It was a resort town in winter, desolate and slumbering, where we waited for the season to arrive and all the beachniks. I wandered the snowy foreshore with Freddy and Annette, toying with frozen sharks and husks of sea-holly. We mused on the grand noon of the last high season. The gardens of the casino… the donkeys… the massed fights on the promenade. Once is never enough.

This trip has put mainstream and alternative poetry into one framework. The related task of putting the lyrics of songs together with poetry in one frame will have to wait for another occasion.

It is no good having an antenna of hermetic purity if there is no signal to be received. Perhaps the pace of assimilation is slow mainly because you have to read so many bad poets and they reduce your sensitivity each time.

There is a stratum of argument which is never silent, which moves rapidly, and which is not relevant to the poetry. There may be people who are rushing this way and that with the arguments but don't get the poetry at all. Other people record the 'frequency map' to help me get there.

This poetry is late in the cultural cycle, deeply original and recondite. It is hard to get to. It strikes me how slowly I assimilate new writers, how few new poets I have discovered and liked in twenty years since 1990. The landscape of poetry acts to hide the things you most want to get to—it is a riddle, *the intricate hills a lament configuration,* as Elisabeth Bletsoe wrote, referring to a famous puzzle. The signal seems to be in all parts of the room except where you are. Taking on a new poet means finding the right part of the room—like adjusting a radio aerial to receive one frequency in a million jamming signals. To acquire the new pattern, you learn what the tempo is and where to put the emphases, so as to reach the pleasurable state. This is a mimetic process, an archaic and a slow one. Having got the pattern, I am trying to record what it is.

With this period, I am trying to get you to retain the difference between Theresa May and Imelda May. This book only became a possibility when I realised that I could write an incomplete work. That is—only fragments from a complete picture which may take fifty years to arrive. Anyway, although the book is overflowing, the themes dealt with do not cover the whole territory of modern poetry, and indeed we could probably produce a list of a hundred themes relevant to that task. The other ninety are missing.

It is noticeable that, the further back you go, the easier it is to make satisfactory generalisations about a period and to put the individual poets in a valid relationship to each other. I just find it easier writing about the 1950s and finding strong patterns in the various pieces. Reluctantly, I translated this into the attempt to write in a fragmentary way about the last twenty years. There was so much going on in the 1970s that brilliant things escaped notice—the phenomenon of crowd-out. Originally there were a hundred or so figures vying for attention. As I became familiar with their work it receded into the background, freeing up the foreground so that my attention could shift to other writers. The 'seventies project' has seen the efforts of connoisseurs—people who delve into the printed evidence of the poetry scene and form aesthetic appreciations of them and even tell us about the findings. Over decades, we came to grasp the poetry of the 1970s and put all the pieces into relation with each other. It is sensible to hope that a shared process of aesthetic infolding will bring us to a full understanding of the period 1990-2010. There is a tier of 'primary readers' but the sheer number of books coming out overloads the tier's powers of assimilation. So what I write is tentative. It is a move in a game which must be played before it is complete. This is the 'partially coded landscape'. The information is already here, so the delay is with the audience, step by step, learning how to read it. I will move the process on by a notch. Thereby making this book obsolete.

New Times, New Sounds

Has anything changed since 1990? David Ashford's *Xaragmata* (pamphlet from Veer), was published in 2013 and this is just about the most amazing stuff we have seen in the last twenty years. Described by Harry Gilonis as 'way beyond weird', the fabric of the poetry goes so far into the recondite, dense, and plain difficult that you can only grasp it through the notes. We were overwhelmed. Sketchy research suggests that it should be 'kharagmata', with a chi not ksi, from a word meaning 'stamp' used in the Scriptures for 'the mark of the Beast' and describing for Ashford the anomalous 6th millennium signs (or quasi-writing??) on tablets from Tartaria in Romania which appear on the cover of the pamphlet. A fascination for mathematics, objects constructed by numbers, and archaeology helps to push this language into the realm of dazzle and darkness. ('Character' is originally the pattern stamped on a coin by a die.) We have a poem about the Mesolithic site on the Danube at Lepenski Vir which describes the mathematical ideas embodied in the shapes of the houses. This is related to the incidental music for radio and television programmes, recorded by Delia Derbyshire in the 1960s, which were also generated by mathematics because they were purely electronic.

> "Roof" over basic low sounds – high shafts of colour
> & cont, high dreamy sound.
> dawn plain sound
> words: colour, stained glass windows, sunlight,
> coloured dreams, clouds etc.
> being chased – along corridors, down stairs, across fields
> falling
> breathing – heartbeat. pillow, sun
> murmuring voices – long mixes, voices out of nothing
> (from 'The Spindle-Whorl')

This is presumably a description of how the sounds of the Radiophonic Workshop were matched to events in narratives. In principle, all the words are from found texts (an interview with Delia Derbyshire in this case). The 'spindle-whorl' also has kharagmata, incisions looking like letters, on it. Ashford's poem about the arrival of the Indo-Europeans (related by David Anthony to a culture of hunters and gatherers moving over a vast area west of the Urals and north of the Caspian which evolved into a pastoral culture) quotes from a reconstructed Indo-European folk-tale, *Avis akvāsas ka*—written by August Schleicher in 1868 but updated in 1997 to incorporate the key changes to the theory made by Kurylowicz in 1927. These lines are therefore in a language which may have been spoken in 4000-3000 BC but which was never written down. David Jones' poems include scraps of Old Welsh, notably, but no-one so far as I know before has deployed Primitive Indo-European. In order to read this poem aloud you would have to decide how the laryngeals were pronounced—a controversial issue. The interest in the point of origin of the European languages coincides with the interest in the origins of European peasant society and the invention of writing—all points on the horizon of knowledge, where haze merges into darkness. We see the first known examples of the cultural systems we use and also a zone where they merge into something else. We hear that Ashford also runs the micropublisher Contraband, which put out Nat Raha's *Countersonnets*, for example.

Xaragmata is something that was not there in 1990. The theme of poetry mutating to take on much much more precise information may be one that writers can follow in the future. Arguably, it has concerned a large number of poets in the past twenty years (and was already occupying J.H. Prynne in the late 1960s).

BIBLIOGRAPHY

see http://intercapillaryspace.blogspot.co.uk/ and http://www.greatworks.
org.uk or http://networkedblogs.com/RWShw for info on recent poetry.

INTRODUCTION
Barker, Hugh and Taylor, Yuval, *Faking It: The Quest for Authenticity in
Popular Music* (London: Faber, 2007)

Partially Coded Terrain. Eight anthologies
Faking It ut supra
Simic, Charles, and Paterson, Don, eds., *New British Poetry* (St Paul, MN:
Graywolf Press, 2004)
Joe Luna essay published at
http://fallopianyoutube.blogspot.co.uk/2012/05/world-is-for-this-on-
poetry-of-jonty.html

EPIPHANY AND VOICELESSNESS
McCardle/ Hugill/ Mooney, *Shuddered* (London: Veer Books, 2009)
Antony John, *now than it used to be, but in the past* (London: Veer Books,
2009)
Rob Holloway, *Permit* (Berkeley, California: Subpress, 2009)
Berger, John, *Ways of Seeing* (London: BBC, 1972)

ARCHIPELAGIC FULFILMENT
Stevenson, Randall, *The Last of England? 1960-2000* (Oxford: Oxford
University Press, 2004)— figure of 2,700 is at p.266
My essay on historicism on angelexhaust.blogspot. Discussion of historicism
in Fuller, Peter, *Beyond the Crisis in Art* (London: Writers and Readers,
1980), pp. 44-67, 70-97) and Gombrich, Ernst, 'The Logic of Vanity Fair
— Alternatives to Historicism in the Study of Fashions, Style, and Taste'
in *Ideals and Idols* (London: Phaidon Press, 1979)
Nietzsche, Friedrich Wilhelm, *Werke*, ed. Karl Schlechta, (Frankfurt am
Main: Ullstein, 1981), Bd. 2, pp. 737 and 835, and Bd. 3, p. 574.

SOME GENERALISATIONS
Figures on published poetry from cuttings in a folder supplied by the Poetry
Library, London.
Brown, Andy, ed., *Binary Myths* volumes 1 and 2 (Exeter: Stride, 1998-9)
Material on depolarisation in A. Duncan, *The Council of Heresy* (Exeter:
Shearsman Books, 2010), which also has a survey of new poetry in the
'90s at pp.154-73. A slightly earlier survey is in *The Failure of Conser-
vatism* (Cambridge: Salt Publishing, 2003), at pp. 317-35. A revised
edition of this volume will appear in 2016 from Shearsman Books.

316

Comments on effects of the new electronic environment in A. Duncan, 'The Tyranny of Space and Distance' at www.pinko.org.

Lucie-Smith, Edward, ed., *British Poetry Since 1945* (1st edition, 1971, is far superior to the 2nd edition.) (London: Penguin Books, 1971)

Duncan, Andrew, *The Long 1950s* (Exeter: Shearsman Books, 2012)

Legends of the Warring Clans. The Poetry Scene in the '90s (by Andrew Duncan, on-line at www.pinko.org) reviews about 40 books coming out in the '90s.

Abbs, Peter, ed., *The Black Rainbow* (London: Heinemann Educational Books, 1975)

THE RECEPTION OF MODERN POETRY

Faking It ut supra

Essay on the singer-songwriter influence in Duncan, *The Long 1950s* (Exeter: Shearsman Books, 2012)

Woods, Tim, *Beginning Postmodernism* (Manchester: Manchester University Press, 2009, originally 1999)

Survey of reception of modern British poetry in Andrew Duncan, *The Failure of Conservatism* (Cambridge: Salt Publishing, 2003), pp. 6-22, and more on-line at www.pinko.org ('Reception Hall').

Jencks, Charles, *The Language of Post-modern Architecture* (London: Academy Editions, 1991)

Stevenson, Randall, *ut supra*

Paterson/ Simic, eds., *New British Poetry, ut supra*

O'Brien, Sean, *The Deregulated Muse* (Newcastle: Bloodaxe, 1998)

Sheppard, Robert, *The Poetry of Saying* (Liverpool: Liverpool University Press, 2003) and *When Bad Times Made for Good Poetry* (Exeter: Shearsman Books, 2011). For more views on indeterminacy see my review of *Conductors of Chaos* in *Angel Exhaust* (periodical: Southend) 15, pp.81-99.

Roy Fisher lines quoted from 'The Only Image' (printed in *The Dow Low Drop* [Tarset: Bloodaxe Books, 1996] p.106)

Chicago Review (periodical, Chicago) issue on British poetry [2007]

MacKillop, Ian, and Sinyard, Neil, eds., *British Cinema of the 1950s : a Celebration* (Manchester: Manchester University Press, 2003)

PARTIALLY NAMED TERRAIN

Information on dates drawn often from the British Library catalogue which may often be based on a questionnaire filled in by the authors.

Found Footage of Self-regard; or, Problems of Individualism

Cogan, Ross, 'In Praise of Lying', in *PN Review* (periodical, Manchester, 2007) issue 177

Karlien van den Beukel poem quoted from *Pitch Lake* (Cambridge: rem. press, 1997), Robert Smith poem quoted from *Angel Exhaust* (periodical, Southend), issue 15.

Stone, Lawrence, *The Family, Sex, and Marriage 1500-1800* (London: Weidenfeld and Nicolson, 1977)

Hauser, Arnold, *Der Ursprung der Modernen Kunst und Literatur: Die Entwicklung des Manierismus seit der Krise der Renaissance* (Munich: Deutscher Taschenbuch-Verlag, 1964)

Hocke, Gustav-René, *Manierismus in der Literatur: Sprach-Alchimie und esoterische Kombinationskunst* (vol. 2 of *Der Manierismus in der Kunst*) (Hamburg: Rowohlt Taschenbuch-Verlag, 1959)

Langley poem from *The Face of It* (Manchester: Carcanet Press, 2007)

Critchley poem from *How to Make Millions* (Cambridge: arehouse, 2005)

Raworth poem from *Collected Poems* (Manchester: Carcanet Press, 2003)

Clare Pollard poem from *Look, Clare! Look!* (Tarset: Bloodaxe Books, 2005)

CRITIQUE OF LITERARY IMAGINATION

Kastan, David Scott, *Shakespeare After Theory* (London: Routledge, 1999)

Dollimore, Jonathan, ed. *Political Shakespeare* (Manchester: Manchester UP, 1994) is a good example of a radical reading of literary classics.

Darlow, Michael, *Terence Rattigan, the Man and His Work* (London: Quartet Books, 2010)

Higgins, Patrick, *Heterosexual Dictatorship: Male Homosexuality in Postwar Britain* (London: Fourth Estate, 1996)

THE CUBE OF NOW

Campbell, James, *The Anglo-Saxon State* (London & New York, NY: Hambledon and London, 2000)

Kristiansen, Kristian, *Europe before History* (Cambridge: Cambridge University Press, 1998)

Gernet, Louis, 'La notion mythique de la valeur en Grèce', in *anthropologie grecque* (Paris: François Maspero, 1968)

B. Catling's *Written Rooms and Pencilled Crimes* printed in *Future Exiles. Three London Poets* (London: Paladin, 1992)

—*Soundings. A Tractate of Absence* (Matt's Gallery, London, 1991)

Pauline Stainer, *The Lady & the Hare. New & Selected Poems* (Tarset: Bloodaxe Books, 2003)

Christopher Logue, *War Music* (London: Faber, 1988)

Stephen Spender, *Edge of Being* (London: Faber: 1949)

Peter Yates, *The Expanding Mirror and Other Poems* (London: Chatto & Windus, 1942)

Brøndsted, Johannes, *Danmarks Historie*, volume 1 (Copenhagen: Politiken, 1962)

Widsith text at http://webcache.googleusercontent.com/search?q=cache:tnwyUSW8El4J:www.soton.ac.uk/~enm/widsith.htm+myrginngas&cd=4&hl=en&ct=clnk&gl=uk

Staffordshire Hoard quotes are from http://www.staffordshirehoard.org.uk/interview/ and http://www.staffordshirehoard.org.uk/commentary/ .

PARTIALLY CODED FIELDS AND BASTIONS OF EXAGGERATION
Nonist press releases
for Matless, and *Electric Eden*: see chapter 13
10th Muse magazine (periodical, Southampton)
Mintern, Charles, *The Forging of Foreignness* (Weymouth Sands: Dodman
   Burrows, 1887)
Andrew Jordan, *Hegemonick* (Bristol: Shearsman Books, 2012)
for Rik Clay: website at http://www.rikclayfoundation.org/rik-clay.html
Wright, Patrick, *The Village that Died for England* (London: Jonathan Cape,
   1995)

CRITIQUE OF INDIVIDUALISM
Ammianus Marcellinus, *Res Gestae* (vol. 3 of Loeb edition, ed. and trans. John
   C. Rolfe; Cambridge, MA: Harvard University Press, 1939)
Lewis, David, *Science and Archaeology* (London: Penguin, 1974)
Information on Kopelev in *Spiegel-Geschichte* (periodical: Hamburg), issue 1,
   2011, p.96.

THE GOTHIC COUNTERPANE
Matless, David, *Landscape and Englishness* (London: Reaktion Books, 1998)
Cocroft, Wayne C., and Thomas, Roger J.C., *Cold War; Building for Nuclear
   Confrontation 1945-89* (English Heritage, 2003)
Showalter, Elaine, *The Female Malady: women, madness, and culture in England,
   1830-1980* (London: Virago, 1987)
Gubar, Susan, and Gilbert, Susan M., *The Madwoman in the Attic. The woman
   writer and the 19th century literary imagination* (Ithaca, NY & London: Yale
   University Press, 1979)
Kossmann, EH, *The Low Countries 1780-1940* (Oxford: Clarendon Press, 1978)
Duncan, Andrew, *The Council of Heresy* (Exeter: Shearsman Books, 2009)
Deutelbaum, Marshall and Poague, Leland, eds., *A Hitchcock Reader*
   (Chichester: Wiley-Blackwell, 2nd edition 2009, originally 1986)

SECRET ENEMY
Rees-Jones, Deryn and Mark, Alison, eds. *Contemporary Women's Poetry*
   (Basingstoke: Macmillan, 2000)
Eagleton, Mary, ed. *Feminist Literary Criticism* (Malden: Wiley-Blackwell, 2011)
Ross, Alan, *British Poetry 1945-50* (London: Arts Council, 1950)
The Poet's Yearbook 1978 (Cleethorpes: Poet's Yearbook, 1978)
Barker, Jonathan, *Poetry in Britain and Ireland since 1970*—a bibliography
   (London: The British Council, 1995)
Kazantzis poem from *Selected Poems 1977-1992* (London: Sinclair-Stevenson,
   1995); her statement in *Contemporary Poets*, 6th edition, edited by Thomas
   Riggs (Detroit: St James Press, 1996)

Mohin, Lilian, ed., *One Foot on the Mountain : an anthology of British feminist poetry, 1969-1979* (London: Onlywomen Press, 1979)

THE PUBLIC FACE OF A PRIVATE ART
Faking It again

Critique of the Government
Axboe, Morten, *Die Goldbrakteaten der Völkerwanderungszeit: Herstellungsprobleme und Chronologie* (Berlin: Walter de Gruyter, 2004)
Bonney: interview in *Don't Start Me Talking*. Piece by A. Duncan in *Silent Rules* (Brighton: Waterloo Press, forthcoming); poem quoted from *Blade Pitch Control Unit* (Cambridge: Salt Publishing, 2006).
Rawnsley, Andrew, *The End of the Party* (London: Penguin, 2010)
Brady interview on-line at http://www.argotistonline.co.uk/Brady%20interview.htm; Brady poem quoted from *Vacation of a Lifetime* (Cambridge: Salt Publishing, 2001)
Marriott quoted from *Hoodoo Voodoo* (Exeter: Shearsman Books, 2008)

MONUMENTAL FORMALISM
Discussion of the history of sampling in Beadle, Jeremy J., *Will pop eat itself?* (London: Faber and Faber, 1993)
Poetry quoted from:
Tony Lopez, *Only More So* (New Orleans, LA: UNO Press, 2011; Exeter: Shearsman Books, 2012)
Giles Goodland, *Capital* (Cambridge: Salt Publishing, 2006); *What the Things Sang* (Exeter: Shearsman Books, 2009)
Matthew Welton, *The Book of Matthew* (Manchester: Carcanet, 2003)
Source on documentary in: Duncan, *Origins of the Underground* (Cambridge: Salt Publishing, 2005) pp. 82-97

PALE AND CRIMSON: ACID FOLK
Young, Rob, *Electric Eden: Unearthing Britain's Visionary Music* (London: Faber, 2010)
Leech, Jeanette, *Seasons They Change, the Story of Acid, Psych, and Experimental Folk* (London: Outline Press, 2010)
Bletsoe poem quoted from *The Ground Aslant*, edited by Harriet Tarlo (Exeter: Shearsman Books, 2011)
Mendoza poem from *Die Fliege* (London: Ninerrors, 2009)
Piece on Holman in *Fulfilling the Silent Rules* (by Andrew Duncan, Waterloo Press, forthcoming).
Holman poem from *Tara Morgana* (Brighton: Scarlet Imprint, 2014)

AFTERWORD
David Ashford, *Xaragmata* (London: Veer Books, 2013)

ACKNOWLEDGEMENTS

Except where specified below, all quotations from original works in this volume have been made under the fair-use rule. Thanks are due to the following for permission to reprint in this volume work that goes beyond fair-use norms:

Rachael Allen, except from the poem 'Goonhilly', as published in the anthology *Dear World and Everyone in It* (ed. Nathan Hamilton, Tarset: Bloodaxe Books, 2013), and since republished in a revised version in the pamphlet, *Faber New Poets 9* (London: Faber & Faber, 2014). Thanks also to Faber & Faber.

David Ashford, excerpt from *Xaragmata* (London: Veer Books, 2013).

Bloodaxe Books for an except from Heather Phillipson's poem, 'Although You Do Not Know Me, My Name is Patricia', as published in the anthology *Dear World and Everyone in It* (ed. Nathan Hamilton, Tarset: Bloodaxe Books, 2013), and since republished in the book, *Instant-fLex 718* (Tarset: Bloodaxe Books, 2013).

Bloodaxe Books for an except from Kate Potts' poem, 'The Runt', from the book, *Pure Hustle* (Tarset: Bloodaxe Books, 2011).

Andrew Duncan, 'The Cube of Now' was first published in *Critical Survey*.

Andrew Duncan: the material on Paul Holman was previously published as an introduction to Paul Holman's *Tara Morgana* (Scarlet Imprint, 2014).

Piers Hugill, excerpt from Section 6.1 of 'Il Canzoniere' in *Shuddered* by Aodán McCardle, Piers Hugill and Stephen Mooney (London: Veer Books, 2010).

Andrew Jordan, excerpts from *EPA Bulletin* issue 1, and from 'News of the World', in *Hegemonick* (Bristol: Shearsman Books, 2012).

Ágnes Lehóczky, excerpt from 'Rememberer' in *Rememberer* (Egg Box Publishing, 2011).

Joe Luna, excerpts from his blog at http://fallopianyoutube.blogspot.co.uk

Marianne Morris, excerpt from 'Who Not to Speak to', published in *Dear World and Everyone In It* (ed. Nathan Hamilton, Tarset: Bloodaxe Books, 2013).

Lesley Saunders, excerpt from 'The Fallen Angels', in *Cloud Camera* (Reading: Two Rivers Press, 2012).

Index

Lightning Source UK Ltd.
Milton Keynes UK
UKOW02f0020260516

274999UK00002B/94/P